ADVENTURES AND RESEARCHES AMONG THE ANDAMAN ISLANDERS

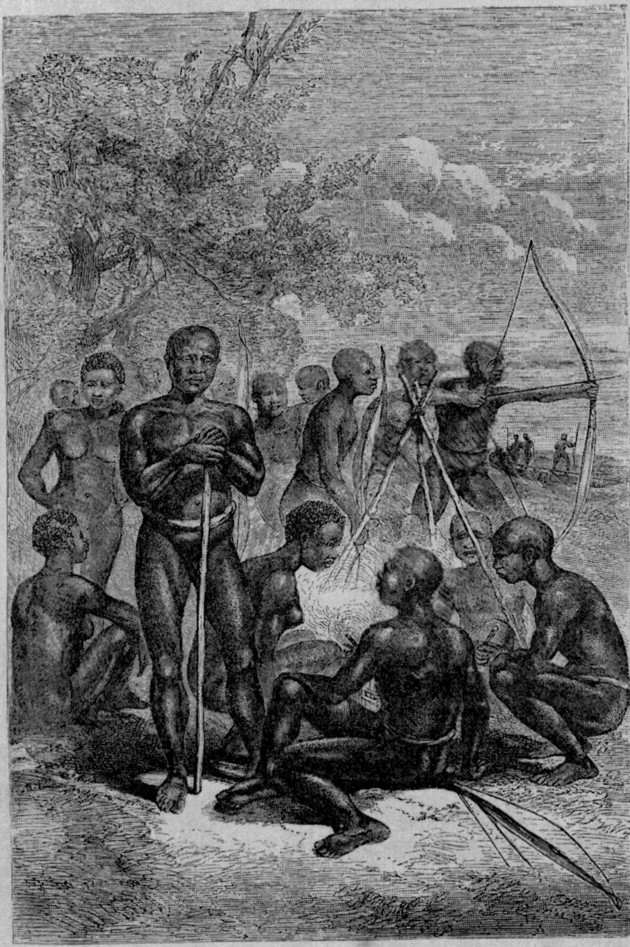

A GROUP OF ANDAMAN ISLANDERS.

ADVENTURES AND RESEARCHES AMONG THE ANDAMAN ISLANDERS

By

FREDERIC J. MOUAT

GYAN

Published by

GYAN

Gyan Publishing House
5, Ansari Road
Daryaganj, New Delhi-110002
Phone: 011-47034999, 9811692060
E-mail: books@gyanbooks.com

Distribution Network
gyanbooks.com
India, USA, Canada, UK, Australia, France

ISBN: 978-81-212-6845-5 (PB)
First Published, 1863

2nd Impression 2023

Printed at: Gyan Press, Delhi.

ADVENTURES AND RESEARCHES AMONG THE ANDAMAN ISLANDERS
Author: FREDERIC J. MOUAT

ADVENTURES AND RESEARCHES

AMONG

THE ANDAMAN ISLANDERS.

BY

FREDERIC J. MOUAT,

M.D.; F.R.C.S.;

SURGEON-MAJOR, H. M. INDIAN ARMY; INSPECTOR-GENERAL OF PRISONS, BENGAL;

F.R.G.S.; F.S.S.; F.S.A.; M.R.A.S.;

FELLOW AND MEMBER OF THE SENATE OF THE UNIVERSITY OF CALCUTTA;

HONORARY MEMBER OF THE ROYAL GEOGRAPHICAL SOCIETY OF BERLIN.

1863.

CONTENTS.

CHAPTER I.

CHAPTER II.

CHAPTER III.

CHAPTER IV.

CHAPTER V.

CHAPTER VI.

ILLUSTRATIONS.

MAP.—The Great Andaman and Ajacent Islands.

ERRATUM.—Pp. 71 and 74, for *anthropological* read *anthropophagical.*

ADVENTURES AND RESEARCHES

AMONG

THE ANDAMAN ISLANDERS.

CHAPTER I.

INTRODUCTORY.

General Description of the Andaman Archipelago—Savage Character of the Inhabitants—The Great Andaman—The Middle Andaman—The South Andaman—The Little Andaman Sighted—Brief Notices of some of the Early Discoverers of this Group—Narrative of two Mohammedan Travellers in the Ninth Century—Their Absurd Description of the Natives—General Belief that the Inhabitants of the Andamans were Cannibals—Mysterious Fate of the Crew of a Ship wrecked on the Coast—Andaman Expeditions against the Nicobar Islands—Capture and Captivity of an Andaman Boy—Expedition under the Command of Captain Blair of the Indian Navy—His Survey of the Great Andaman—His Report addressed to the Marquis Cornwallis—Selection of a Convict Settlement—The Coral Reefs—General Accuracy of Captain Blair's Survey—His Speculations as to the Origin of the Natives and their Peculiar Character—Colonel Colebrooke's Account of the Andamans—Discovery of one of his Manuscript Journals—Visit to Chatham Island—Constant Hostility of the Natives—Colonel Colebrooke's Paper in the Asiatic Researches—Occasional

Notices—Account of the Andamans in the Calcutta "Monthly Register"—Port Cornwallis visited by Colonel Syme—Exaggerated Reports of the Climate—Port Cornwallis appointed the place of Rendezvous for the Fleet and Army in the First Burmese War—Reported Discovery of Gold—Death of Dr. Helfer—Peril of Two Troop Ships —Works on the Andamans—Occasion of the Present Work.

NEAR the centre of the track of one of the greatest highways of commerce, traversed by the ships of the most civilized and enlightened nations of modern times, lie a small group of islands, the name and position of which may be found in the map, although our knowledge of them is in general very limited. Forming an almost invisible dot on the map of the world, the civilization both of the East and of the West has passed them by without in any way affecting the condition of their inhabitants. In these islands man is probably still in the same condition in which he was when they were first settled—a state not only simple and primitive, but lower even than that of the natives of those remote islands of the sea that lie far beyond the bounds of civilization. Their inhabitants acknowledge no law to restrain and guide them in life. Not only have they no knowledge of a supreme Being, but they are even destitute of such a rude system of religious faith as is generally found even amongst men in the most savage state. Their language is harsh and disagreeable, in an imperfect state of development, barely sufficient for the expression of their few and simple wants. Totally ignorant of agriculture, they have no means of making provision for the future, and must be satisfied with such fruits and herbs as the earth spontaneously produces, or with the shell-fish they pick up on the shore. Their habitations are of that primitive and simple construction which suffices for the necessities of savage tribes constantly moving from place to place.

The Andaman Archipelago, the group of islands to which we allude, is situated in the Bay of Bengal, near the meridian of 93 deg. E., and between the 10th and 15th parallels of North latitude. The largest and most important of the islands is that termed the Great Andaman, the configuration of which is remarkable in one respect, namely that, consisting of three great tracts of land, divided from each other by narrow passages, it forms apparently one great island. About twenty miles to the southward is situated a second island, which, being considerably smaller than the other, is termed the Little Andaman. The surrounding waters are studded in many directions with numerous small islets, many of them exceedingly pretty and picturesque in appearance, rising as they do like beautiful oases in the wild waste of ocean that lashes their rocky shores. All of them are clothed with the richest tropical vegetation, which, from the level of the lowest swamp to the summit of the highest hill, grows in that unrestrained profusion in which Nature indulges in such climates. The entire group is surrounded in every direction by a natural fortress of coral reefs, which, extending for many miles, guards the approach to the islands, and in stormy weather, or in dark nights, renders it a matter of no little difficulty, and attended with considerable danger, to attempt to land upon them.

The inhabitants of the Andamans have always been considered one of the most savage races on the face of the earth, whom civilization has yet found it impossible to tame, or even almost to approach. From the earliest records we have, down to the most recent descriptions of their appearance and character, all accounts agree in this unfavourable representation of them. With such an unenviable reputation, and the opportunities of obtaining an accurate knowledge of them having been hitherto so few and unfavourable, much has never been known with regard to their actual condition, their habits and modes of life, or their origin and peculiar characteristics. The study of the race to which they belong also involves one of those ethnolological problems which yet remain to be solved; and although we may not be able to settle the question, it may at any rate be in our power, by means of the personal observations we have had an opportunity of making, to furnish some data by which a solution may be rendered easier to other inquirers.

In giving a more minute description of the Great Andaman, it may be observed that its western section is about forty-four miles in length, while its breadth may be computed at about an average of fourteen miles. In this part of the island is the magnificent harbour called Port Cornwallis, which, being locked in by land, affords a secure refuge for ships. The surface of this spacious natural harbour is diversified by several small islands, in one of which, in the year 1791, a place of refuge for such mariners as had the misfortune to be shipwrecked on that dreaded coast, and a burial settlement for those who sank under their hardship, were founded. They were discovered, however, to be in several respects unsuited for the purpose intended, and in the course of a few years were ultimately abandoned. The principal reasons for taking such a step, after a good deal of trouble and expense, were the extreme unhealthiness of the locality that had been selected, and the great additional expenditure that was requisite in order to supply those temporarily settled there with the various necessaries of life.

The Saddle Mountain is situated to the southward of Port Cornwallis, at the distance of a few miles. It rises to a considerable height, and forms the highest point to be seen in the whole group, its elevation being about 2,400 feet. On a favourable day, when the atmosphere is clear and cloudless, it is visible to the practised eye of the mariner at a distance of twenty leagues from the land.

The middle division, known as the Middle Andaman, is separated from the northern portion of the island by a narrow strait. It is somewhat larger than the latter, extending in length to fifty miles, and being fifteen miles in width. The narrow strait is quite innavigable, and on examining it we found that, at a distance of six miles from its eastern outlet, it became a mere mud marsh at low water. At its north-western extremity, on the other hand, it was ascertained that it opened into a fine broad expanse, forming an excellent and capacious harbour, with secure anchorage for ships, at the extremity of which is Interview Island, one of the largest detached islets of the whole group.

The South Andaman is forty-three miles in length,

and its average breadth about the same as that of the Middle division. On its eastern side there are two commodious harbours, to which the names of Port Meadows and Port Blair have been given. There are also two harbours on its western coast, distinguished as Port Mouat and Port Campbell. The strait by which the Southern Andaman is separated from the Middle is navigable throughout its whole extent; and near its western extremity is an extremely fine harbour, which has only recently been discovered by Major Haughton, the second superintendent of Port Blair. On the southern side of the South Andaman, from which it is separated by Macpherson's Straits, another small island is situated. It is known by the name of Rutland Island, and is nearly ten miles long, by four broad. The northern extremity of this island rises to a considerable height.

In the course of our voyage we sighted the Little Andaman, but after due consideration did not deem it advisable to land and examine it. In the first place, we knew that it contained no good harbours at which we could conveniently land, in order to carry on any explorations in the interior; and what weighed most with us, we were aware that it possessed none of those requisites of which we were specially in search, and was in no way adapted for a settlement to which convicts might be safely conveyed, and where they might be profitably employed.

Many conjectures, more or less probable, have been formed regarding the knowledge which the ancient geographers had of these islands. An opinion has been expressed by some modern writers, that with the Nicobars and some smaller islands, they were included by Ptolemy under the general appellation of the *insulæ bonæ fortunæ*. At that distant period, as now, they were supposed to be inhabited by a race of Cannibals, formidable not only to their enemies, but to all who approached their coasts—a sort of dreaded "anthropophagi, whose heads do grow beneath their shoulders."

It is not, however, till a period long posterior to the time of Ptolemy, that we obtain any information regarding them that can be considered authentic. Probably the first historical account we have is that contained in the narrative of the travels and adventures of two Mohammedan wanderers, who, in the ninth century, traversed great part of India and China. Their description of the islands, which they may have personally visited in the course of their travels, although it is not certain, was afterwards translated, and is quoted in Pemberton's Collection of Voyages and Travels. Their narrative gives a remarkably striking, though doubtless exaggerated representation of the natives. Their appearance is described as something truly frightful. Black in complexion, and with coarse frizzled hair, their countenances had a hideous and ferocious aspect, the effect of which was heightened by the fierce glances of their dark restless eyes. Their feet are described as huge and misshapen, no less than a cubit in length. They had no sort of garments to cover themselves with, but went about perfectly naked. The food in which they chiefly delighted was human flesh, which they tore up almost like wild beasts, and, ignorant of even the simplest form of cookery, devoured raw. It was believed that they possessed no kind of vessel on which they could venture out to sea, their intelligence being so limited that they had not then formed the notion of shaping for themselves canoes, even of the simplest form. This was considered a fortunate circumstance for the voyagers in these remote seas, for the natives might otherwise have lain in wait for them like pirates, or rather like the most ferocious beasts of prey, to supply themselves with stores of human flesh for the horrid banquet of blood in which it was their delight to indulge.

Ships were occasionally driven, by stress of weather, towards these unfrequented shores, or constrained to anchor near the coasts, for the purpose of procuring water; and when such was the case, it was rarely that they were permitted to sail away again without leaving a greater or less number of their crews behind, in the hands of their merciless captors, for such as, ignorant of the danger they incurred, ventured to land, scarcely set their feet upon the shore, before they were captured and dragged into the interior to encounter the horrors of a fate, of which death was the least.

We should not of course judge, from this absurd account, that the narrators themselves had ever visited the islands, or that they had any personal knowledge of their inhabitants. Their exaggerated description is probably made up of the rumours which were at that period current in the Eastern seas—rumours which, doubtless with some foundation in truth, were, at the same time, so highly coloured by the terror or credulity of imperfect knowledge, as to render them in many respects unworthy of belief. The Andamanese were, no doubt, sufficiently formidable and horrible, but when the imagination draws pictures under the influence of terror, we must hesitate before we can accept its representation as a faithful one.

There is another account of the Andaman Islands and their inhabitants, which dates from the early part of the reign of William III. This was the time when Aurungzebe was ruling the Moguls, and when the new and old East India Companies were carrying on those struggles for monopoly which ended in the formation of that grand corporation of merchants, which, after founding and ruling, *tant bien que mal*, one of the mightiest of Eastern empires, has recently become historic. The maritime adventurers of England, excited by the wildest rumours of the exhaustless riches of India, then fitted out ship after ship, in which they undertook this distant voyage, to return to Europe laden with the shawls, the silks, and precious stones of the East.

As mariners became better acquainted with the navigation of these seas, the Andamans were more frequently visited, and our knowledge of them begins to be more trustworthy and accurate. The more recent accounts that have reached us, however, are scarcely more favourable to the inhabitants. In the long period that has elapsed since the account of the Mohammedan travellers was given to the world, their moral and social state appears to have made little or no progress. They are still the same wild and untutored children of savage Nature. Invention, however, has so far been busy that they have learned to construct canoes, and sallying forth in them, to capture and slay all who are so unfortunate as to fall into their power. We have the same horrible accounts of their cannibal propensities. Their character is described as at once so fierce and fearless that they swim off to such vessels as approach their shores, and, regardless of the number of their crews, and their superiority in arms—not intimidated even by firearms, dealing death so mysteriously—they attack them boldly with their rude weapons, and maintain the unequal conflict as long as they have life and strength to inflict injury upon their enemies.

In Hamilton's account of the East Indies, allusion is made to the wreck of a ship, the crew of which, there is only too good ground for believing, were devoured by these untameable and merciless savages. This vessel, it appears, had set sail from Malacca, some time towards the latter part of the sixteenth century, and had made a prosperous voyage until she arrived in the vicinity of the Andamans; when, as ill fortune would have it, she drifted into a powerful current, against the force of which it was vain to strive; and being carried by the waves towards the threatening rocks that guarded that inhospitable shore, she was dashed upon them, and in a short time went to pieces. This sad event happened in sight of another ship, by which she had been accompanied during a considerable part of her voyage. The crew of the latter were spectators of the miserable fate that had befallen their fellow-voyagers; but being themselves in difficulties, and all their skill and energy being required to preserve themselves from the same fate, they were unable to render any assistance either to the ship-wrecked vessel or its crew. As none of these unfortunate castaways were ever seen or heard of again, there can be little reason for doubting that if any of them succeeded in reaching the land, they must have met the fate of so many other unfortunate voyagers, who, driven by stress of weather, or ignorant of the dreadful reports circulated regarding the natives, had suffered themselves to fall into their hands.

The narrator of this lamentable incident seems afterwards to have fallen in with a native of one of the Andaman Islands. Being at Acheen in the year 1694, he observed a man about forty years of age, whom he recognised as one of these "cannibal islanders." He appears to have been able to converse with him, and to have been successful in obtaining some information regarding the customs of his native tribe. Among other things, he was told that, in order to obtain food for the gratification of their horrid appetite, the savage Mincopies were in the regular habit of fitting out expeditions against the Nicobar Islands. A considerable number of the Andamanese having assembled at some appointed locality, in a large fleet of small prahus, they would then proceed against their more peaceful neighbours, numbers of whom they would mercilessly slaughter, and then carry off as many as they could capture alive, reserving them for a more hideous and appalling fate.

The inhabitants of the Nicobar Islands being of a more gentle and peaceful character than their Andaman neighbours, they were generally overcome without much resistance. But on one occasion despair seems to have inspired them with a greater amount of resolution and vigour than they usually displayed, and they formed the determination to unite their scattered bands, and present a bold front to the invader. The result was, that the aggressors, unprepared for so heroic a resistance, were conquered in their turn, and no quarter being given to them by their victorious enemy, immense numbers of them were slain.

The Mincopie just mentioned, from whom this information was obtained, was then a boy of about ten or twelve years of age, but he had already been accustomed to follow his father on the warlike expeditions in which he took a part. On this occasion, along with several other prisoners, he was captured and carried into captivity, his tender years alone saving him from the death which was the lot of so many of his fellow-islanders. He was kept about four or five years at Nicobar, being detained all that time in a state of slavery. Ultimately having been taken to Acheen, he was there delivered into the hands of new masters, who gave a quantity of cloth, knives, and tobacco in exchange for him.

A considerable change now took place in his position. His new masters being Mussulmans, they were anxious to convert him to their faith; and, having instructed him in its principles, he gratified them ere long by acknowledging his conversion to Mohammedanism. The master whom he served was so pleased at this, and with his general character, that on his death he left orders that he should be manumitted, and he was accordingly once more a freeman. A very natural desire now arose in his mind. It was long since he had seen his native land, and his kindred, from whom he had been separated by the fortune of war. He was anxious, therefore, to return to the Andamans, again to renew the ties that had been so long broken. As the season was favourable—for in the early part of the year the weather is always moderate and settled in these latitudes—he resolved at once to gratify an inclination which every day became more intense.

Few preparations were necessary before venturing to sea. The distance between the Andamans and the Nicobars is not great, the latter lying about seventy-two miles to the south. The nearest of the Andamans is said to be perfectly visible from a small island lying near Acheen. At this small island he embarked in a boat or canoe. Being alone, he had considerable difficulties to contend with; all of which, however, he successively surmounted, and soon experienced the joy of finding himself ashore on the Lesser Andaman. To the Andamanese, who had been drawn to the beach by his arrival on their island, he made himself known, and being recognised by his friends and relations, he was joyfully acknowledged. As he had long been given up for lost, the supposition being that he had perished in the fight in which he was taken captive, the welcome with which he was received was so much the more joyous.

His countrymen, of course, were eager to learn the history of his adventures during his long absence from among them; and as he had not forgotten his native tongue, though he was so young when taken prisoner, he was able to gratify their curiosity. He also endeavoured to communicate to them some portion of the knowledge he had acquired during his residence among a comparatively much more civilized race. His countrymen, as we have already remarked, were very ignorant and degraded. Their ideas were few, and their knowledge as limited as it could well be. They were totally unacquainted with spiritual truth of any kind. They had no kind of worship, not even the most gross, being entirely ignorant of the being and nature of a God. He accordingly endeavoured to communicate to them that idea of a Supreme Being which he had learned from the faith he had adopted. But their minds were obscured by long ignorance. No ray of light could penetrate the darkness in which their undeveloped intellects were shrouded; and at last he had to give up all attempts at instruction of any kind, as an utterly hopeless task.

After he had spent some time—about a month or two—among his countrymen and kindred, the restless disposition with which he must have been endowed, again awoke in him the desire of change, and he was now as anxious to return to the Nicobar Islands as he had formerly been to get away from them. His kindred, however, were jealous of him; they did not wish to lose him; and he was permitted to revisit the neighbouring islands only on one condition—he must promise faithfully to return. This condition being, of course, assented to, he was allowed to take his departure.

Having acquired, along with his other knowledge, some idea of articles that were valuable in commerce, he took with him a considerable quantity of quicksilver, with which he revisited the Nicobars. At the period he was seen and conversed with by the English voyagers to whom allusion has been made, he had passed several times between the two groups of islands, and he asserted that quicksilver could be obtained in considerable quantities in some of the Andaman Islands. Some Mohammedan Faquirs expressed an anxious desire to accompany him in some of his voyages, but they found it impossible to persuade him to allow this. So great, he asserted, was the ferocity of his countrymen, that even with such protection as he was able to afford, he could not assure them of their safety when they had once landed on the shores of any of the islands.

A considerable portion of the account of this Andaman adventurer was communicated to the narrator by a Syad in whose company he was seen when going as a passenger to Surat.*

Any knowledge we possess of the Andamans after this period is only to be derived from the short notices communicated by occasional voyagers who ventured to

* Hamilton's Account of the East Indies.—Pinkerton. Vol. viii., pp. 430-1.

touch at them. Indeed, almost a complete century elapses before we are able to collect additional information. During this long period they may be said to disappear altogether from the view of even the most curious inquirer.

Our information now becomes more trustworthy. In the latter part of the eighteenth century, two able men were sent to examine minutely the Andaman Islands, to survey their surface, and to collect as many important details concerning them as possible. The one was Captain Blair, one of the early hydrographers of the East India Company, and the other, Colonel Colebrooke, the Surveyor-General of India; by both of whom—men of great practical experience in operations of this nature—the islands were carefully surveyed. The operations, which were conducted under their superintendence, were finished in the year 1789.

Reports, minutely describing the method and results of their operations, were afterwards prepared by both officers, and submitted to the consideration of the proper authorities. Captain Blair's Report was ready in June, 1789, and was addressed to the Marquis Cornwallis, who, at that time, held the office of Governor-General of India. It not only contained a minute and accurate account of the survey conducted under the superintendence of that able and enterprising officer, but it was also illustrated by a chart in which the situation of most important localities was distinctly marked, accompanied with a plan of three harbours which he had surveyed and found to be secure places of refuge for the shipping that stress of weather or other causes might drive on the Andaman coasts.

The Report merited and obtained much praise for the clearness with which it was written, and the intelligible manner in which the various operations of the surveying party were described. The chief geographical features of the islands were delineated with a fidelity that has secured the approbation of subsequent explorers, for whom, indeed, in many important points little was left to do, unless it might be, in some cases, to fill up the details, the great outlines of which had been already sketched by a careful hand.

In one respect, Captain Blair's Report differed from all previous accounts of the islands. The inhabitants were described in such a manner as to leave a much more favourable impression on the mind of the reader, as to their character, manners, and customs, than the narratives of any former writers were calculated to impart. So favourable, indeed, was the impression conveyed, that it led the authorities to take measures for the formation of the first settlement on the Andamans. This settlement was in the southern island, and was originally known as Port Cornwallis—a name which was some time afterwards changed, that of Old Harbour being substituted for it, which in course of time also disappeared, the settlement being now known, in honour of the able officer by whom the island was surveyed, as Port Blair.

The necessity of a suitable penal settlement, to which the more heinous offenders who had been convicted by the judges on the Continent of India might be transported, had already begun to be felt, and those interested in the matter had turned their attention to the different localities that were thought likely to answer such a purpose, in order that the most suitable one might be selected. The impression in favour of Captain Blair's proposed settlement created by the able and complete manner in which he had performed his previous task was so strong and so general, that the establishment and regulation of the first convict colony was entrusted to him. With this important government service was also associated that of forming a harbour of refuge, to which European ships overtaken by storms in that part of the Bay of Bengal might betake themselves with safety, and in which such mariners as had the misfortune to be cast helpless ashore might find protection and care.

In order to fulfil the important mission with which he was charged, Captain Blair sailed from Calcutta in the month of September, 1789. The expedition under his charge was not on a large scale, the number of artificers and labourers by whom he was attended being limited. They were accompanied by a few Sepoys as a military guard to protect them, or at least to aid them in protecting themselves while engaged in their laborious and in some respects dangerous task. The chief of the undertaking was also directed to proceed with his surveying operations as soon as the vessels in which the expedition was conveyed could be spared from the service of the newly-established settlement.

On this occasion Captain Blair completed some portions of his survey which previously he had not had opportunity or time to execute. He sailed entirely round the Great Andaman, making in the course of his voyage several useful and important discoveries. Among the most so was that of a large and spacious harbour, admirably adapted for the safe anchorage of ships. Numerous inlets, by which the shores of the island were penetrated, were discovered and surveyed. Not the least important service he rendered to the commercial marine compelled to navigate these seas was the care with which he fixed the position, and described the figure and extent of those dangerous coral reefs by which the shores of the islands are in so many places rendered more than usually dangerous. The harbour which, as we have previously stated, now bears his name, he examined with the utmost care and minuteness, afterwards giving a detailed report of all his operations.

On the occasion of our visit we went over much of the ground that he had previously explored, and found that all his observations, even down to the minutest particulars, were scrupulously accurate. Indeed, it is impossible to estimate too highly the services his labours have rendered to that portion of the mercantile community whose ships traverse these latitudes. Not only were all hydrographic details noted with his unfailing minuteness and accuracy, but he communicated to the public many valuable observations on the peculiar difficulties that render the navigation of this part of the Indian sea so much more than usually dangerous. They were accompanied by sailing directions, the practical value of which may be estimated from the fact that to this day they continue to be consulted by all who require such trustworthy directions as will enable them to carry their vessels in safety through the dangers by which they may find themselves encompassed. Nor are the various incidental observations which he noted down while engaged in the performance of his more immediate duties to be passed over as of little interest or value, as in many of them we are made acquainted with facts of considerable practical importance.

His general description of the Andaman Archipelago is at once accurate and vivid. He draws the attention of the reader of his Report to the number and variety of the islands, and to the diversity of their appearance —the rugged cliffs by which they are defended against the encroachments of the ocean, and the luxuriant forests by which the various prospects in the interior are rendered so picturesque and attractive.

Captain Blair now found reason to modify the opinion he had expressed regarding the natives, as he found by experience that they were quite as rude and uncivilized as all preceding reports had concurred in representing them. From inquiries which he instituted, he came to the conclusion that the inveterate, deep-rooted hostility with which they regarded all strangers who approached their coasts, had its origin in the fact that they had once been in a state of slavery, and that the remembrance of their sufferings, which nothing could efface, was so vivid as to produce those feelings of enmity which nothing but the blood of all whom they regarded as their foes could assuage.

The traditions which have been preserved with regard

to the original peopling of the islands, do not carry us back to a very remote period. One of the very earliest ascribes their original occupation, at least by the present race of inhabitants, to some period about the commencement of the sixteenth century, when it is said a Portuguese ship, laden with slaves, was wrecked on the coasts of one of the islands while on her voyage from Mozambique. Apart altogether from the inherent improbability of such a story as this, it is known as a matter of certainty that the Andaman Islands were inhabited so early as the ninth century. Colonel Syme hints that the Arabs, who are known to have navigated the Indian Ocean as early as the seventh century, and who, in the course of their voyages, had not only explored the Chinese seas, and sailed round the immense continent of India, but had also acquired a knowledge of most of the islands of the Eastern Ocean, might, by some such accident as that ascribed to the Portuguese vessel, have peopled the Andamans with their present race of inhabitants, whom, however, he describes as negroes, a race not precisely resembling Arabs in their general features, form, and constitution.

The ethnological researches, however, of modern times, which have thrown so much light on inquiries of this nature, are entirely opposed to this supposition, on grounds the nature and force of which will be referred to hereafter. The Malays, who were accustomed to trade with the islands, for the purpose of procuring the birds' nests with which they abounded, are known to have been in the habit of kidnapping the natives, carrying them away with them, and either reducing them to the position of slaves among themselves, or selling them to others.

The character of the Malays is well known in the Eastern seas. Cruel and vindictive in their disposition, they delighted in inflicting on all who fell into their power the most cruel torments, and such as ventured to oppose them in the execution of their merciless projects had only one doom to expect. Captain Blair is of opinion that it was in consequence of the ill-treatment which they met with from these merciless pirates that the Andaman character became in many respects, and particularly in some localities, greatly changed for the worse. The people in the neighbourhood of Old Harbour, he found quite ready to reciprocate acts of kindness, when they saw that their white visitants came amongst them with no feelings of hostility. They showed themselves susceptible of impressions for which they had hitherto gained no credit. When confidence was established, they appeared happy in the enjoyment of intercourse with the strangers, and hence he thought he was not rash in concluding that the bad qualities, which they had no doubt often displayed in their intercourse with strangers and with the neighbouring islanders, were not, as it were, the foundation of their character, but in a great measure the result of the cruel treatment which they had themselves experienced from others, and particularly from a race so malicious and vindictive as the Malays.

Highly as the account of Captain Blair is to be recommended for its minuteness and accuracy of description, that of Lieutenant, afterwards Colonel Colebrooke, may be regarded in some respects as superior to it. When it first appeared, it was by far the most detailed account of the islands that had yet been given to the world. Its circulation, however, was confined mainly to those who took an interest in the progress of geographical discovery in the East, the work in which, in the year 1795, it was published, one of the early volumes of the Asiatic Researches, not being accessible to the public generally.

The value of the Colonel's information was greatly enhanced by the original illustrations of Andaman scenery by which it was accompanied. As he was an accomplished draughtsman, he was able to represent accurately the appearance of the natives, their abodes, their manner of life, and the various instruments of a warlike and domestic nature of which they made use.

Some of his original water-colour sketches are still in the possession of his surviving relations, by whom they are no doubt highly valued. They are characterised not only by that artistic delicacy of touch which the Colonel was known to possess, but also by an accuracy of detail which, even at this distance of time, can be recognized by those who are familiar with the appearance of the islands, and the more prominent features of their scenery, so exact is the presentment of the landscape which they give, and so small the appreciable change, after the lapse of so many years, in the distinctive features of the places represented.

A very valuable discovery was made some time ago in the course of some examinations which certain *employés* had been directed to make amongst the records in the office of the Surveyor-General in Calcutta. In the course of their researches, they came upon one of Colebrooke's manuscript works, which proved to be a journal that he had written during his first voyage to, and exploration of the Andaman Islands. As the manuscript was found to contain much original and valuable information, it was published a few years ago in the twenty-eighth volume of the Selections from the Records of the Government of India. The voyage was undertaken with the object of fixing the true geographical position of the islands, a duty which he accomplished with an accuracy not inferior to that manifested in the hydrographic survey assigned to Captain Blair.

The manuscript account of Colebrooke's survey is diversified by many light and amusing details. In the course of his voyage, the vessel visited the Diamond Islands, lying near the Tenasserim coast, which have always been remarkable for the number of turtle frequenting their shores, offering valuable prizes to the adventurous mariner. Diamond Island might be appropriately designated the Alderman's Ward of the Bay of Bengal. Lord Mayor's banquets need never be without their characteristic dainty while a locality with so abundant a supply is within the reach of our merchant vessels. In the short period of three days, Colonel Colebrooke's crew secured no fewer than one hundred and two of those valuable natives of the Eastern seas. Their dimensions and condition may be imagined from the statement that one of them was found sufficient to supply a ship's company of a hundred and eighty-five men with an ample supply of food for a day. Notwithstanding the rich harvest they had been so fortunate as to secure, it was with reluctance that they found themselves under the necessity of leaving behind fifty or sixty more which they might have easily appropriated. No doubt all who cast their parting looks upon them were calculating in imagination what they would realise for the kitchen of the Mansion-House. But the capacity of even the largest ships is limited, and there was no space for stowing away any more of them.

On the 25th of December, Colonel Colebrooke's expedition visited Old Harbour, Chatham Island, on which they landed, and were warmly welcomed by Blair and his companions, who had lately erected a small house of wood and canvas. This, however primitive and modest might be its accommodation, was still an agreeable change for those who had been for some time confined to those wooden walls within which they had been rudely buffeted by the waves.

Captain Blair's small party had been very active during their short stay. They had cleared some space in the vicinity of the harbour of the luxuriant vegetation by which it was encumbered, and had marked out the boundaries of a small garden, in which, as an agreeable diversion after their other labours, they had already commenced horticultural operations.

In company with Commodore Cornwallis, they made

preparations for an excursion up the harbour. In the barge with them was one of the natives of the Andamans, whom they had captured in a skirmish. The poor fellow unfortunately bore on his person a mark that would doubtless remind him for all time to come of the superiority of European arms over the primitive weapons of his fellow-countrymen. Notwithstanding this memento, the loss of one of his eyes by a pistol-shot, he seemed to bear no grudge to his captors; for he was evidently satisfied with his position, confident and fearless in his intercourse with all on board; his appearance being that of a perfectly quiet, cheerful, and contented man.

The progress of the barge was observed by numbers of the aborigines, who watched its movements from the shore. As they had no knowledge of the object for which their white visitors had come, it is no matter of wonder that their suspicions were excited, as was evident from the hostile attitude which they assumed as the vessel gradually approached the position they had taken up. On the barge entering the harbour, their manifestations of hostility became too plain to admit of any doubt as to the feelings with which they regarded the strangers who had ventured among them.

When it was necessary for the boats to approach the shore, that the sailors might land for the purpose of obtaining a supply of water, the natives were always ready to drive them back by showers of stones and arrows. As the men, in compliance with the desire of their superior officers, were unwilling to have recourse to extreme measures with them, this reluctance to attack was regarded as fear of their prowess; and their daring growing in consequence of this conviction, they even ventured to approach the ships at anchor near the island. As they persevered in these attacks, it became necessary to resist them, and some skirmishes ensued. A native being at last killed in one of them, his companions, filled with alarm, took to flight, setting up most doleful lamentations for the loss of their countryman.

The party being now left at peace, they proceeded with their exploration of the harbour, and having sailed up a salt creek at its extremity, they then returned, again landing on their way back to examine a small solitary hut which they had remarked on the shore. No inhabitants, nor any living creatures, were found in it, although there was evidence of the former presence of natives in the quantity of bones of the white hog which were found suspended from the roof by strings. The floor was also strewed with a numerous collection of the shells of oysters, muscles, cockles, and other shellfish, on which the inhabitants had probably banqueted, for these form their principal articles of food when they can no longer procure that luxury in which they are reported to delight.

At another point, on turning his attention inland, one of the party discovered a native seated aloft on a tree. It was not long before the recognition was mutual, for he began making a great noise, probably to warn a number of the other natives, who were observed at the foot of the tree, and at least one of whom was conjectured, from the sound of her voice, to be a woman.

He then lost no time in descending from an eminence which he no longer considered consistent with personal safety, making his way to *terra firma* with all the speed and agility of a monkey. The English being anxious, not only to attract their attention, but also to acquire their confidence, and make acquaintance with them, all sorts of friendly signs and gestures were made to induce them to remain. Two or three cocoa nuts were also thrown to them as tokens of friendship, which they were not so prompt in appropriating as it was anticipated they would have been. Their uneasiness was probably excited by the vicinity of the boat to the shore, for they were suspicious to an inconceivable degree. The sailors therefore rowed off to a greater distance, on which one of the natives ventured to approach the object of his desire, still, however, looking about him with caution, as if he expected every bush to conceal an enemy. His suspicious movements excited much amusement, resembling, as those who are familiar with their habits know, the movements of a crow in similar circumstances—first hopping towards a coveted morsel, then retreating timidly from it, but still with his eye fixed upon the pleasant bait, which at last he snaps up, and flies victoriously off with,—such were the movements of this wild savage, until, getting within arm's length of the tempting object, he snapped it up in a moment, and was off like a cannon ball.

In the afternoon of the same day they saw another native wandering about on the shore, who, being either less timid than the one just mentioned, or not aware of their approach, was accosted without difficulty, stopping, though at a little distance, to hold a short conference with us. He was a man of middle height, and tolerably well-shaped; one whom nature had not treated amiss, but who, indulging the strange taste of the savage for adornment, had rendered himself a most disagreeable object to look upon. Some kind of red earth had been rubbed into and over his woolly head; and the remainder of his body was smeared, in the way of ornament, with mud. Round his neck and left arm he wore ornaments resembling a fringe of dry grass. He was very cautious in not allowing the distance at which our interview had been commenced to be at all diminished. The fear of being kidnapped was evidently ever present to his mind, and his knowledge of us was too limited and too recent to inspire him with any confidence. Every one of the party, therefore, was kept at the distance he chose to assign, although in all other respects he seemed quite free and easy, and to enjoy the conversation by signs and nods, and gestures, which evidently amused him not a little. The only arms, either offensive or defensive, which he carried with him, were a bow and arrows, which he readily consented to exchange for a knife. He had, under his arm, a small wicker basket, in which he deposited everything given to him—among other things, some handfuls of biscuit—which he was observed to devour with avidity, immediately after we had taken leave of him, and resumed our places in the boat.

On the 27th of December an event occurred which

showed that the benefits of civilization were not appreciated by the savage mind, and that even after experience had made him acquainted with the two modes of life, he still preferred his own. A native had been received on board of one of the English vessels, and was in every way well-treated—among other things, a suit of sailor's clothes having been given to him, which he constantly wore, apparently pleased with his appearance in them. Indeed, the impression was that he was quite reconciled to the change in his condition, and had some notion of the benefits it secured to him. So sure did the officers and crew feel of this, that he was allowed to enter a boat and go ashore, although it was the intention of the party to land at a point where a group, consisting of several natives, was visible at the time. As the boat approached the land, he gave some indications of his joy at seeing them, which being considered only natural, little notice was taken of it. But all eyes gazed with an unequivocal expression of astonishment, when, at a short distance from the beach, he suddenly leaped out of the boat, swam and waded ashore, and then ran off full speed in the direction of his countrymen. So rapid was the whole performance, that he was far beyond their reach before any one thought of making an attempt to detain him. As he approached his old friends, however, instead of joyfully greeting and receiving him, they stared with undisguised astonishment, and seemed inclined to resort to hostile measures against him. The fact was, that fully equipped as a Christian,—in a sailor's hat, jacket, and trousers,—they did not recognize him. He seemed to become at once conscious of this himself, for in a moment he snatched off his hat, and flung it to the ground, whipped off jacket, trousers, and shirt, and stood displayed *in puris naturalibus* before the ladies and gentlemen of his tribe. The transformation was complete, and he was apparently recognized with as much joy and satisfaction as that with which the little boys and girls greet the change which introduces the Clown in a Christmas pantomime.

The escape of the "noble savage" was evidently a matter of hearty congratulation among them all. Without giving a thought to those he had left behind, he scampered off with his recovered friends, and they soon all disappeared in the woods together.

The exploring party, in the course of their rambles, again fell in with the native who had bartered his bow and arrows for a knife. He seemed quite as disposed for a little conversation as on the former occasion, the nature of a civilized gossip being to some extent grafted on that of the silent savage. The party came upon him unexpectedly as he was sitting by a fire among the rocks, intently watching some shell-fish which he was roasting. He had companions this time—a woman and a little girl—both like himself perfectly naked, unless the usual thick coat of mud can be considered any substitute for clothing. These took no part in the short conversation held with their male companion, but remained at a little distance, eyeing the strangers in such a manner as showed that their fears and suspicions had not been altogether quelled. After this occasion very little intercourse was held with any of the natives, for they were evidently disposed to indulge in some of their more mischievous tendencies, and made unequivocal demonstrations of their hostility.

The paper of Colonel Colebrooke, in the volume of the Asiatic Researches, is altogether a very valuable one. It is full of the most useful information, diversified with interesting anecdotes. A more satisfactory account of the physical character, vegetable products, and general scenery of the islands, is nowhere to be found. At the time of its appearance it contained much that was altogether new respecting the appearance, manners, customs, dwellings, canoes, arms, and implements of the inhabitants. To his paper is appended a brief vocabulary of the Andaman language, to which little that is new has since be added. We endeavoured with its aid to make ourselves understood by some of the natives whom we captured; but the attempt was a mortifying failure, for we were unable to make any of them comprehend a single word we used. As Paddy said to the Frenchman, when he asked for the "loan of a gridiron," they did not understand their own language. "No," probably they might have replied, with Claude Melnotte "not as you pronounce it." Indeed, there can be little doubt that our want of success was principally owing to our defective pronunciation, correctness in which is always one of the best tests of a professing linguist's mastery of a language.

Occasional notices of the Andaman Islands and their inhabitants have appeared from time to time in the Indian and other periodicals of the day. Generally they contain little or nothing that is new, their statements being derived or abridged from those of previous travellers and writers. Any new account, the genuine production of one who has visited the islands, serves only to confirm the previous descriptions of the group, the luxuriant beauty of the scenery, and the savage, inhospitable character of the inhabitants.

In the *Calcutta Monthly Register*, for November, 1790, is contained a brief account of the Andamans. The article is written with considerable ability; and although it can scarcely be said to do more than corroborate the statements of Blair and Colebrooke, yet as the periodical is scarce in England, and the number long out of print, I reproduce some portions of the sketch, which are so short and graphic that they cannot fail to gratify the intelligent reader:—

"The Andamans are on the eastern side of the Bay of Bengal; they bear about south half west of Point Negrais, about 130 miles distant. The Great Andaman extends in length, north and south, about two degrees and a quarter of latitude; viz., from 14° to 11° 45′ North. The Little Andamans are a cluster of islands in the latitude of about 10° 30′ North. The longitude of the Andamans is about six hours and eight minutes east of London.

"These islands, from their situation and appearance, had long been considered by navigators as possessing no importance; they were, therefore, little known or attended to by our eastern rulers. Pulo-Penang had been given by the King of Quida to Mr. Light, and by him to the Honourable the East India Company; and a settlement had been recently established there, when the Honourable Commodore Cornwallis, with the squadron under his command, arrived in India.

"Shortly after the Commodore's arrival, the harbour of this new settlement, and that of the Great Andaman, were minutely and accurately surveyed, by order of the Supreme Government, and the proper officers ordered on that duty; but the particulars of their official reports, or the consequent intentions of Government, have not yet been made public.

"Port Cornwallis is situated on the eastern side of the Great Andaman, and is discovered to be a noble, capacious harbour, with most excellent anchorage, and capable of containing three hundred sail of ships of the largest size or greatest burden.

"The face of the country is covered with lofty trees and thick underwood, the former affording most excellent timber, either for domestic uses or ship-building. The soil, however, is excellent; and if we may judge from the experiment made by the gentlemen of the fleet, who cleared a spot of ground, and, upon sowing various seeds, found them thrive beyond their expectation, it is capable of bringing all vegetables to as great perfection as any other part of India can boast.

"From the temperature of the climate, we are led to imagine that upon a further trial we shall rather be induced to confirm than to alter this opinion. During the south-west monsoon, a cool steady breeze constantly predominates; and at the other part of the year, when the north-east monsoon sets in, the wind is sometimes intensely sharp during the night, but decreases into a gentle sea-breeze during the day. As a convincing proof, however, of the salubrious air and healthy atmosphere with which heaven has blessed this hitherto forlorn part of the globe, we need but instance that out of two hundred men belonging to a ship upon this voyage, towards the close of last year, there was not a single invalid; but, on the contrary, several who had left Bengal with troublesome complaints, were completely restored to health very shortly after their arrival.

"The manner in which these islands were peopled is a matter of mere conjecture. We are told that when the Portuguese had a settlement near Pegu, two of their ships, with cargoes of slaves on board, amounting in number of men and women to 300, were cast away there; and as the inhabitants are of the Coffree caste, it must be allowed that probability favours this opinion or conjecture. They are a strong, robust set of Coffrees, and in their appearance and mode of living resemble much what Cook describes to us of the inhabitants of the south-west part of New Zealand. Both men and women go entirely naked; the former armed with bows and arrows, which they employ in shooting fish for their subsistence. In this instance we perceive a want of instinct which neither fails the rude inhabitants of New Holland, the simplicity of those of the Sandwich Island, nor the gloomy, uncultivated mind of the Nootka Sound men, who all employ some kind of a hook and line for the purpose of catching fish. The women, at low water, wade the mud flats, and search the reefs for cockles and other shell-fish; and as the tide rises, they retire to their huts to roast this casual provender. When a supply of fish fails them, they roam into the woods in quest of wild hogs and rats (the only animals that were perceived in that country), and which they are sometimes fortunate enough to procure, as the bones about their huts testify. These are, however, by no means plenty, and it is to be supposed, from the few that were seen by our people, that they are a *dernier ressort* when the calls of hunger are very pressing.

"So far we have been able to give a brief account of the origin and manner of living of these people, who are probably destined by the hand of Providence to come under our protection, and to participate in the blessings of civilization. The shyness they have hitherto shown, and the want of confidence they have betrayed, may easily be accounted for; nor is it to be doubted but that when once they experience the advantages of commerce and the benefit of our friendship, our intercourse will be permanent; and that they may be taught to enjoy the fruits of a well-directed industry and a civilized government."

Port Cornwallis was visited by Colonel Symes, on his way to Ava, in 1795. In the absence of Colonel Kyd, the governor of the settlement, he was received by Captains Ramsay and Stakol. In the evening, Colonel Symes and the party accompanying him were conducted over the grounds that had been cleared in Chatham

Island. They walked round them, making a circuit of a little more than a quarter of a mile, the path they selected being partly along the beech, its beautiful silver sands reflecting the glorious crimson rays of the setting sun, and partly by a path leading through those dense masses of brushwood that encumber the island, and among the gigantic trunks of the huge trees that had recently fallen before the blows of the woodman's axe. They were also conducted to a small garden, which had been laid out with great taste, and carefully cultivated; but the crop it yielded—a very scanty one of Indian vegetables—formed but an insufficient reward for all the labour they had expended on it. The settlement was established on an eminence of moderate height, which rose abruptly from the margin of the sea. The houses of the Commandant and officers appeared to be extremely comfortable, as were also the huts inhabited by the inferior classes of settlers. In the construction of the former, stone and planks had been employed; the latter were formed of mats and clay, thatched with the leaves of the rattan. The whole colony, including guards and convicts, numbered seven hundred souls.

The situation of this original settlement rendered it a very pleasant and attractive place of residence, for nothing could be more picturesque and romantic than the scenery amidst which it was established. The great defect was the character of the people, the barbarism of whom was described by those who were settled among them as transcending all that had ever been experienced of savage life in any other part of the world. It is quite possible that when European settlers come to look upon their native neighbours with anything but a favourable eye, exaggerated reports are easily raised and circulated, particularly among the servants and workmen, sailors and soldiers, if any. But, making all such allowances, it is strange how completely all accounts of the Andamanese, at all periods in which we have any information regarding them, agree in representing them as the *ne plus ultra* of all that is savage and barbarous in life, character, and manners. Some ideas regarding a form of religion which they were said to hold were circulated, and credited by such as take such statements on trust; but a careful inquiry instituted on the spot proved that they were apocryphal. The dislike that was entertained for the people, and the aversion which all but the most self-sacrificing felt for settling in a place where there were so many dangers, led even to the creation and circulation of the most unfavourable reports regarding the climate—all highly exaggerated. It was said, for instance, that the rains descended in torrents for eight months in the year, that the settlers were eaten up with scurvy during the dry months, from December to March, and that during the remainder of the year, the incurable agues, and other painful diseases arising from the insalubrious atmosphere, rendered the place a perfect purgatory, fit to be used only for such a purpose as that originally intended, viz., a convict settlement, for the punishment, or rather torment, of the most profligate and abandoned criminals.

A considerable period must now elapse before anything more is heard of the Andamans, the perverse barbarity of the natives, which no assurances of friendship could subdue, having apparently induced the inhabitants of all the civilized parts of the world in their vicinity to leave them to their own devices. Their former reception of strangers had in no single instance been encouraging, and no one therefore felt tempted to venture again on expeditions which had already proved so fruitless of any good result. Only the occasional account of some shipwreck, accompanied with circumstances of unusual barbarity, reminded the world, from time to time, of the existence of these dark places of the earth, truly the abodes of cruelty.

In the year 1824, the fleet which carried the army of Sir Archibald Campbell to Rangoon in the first Burmese war, assembled at Port Cornwallis, in obedience to the order which appointed that locality as their general rendezvous; and the few incidents of interest that occurred during their short sojourn are very briefly referred to by Snodgrass and Havelock, the latter of whom at that time held the appointment of adjutant to the 13th Regiment of Foot. But all attempts to hold intercourse with these wild and suspicious savages proved vain. Their forests were impenetrable, and nothing could tempt them to venture beyond their precincts, where alone they considered themselves in safety from so numerous a host of armed visitors.

In the year 1839, the Andaman Islands again come under our notice in a new aspect. A report had obtained circulation that the beds of the streams, the soil, the rocks, abounded with the precious metals. Accordingly Dr. Helfer, a Russian *savan*, who at that time happened to be in the temporary service of the government of India, buoyed up by the belief that gold was to be found in abundance, visited the islands to prosecute a search which he had every reason to believe would be successful. He was prevented, however, from carrying his adventure to a successful issue by the lamentable fate which befell him. He had begun his explorations a little to the northward of Port Cornwallis, landing on the island every day in a boat under the charge of Lascars. There appears to have been an element of rashness in his disposition, and he despised the rude natives too much to take such measures of precaution as were necessary to secure his own safety. The consequence was, as might have been expected, that one day, on landing, he was attacked by the savages, and in the skirmish which followed had the misfortune to lose his life. Rash and headlong himself in venturing into scenes of danger, without taking such precautions as a wise prudence would dictate, his unfortunate death was also in no small degree to be attributed to the cowardly abandonment of the Lascar crew of the boat in which he landed.

In 1844, two troop ships, the *Briton* and the *Runnymede*, with detachments of the 50th and 80th regiments of foot on board, were driven close to the islands by stress of weather, and all the means that were taken either to keep them out at sea, or to obtain timely entrance into a secure haven, proving unsuccessful, they were driven hopelessly, at the mercy of the waves, towards the shore of one of the islands of the Andaman archipelago, where, despite all the efforts that were made to avert such a fate, it appeared impossible to avoid utter destruction. According to all accounts the night was intensely dark, and, from the impossibility of making out where they were, their position appeared hopeless. The tempest, too, before which they were driven, was one of those tremendous hurricanes the fury of which mariners must occasionally face in navigating these tropical seas. Most must have seen that an ocean death was their unavoidable doom, for what hope could men entertain, driven before a tempest loud enough almost to wake the dead, and in a darkness so intense that they could not see each other's faces, or their own hands held up close before their eyes? In one of the ships, on board of which was the narrator of this calamity, the deck was crowded with bands of soldiers, useless in such circumstances; to move was impracticable, and the men were therefore sent to their berths, to await in silence and resignation what appeared to be their certain doom—for, from the dashing noise caused by the terrific strife of the elements, no human sound could be heard. The soldiers, seeing that their fate was to all appearance inevitable, submitted with the implicit obedience of military discipline, and each one was allowed to give himself up to those meditations with which he thought it most becoming to meet death. Suddenly what appeared to be a tremendous lurch was made by the vessel; then all movement ceased. After a moment of anxious expectation, a deep awe fell upon every one, for it was believed that the doomed ship was foundering. This, however, was a mistake. The vessel remained still and motionless, as if suddenly arrested in her headlong career to destruction. Most thought that daylight would never appear to them again, and yet with what trembling anxiety was it awaited by all! Those only who have lived through such a night of peril can imagine what their feelings must have been—the alternations of hope and despair that by turns reigned paramount. The first streak of dawn enabled them to see a sight the reality of which they could scarcely credit, so different was it from all they had imagined—from the appalling death they had dreaded. The vessel appeared to be surrounded, not by an ocean of waves, but by an ocean of leaves. The branches of the giants of the primeval forests, interlaced with each other, spread over the deck of the motionless ship, which, as they afterwards discovered, had been driven right over a dangerous reef into that interminable jungle, in the midst of which there is safety even from the mighty force of the tornado. Presently the curtain of night was altogether withdrawn by the rosy fingers of morning. The spars of another vessel, hard and fast on the outer edge of the reef, were perceived, and unspeakable was their joy when her decks also were seen to be crowded by the daring warriors who afterwards shared with them the scarcely less deadly perils of the great battle-fields of the Sutlej.

Although the troops on board the two ships, thus marvellously delivered from almost certain destruction, were some hundreds in number, all well armed, and perfect in discipline, yet such was the savage fury of the natives that they hesitated not to attack small bands of them. The restless savages, concealed themselves by the impenetrable forest, were constantly on the watch for opportunities of attack, and any one who was so inconsiderate as to straggle a short distance from his companions became their inevitable aim, and was shot at with their long arrows, which inflicted troublesome, painful, and, in some cases, dangerous wounds. Every attempt was made to conciliate them, but the unyielding obstinacy of their dispositions appeared invincible.

The accounts of the Andaman Islands contained in works on Geography are evidently borrowed from the sources above mentioned, occasionally, as will be seen from the following references, embroidered by the fancy of the writers. In Meyer's "Grosse Conversations Lexicon," they are represented to be mountainous, covered with forests of teak, turpentine, and the purple Dracona, which is said to afford excellent materials for ship-building. The inhabitants are described as small, ugly, uncivilized negroes, and very warlike. In Bergham's "Conversations Lexicon"—the Leipsic edition of 1854—the islands are said to be rich in minerals and metals, and their luxuriant forests to afford excellent building timber. Mention is made of the unsuccessful attempts to colonize them by the English, while speculations are hazarded as to the issue of later efforts of the Dane and French, showing that they have been grouped with the Nicobars, from which they are as distinct as Denmark is from France. In the *Encyclopedie des Gens du*

Monde, monkeys and parroquets are said to abound, and the inhabitants, who are represented with woolly hair and flat noses, are described as being partially clothed.

The continually recurring outrages committed by the natives of the Andaman Islands on such shipwrecked mariners as had been thrown by the tempests on their inhospitable shores, were at length carried to such a formidable extent that the Government of India was imperatively called on to interfere. In the year 1855, therefore, when this matter became so urgent that it could no longer be neglected, the measures proposed as a remedy for the evil were taken into consideration without any further delay. The object in view was not only to make the islands safe asylums for those who had the misfortune to be wrecked on their coasts, but also to utilize them in such a way as would prove ultimately beneficial to the inhabitants themselves, supposing their suspicious fears overcome, and their confidence gained. Two plans were accordingly proposed. One was the formation of a harbour of refuge on a suitable part of the coast, the expediency of which was generally admitted. The second was the establishment of a penal settlement on the principal island, in the most advantageous locality that could be selected. The advisability of carrying this proposal into effect was under discussion in the Indian Council at the time when the late dreadful mutiny broke out in 1857. Startling the world by its sudden, savage, and unprovoked nature, its immediate effect was to lay all such useful measures and plans in abeyance for the time; and it was not until the neck of this treacherous rebellion was completely broken that the subject was again submitted to the Councils of Government, in circumstances that rendered a speedy decision necessary. A settlement was now required to which those misguided agents of the late mutiny, whose crime, however great, was not attended with circumstances of such unpardonable atrocity as rendered imperative the forfeiture of their lives, might be transported. There were many whose hands had not been actually imbued in blood, yet who, from the share they had openly taken in the revolt, could not with safety be included in any measure of amnesty, however comprehensive, until either the last traces of disaffection had entirely disappeared, or the natives of India were thoroughly convinced that any further attempt at rebellion against the authority of England must infallibly be put down. It was believed that the transportation of these mutineers to the Andaman Islands would be an adequate punishment for the crime of which they had been guilty. There was something poetical in the retributive justice that thus rendered the crimes of an ancient race the means of reclaiming a fair and fertile tract of land from the neglect, the barbarity, and the atrocities of a more primitive, but scarcely less cruel and vindictive race, whose origin is yet involved in such a dark cloud of mystery.

To the combination of these causes is due the visit which I paid to the Andaman Islands in 1857, some of the more prominent incidents of which I propose to narrate in the following sketch of my proceedings.

CHAPTER II.

The Month of November, 1857—Events in India—The "Black Watch"—State of Feeling among the European Inhabitants during the Mutiny—The Author appointed to the Charge of the Andaman Expedition—Dr. Playfair and Lieutenant Heathcote—Last Evening in Calcutta—Lady Canning—The Governor-General—The Telegraphic Despatch—Preparations for the Expedition—Paucity of Records of Former Expeditions—The Steam Frigate *Semiramis*—Captain Campbell—Goa Musicians—The Scotch Bagpipes—Sandy's Peculiarities—Arrival at Moulmein—Pleasant Scenery—Monsieur Mallitte, our Photographer—Attentions of the Commissioner of the Province—Burmese Pioneers—Savage Implements of Destruction—Experiments with Poisoned Arrows—Information communicated by an Amateur Traveller—An Old Lady's Fears—The *Pluto* ready for Sea—Departure from Moulmein—A Crew of Various Nations—Sailors' Yarns—Opium-eating Malays—Sea qualities of the *Pluto*—Exaggerated Ideas respecting the Mincopies—The Island of Narcoudan—Character of the Scenery—Profuse Vegetation—Saddle Hill—Remains of Blair's Original Settlement.

The month of November, 1857, was distinguished by the number of important events which took place within that short period, all of so stirring a nature as to produce no small amount of excitement among the English community in Calcutta. The expectation of all constantly strained for the reception of news relating to the fate of hundreds of their fellow-countrymen, and, in many cases, of their nearest relatives, it was with an amount of enthusiasm that has rarely been paralleled that a series of historical events, on which depended the safety and preservation of our Anglo-Indian empire, and of the devoted soldiers who were freely venturing their lives to maintain the authority and *prestige* of England in some of its finest provinces, were made known in rapid succession, within that limited space of time, to the English inhabitants of the capital of India. Delhi, which was regarded by the natives with so much veneration, had fallen before the victorious arms of our troops, who signalized themselves by many an act of valour and devotion. In every field of battle where they had met the mutineers, however great the odds, they had overcome them. The beleaguered garrison of Lucknow, in almost daily apprehension of the same fate that had befallen the unhappy captives of Cawnpore, was for a time relieved by the heroic band that followed the devoted Havelock and the chivalrous Outram, who has but recently paid the penalty of a life of devotion in the military service of his country. The last descendant of the long and illustrious line of the Mogul Emperors, the pensionaries of their conquerors, was now a captive in the hands of British troops. The infamous author of the massacre at Cawnpore, and the ubiquitous Tantia Topee, were now wretched fugitives, fleeing from the fate they had merited by their treachery and cruelty. Everywhere the troops of the rebels were defeated—they were without leaders on whom they could depend; they were harassed by disputes among themselves, and the glowing hopes with which they had renounced their allegiance as soldiers, and thrown themselves into the mutiny, had faded before the successive defeats which they met with at the hands of comparatively small bodies of English troops.

About the same time, after the conquest of Delhi had been achieved, an avenging column marched from that city, with the intention of joining the small army that followed the Commander-in-Chief, and striking the decisive blow by which the conquest of Oude was to be achieved. Another column of troops was in Central India, where, under the command of that able general, Sir Hugh Rose, it was baffling the enemy by feats of strategy which recalled to the memory of all who were familiar with the Indian exploits of the Great Duke, his early career as a leader in the same country. How often, at that period, were the inhabitants of the metropolis of British India excited to the expression of their patriotic enthusiasm by such military spectacles as few of them had ever witnessed before! The city was all aglare with the pride and panoply of glorious war. Regiment after regiment of noble-hearted warriors, glowing with the hope of effecting the deliverance of their beleaguered countrymen, and of avenging the murdered victims of Cawnpore, were marched off without delay, as soon as they arrived from England, to complete the great work for which such commanders as Nicholson and Niel had shed their blood, and for the successful issue of which there was not a man that was not willing to expend the last drop of his own. There were seen in military array, drawn up before admiring thousands, the kilted giants of the Black Watch, and "all plaided and plumed in their tartan array," the distinguished regiment whose "thin red line" had checked the advance of the Muscovite cavaliers at Balaclava. These troops, clad in a costume so novel to the inhabitants of Eastern countries, were gazed on with mingled feelings of wonder and fear by crowds of the astonished natives, among whom all sorts of incredible rumours were circulating respecting them, and who could not believe that they belonged to the same race whom they had been accustomed to see daily in the streets of Calcutta and other cities of India. When at last their pipers struck up the notes of some warlike tune that was strange to almost every ear that heard it, and, in obedience to the word of command, the whole body marched off with steady tread and stately mien, the wailing yet martial notes of the pibroch sounding along the quays of the city of mourning, they were greeted by the friendly farewell of thousands in whose hearts the very sight of their determined countenances and martial demeanour had inspired a certain confidence that in good time they would be able to render a satisfactory account of the expedition on which they were sent.

Yes, at this time, as we well remember, dismay, uncertainty, and anxiety had given way to hope and confidence. Our troops, though few in comparison with the numerous bands of our dingy enemy, were in every way so superior to them, in personal strength, in military discipline, in arms, and in *morale*, as it is termed, that we felt it was no presumptuous confidence by which we were inspired, but a well-founded rational hope. Peel's guns, managed by his dauntless sailors, had shaken the walls of the palace in the plain, and had startled the timid inhabitants of the densely peopled bazaars that extended a considerable distance along the banks of the muddy Hooghly. The gloomy misgivings which, at the commencement of the revolt, many could not but entertain, were now experienced only by those whose reckless folly had caused it. We had dismissed all those melancholy forebodings which had so long thrown a veil of mourning over all the circumstances and relations of our lives. We could look with confidence into a future which no longer threatened us with calamities that were magnified by fear and uncertainty.

The state of feeling prevalent at this time in the minds of the European inhabitants of the City of Palaces, few who were then resident in it can ever forget; for there were few that were not personally affected by the recurring events of each day. Many a pale face was encountered on the street—many a trembling lip saluted you in the house; for the numerous fugitives from scenes of horror, almost unparalleled in their cold-blooded atrocity, could not, even in the midst of their newly-born joy and confidence, dismiss from their minds the remembrance of scenes that had nearly frozen the life-blood in their veins. The assurance of safety, the freedom from fear, that all felt, was, in numerous cases, combined with sad and gloomy recollections. The names of Cawnpore, Futtighur, and of other places, were associated in the minds of many a mourner with the names of those dearest and nearest to them, who had perished in these scenes of horror. The atrocities by which these localities had been distinguished were well calculated to make the blood of even the boldest flow back from the face, and leave the cheek pale and livid. Even in the minds of those who gazed with admiration and confidence on the departing forms of the devoted soldiers, clouds of misgiving would arise to darken their joy, and to mingle their confidence with fear. Many had kinsmen in these hosts of warriors, and how soon might the exultation with which their departure for the deadly arbitrement of war was regarded, be changed into the sorrow with which the news of death, or of captivity worse than death, would be received. All felt that any hour might bring the most melancholy news—that the heart that now exulted in the hope of national victory, might ere long be called to mourn the death of husband, brother, or other near relative. Still, on the whole, the general feeling was one of joy. Human nature is fortunately so constituted, that it can enjoy the present sunshine, even though it knows the cloud that threatens disaster or death is about to break overhead. All were ultimately inspired by one general feeling of confidence, and only a few brooded perseveringly over the losses, the disasters, the misfortunes, which, though they might undoubtedly come to them, were yet but mere possibilities.

However, whatever might be the feelings of the heart at such a moment, no face betrayed any mark of craven fear. In that comparatively small community of Europeans, there was not one to whom the term coward could be applied. All felt that the revolt must be suppressed, and every foot of the country regained, no matter at what cost of blood or treasure. No voice counselled half measures. Every effort that was requisite to secure our superiority must be made with vigour and without delay. Such was the feeling of all in whose veins flowed English blood—from the calm, dauntless, noble-minded ruler of the country, the representative of the Empress Queen of Hindostan, to the humblest individual of the Saxon race. The manhood of the representatives of England in India was fairly roused. If there were pale faces, the pallor arose from no feeling that a brave man need disavow. The determination to face any peril, however imminent, was universal, and to despair of their country in almost any circumstances that could have occurred, would have been regarded as a disgrace—almost a crime.

It was at such a time, so absorbing to all who take any interest in the affairs of their country, that I was called upon to undertake a distant voyage. So completely was I pervaded by the feelings which I have just described as universal, that I might have wished to remain at the great seat of Indian government, especially at a moment when decisive and interesting information from the scenes where warfare was still carried on was expected. But, however anxious I may have been to hear at the earliest possible moment of the release of the heroes of Lucknow, as a public servant my duty was to render instant and uncomplaining obedience. When, therefore, I was summoned, at a few hours' notice, to form part of an expedition which was to proceed without delay to the Andaman Islands, I immediately directed all my energies to the fulfilment of this duty, and to making preparations for my departure without loss of time.

The object of the expedition which I was called upon thus suddenly to join was to explore the coasts of these islands of the Indian sea, to examine how far they were adapted for the establishment of a convict station, and to select a suitable site for such a settlement. It was my good fortune, in this enterprise, to be associated with able, intelligent, and agreeable associates, and I could therefore undertake it with the confident hope of bringing it to a successful issue. My colleagues were Dr. George Playfair, of the Royal Army, and Lieutenant J. A. Heathcote, of the Indian Navy; and I am sure I can be guilty of no indiscretion in affirming that no army or navy in the world could have produced men better fitted by their talents for the tasks specially assigned to them. Their scientific ability was undoubted, and their practical skill had been more than once put to the test, and with the most successful results. Nor was their personal character less worthy of all the approbation that can be bestowed upon it. I have never met with men more noble-hearted, more self-sacrificing, or of more kindly disposition; and I need hardly say that my satisfaction in being associated with two such officers was almost—I should rather say entirely—unalloyed. I knew that no enterprise was too arduous for them, and that the prospect of danger would rather increase than impair their energy and devotion.

My last evening in Calcutta was spent in the society of the Governor-General and his kind-hearted and accomplished lady. Alas! it is only a few years since, and they are now both no more! To my certain knowledge they are both mourned throughout our Eastern empire with a depth and intensity of sorrow, with feelings of such deep personal regret as are seldom felt for those who have occupied a station so exalted, their authority, although only derived and representative, exceeding that of many European kings and rulers.

I can scarcely trust myself to speak of the lamented Countess Canning. Her popularity in India was, as it deserved to be, unbounded. Every one who has ever had an opportunity of coming in any way in contact with her can only have words of praise to bestow in speaking of her personal character. All were immediately attracted by the matchless grace and elegance of her manner, and the kindness beaming in her eye at once won the homage of every heart. Not only did she possess the lighter accomplishments that enhance the beauty and dignity of the female character, but she had evidently applied herself with no little zeal and diligence to severer studies, and had amassed much of that useful knowledge which strengthens and elevates the mind. Every one who was admitted into her presence she received with the most refined courtesy; and none could converse with her long without perceiving that all the other excellencies of her mind and heart were enhanced by that Christian grace which is the crowning beauty of an elevated female character. The virtues she manifested in her intercourse with society were evidently not assumed, as mere means of attraction in the circle in which she moved; but were the natural outgrowth of her character, the root of all that was beautiful in her life and intercourse being within. Never will the memory of her inexpressible sweetness of disposition fade from the memory of those whose misfortunes she endeavoured to alleviate, and the smile with which she showed her sympathy in the happiness of the more fortunate is impressed equally indelibly on their hearts. No doubt, like all human creatures, she had her weaknesses, but she knew how to conceal, to overcome, or extirpate them. Never did her innate kindness more delight in alleviating the sorrows of the unfortunate than during that fearful mutiny which overwhelmed so many once happy and prosperous families with unexpected calamities. The sympathies of her noble nature were a source of joy and comfort to all during that period of trial and probation, and in many a grateful heart is the recollection of her unwearied goodness cherished with a devotion equal to that with which the pious Catholic regards the patron saint whom he believes to be his constant guard and guide amidst all the temptation, sin, and sorrow through which he must pass on his way to a better and higher life

The character of her gifted husband shone no less conspicuously for its many excellencies. While the wide grasp of his intellect, and the firmness of his moral character, fitted him for the rule of such an empire as that of India, as was fully testified by his conduct during the unparalleled difficulties against which he had to struggle, he shone with no less lustre in more limited circles; and his easy manner, well-informed mind, and benevolent disposition rendered him at all times a pleasant companion among his equals, or among those whom his kindness led him to treat as such; while his practical sympathy with those who required his assistance has often lifted the load of trouble from many an afflicted individual or family. Indeed, cases might be cited in which the munificence of his private charity seemed almost to degenerate into prodigality. And yet I cannot help thinking that but scant justice was bestowed either on his opinions or his acts, and especially when the regular course of civil government was arrested by the mutiny. Many, however, who then expressed their disapprobation of his measures have since seen occasion to change their opinion, and have freely acknowledged the error of judgment into which they had allowed themselves to fall. It was impossible, indeed, for any liberal and enlightened mind not to admire the calm dignity of demeanour which he displayed at a time when the firmness of even the most resolute men was put to so severe a test. In the hour of India's greatest trial, when the burden of his responsible and almost kingly office weighed with such unusual severity upon him, no one can venture to assert that Lord Canning, by any display of weakness or unworthy yielding, ever showed himself incapacitated for the exalted office which it had pleased his Sovereign to entrust to him. At that period he might without any impropriety have adopted the well-known motto of an ancient Scottish family—for, in the rapid whirl of events, who can say that Lord Canning was ever found to be anything but "aye ready?"

It cannot be denied that there was a certain outward coldness in his manner. This, which with many people is a mere constitutional peculiarity, was too generally regarded as a sign of a nature warmed by no lofty or generous emotion, and that could not be stirred up to the performance of any great decisive deed. It was asserted that he must be a stranger to that deep sense of responsibility which in more ardent natures is the source of great deeds, when once they see that the exigencies of the times demand prompt and fearless measures. In reply to such hasty accusations it is sufficient to say that all who were admitted to his intimacy must soon have seen that the necessities and demands of his position, as the ruler of many millions of men, at the time of an unexampled crisis in the history of the country, was with him an ever-present, all-pervading thought, which not all the apparent coldness of his impassive character could conceal. Those who represented him as unmoved by the dreadful nature of the mutiny raging in India, as he was represented in correspondence read before the House of Peers at the time, knew little of his genuine character, of the warm-hearted, anxious, laborious man, who made no unnecessary display of the feelings by which he was animated. Lord Canning was no cold-blooded, lifeless automaton, and those who described him as such can have had no real knowledge of the man, and must have founded their opinion on grounds that were far from justifying it. If his character showed no trace of that hasty impulse which gives birth to inconsiderate actions, it was equally removed from the stolid apathy or indifference to which nothing can communicate the breath of life, or one spark of genuine emotion. No man really could have a more sensitive or humane heart; but he was at all times master of himself, and had complete control over his feelings—an invaluable characteristic in a position so responsible and exalted as that to which he was called.

At Government House it was customary to retire after dinner to the small drawing-room, which all, who have had the privilege of seeing it, know to contain many objects that cannot be surpassed for elegance as specimens of art, bearing testimony to the rare accomplishments and refinement of its usual occupants. It has been my good fortune to enjoy opportunities of conversing confidentially with Lord Canning in that favourite sanctum, and it is therefore in my power to bear ample testimony to the interest which he took in all that referred to the government of the country, the amelioration of its condition, and the security of all classes. On one occasion I had a long conversation with him regarding the conduct of the expedition which was committed to my charge. The Governor-General, worn out by a day of toil and anxiety in the performance of his official duties, the burden of which, I believe, none but such as have experienced it can realize, gradually sank back on the sofa, overcome by exhaustion, and fell into a soft, deep, silent sleep. I narrowly watched the changing expression of his features as he calmly slumbered, now totally unconscious of the presence of any one that could watch him. It seemed to me that the expression of his countenance during that calm slumber could only be compared to the appearance of a bright clear sky diversified by the lights and shades produced by the rapid flight of thin fleecy clouds between it and the spectator. At times the severer impress of his features appeared to indicate that some important thought having reference to the cares and responsibilities of his office was disturbing the calm serenity of his visage. Although the expression of anxious thought was only momentary, one could not help imagining that it presented a type of the state of that mind during the long hours of day, when it had unceasingly to revolve on matters pertaining to the destinies of a great continent. In a few moments my observations were disturbed by the appearance of a native servant, who, entering the apartment with the noiseless, stealthy manner of his race, approached his slumbering Lord. I saw that he was the bearer of a telegraphic dispatch, marked *urgent and immediate.* When the man saw that the Governor-General was asleep, he seemed at a loss what to do. Influenced by those feelings of respect with which the natives of the East regard all who exercise authority, he did not dare to awake the mighty ruler of millions of his fellow-creatures, to whom the important missive was addressed, and before whom he stood with folded hands and bended head, a patient monument of Asiatic humility and awe. As the matter of the message might be of infinite importance, affecting perhaps the life or death of individuals, I considered it necessary, although with considerable reluctance, to awake him. I therefore came near, and touched him lightly on the arm. He awoke immediately. The return to consciousness seemed to be instantaneous and complete. Reason appeared at once to resume her usual calm and certain sway. There was no hesitation, no uncertainty, no gradual collecting of the faculties, but with the self-possession of one who had renounced all self-indulgence, and who suffered no procrastination either in himself or others, he was at once ready for the transaction of business.

The dispatch was immediately delivered to him, and when he had glanced over it, I took the liberty of asking if it contained any information as to the capture of Lucknow by Sir Colin Campbell. This was a point on which I was very anxious for authentic information, as I had many friends there, of whose fate I was desirous to hear. His answer was kind and considerate, though cautious, as it ever was to those who approached him with similar inquiries.

Lord Canning's administration of our Indian empire has been much and variously canvassed, and on such a subject, all the documents concerning which have not yet been made public, it would certainly be premature to pronounce a decided opinion. His removal from the toils and cares of an anxious life, at a most perilous period of Indian history, has been so recent, that we must be content to wait a little for the means of pronouncing a calm unprejudiced judgment on one who occupies the most prominent place in so important a period of history.

As it was through Lord Canning that I was selected for the conduct of the expedition to the Andaman Islands, and as I was thus brought into immediate contact with him, I hope this allusion to the character and services of a nobleman who in some respects has not obtained strict justice from his countrymen in England, may not be deemed inappropriate. If Lord Canning were still alive, I might not have considered it necessary to say anything; but as his administration of India, during the severest period of trial to which our authority in that country was ever exposed, is now matter of history, I have been eager to seize this opportunity of paying a passing tribute of respect and regard for the memory of one whom I consider to have been both a great and a good man. It might be deemed altogether out of place for me to dwell upon his character in any other point of view than that of a ruler, although in many other respects he excited the admiration of all who were admitted to familiar intercourse with him. In the midst of great and pressing duties he had found time to cultivate his abilities as a scholar, and his attainments were such as would have done no discredit to one whose time was not engrossed by the harassing duties which a high political position necessarily imposes. His scholastic acquirements, his singular refinement of feeling, his inflexible adherence to justice, his discriminating humanity, and his untiring devotion to duty, all united in the formation of a character at once so dignified and accessible, so just and merciful, as is only seen in the purest and most upright rulers, of whom a Washington may be regarded as the type.

It is now time to pass to the more immediate subject of this work. The urgency of the expedition was such that I was allowed only a short time to make the necessary preparations; and the few hours at my disposal were therefore devoted to the collection of the necessary photographic materials, and inquiry after such information regarding the Andamans and former expeditions to them as was likely to be useful to me. The latter, as will have been seen from the statements in our introductory chapter, was but scanty, and with the exception of that contained in the reports of Blair, Colebrooke, &c., most of it of no real value or importance. The admirable chart, however, of Captain Blair, I found of infinite service, and the accuracy of his survey was afterwards fully confirmed in most important particulars by our own observations.

I had entertained the hope of being able to procure a larger number of former records, and of works previously published, than I was able to discover. Either, however, the time at my disposal for the prosecution of the necessary researches was too limited, or all that was of much interest must have disappeared, for little that I could avail myself of in the way of really practical and useful information was forthcoming. In reality, with the exception of the papers published in the Asiatic Researches, of one of which I have given a *resumé*, we were left almost without anything that could be of the slightest service to us as a guide in the conduct of the present expedition.

We were fortunate in having a comfortable and convenient vessel in the steam-frigate *Semiramis*, which was selected for the conveyance of the expedition, although a good many years must have elapsed since her keel was laid, and she was in no way to be compared to the scientifically-constructed vessels, both lighter and stronger in their build, that have been launched since her prow first divided the foam-crested wave. She was a favourable specimen of the fast disappearing tribe of wooden steamers propelled by paddles. She was built of teak, and her saloons and cabins were sufficiently spacious to be comfortable, in the limited sense in which that word can be used as applicable to the condition of those who must make their home for a time within the wooden walls of an old steamer. I am informed that she has since deposited her timbers somewhere on the coast of Africa—doubtless from a well-grounded conviction that, as she was so far behind these go-a-head times, it would be more becoming to shelve herself with dignity on the first suitable occasion rather than be compelled to expose her many deficiencies in the presence of the Warriors, Monitors, and Merrimacs, who might ere long show their colours, even on the seas with the navigation of which she had long been familiar.

We embarked in this ship on the 23rd of November. Our captain, one of the wide-spread tribe of Campbell, whose name so frequently occurs in army and navy lists, was a seaman of more than ordinary ability, and enjoys the reputation of having been one of the first Euphrates explorers. We experienced from him all the kindness and good feeling that could be anticipated from a genuine sailor. His hospitality knew no bounds, and as he knew that landsmen find it no easy matter to make themselves at home on the sea, he did everything that kindness could suggest, or ingenuity discover, to make our position as his guests not only comfortable, but desirable. Nor were his services confined to the period during which the voyage lasted, and we were passengers on board his vessel, but his protecting care followed us afterwards in our wanderings over the Andaman Islands; for it was from him we obtained an efficient guard to protect us from the natives, whose disposition we afterwards found, to use the expressive phrase of Bailie Nicol Jarvie, to be rather on the "north side of friendly."

The moment the ship was ready for sea, the steam was got up, and we started on our voyage across the Bay of Bengal. We were happily in the best of spirits, for the expedition was one in which all who were engaged as principals took a great deal of interest; and it was fortunate for ourselves we were so, for our progress was very slow, and as we watched the tardy motion of the vessel, cutting her way deliberately through the waves, we calculated with a feeling akin to disappointment the long time that would necessarily elapse before our destination should be reached, and we should once more set our feet on land, even though we were menaced with perils among those whom our predecessors had taught us to regard as a race who, if their heads did not grow between their shoulders, were at any rate little better than genuine anthropophagi.

The ship's company had, by some good fortune, a fair proportion of musical amateurs, and from these was formed a band of serenaders, whose strains at occasional intervals relieved the tedium of the slowly-passing hours. The musicians were all natives of Goa, a peculiar composite race, who supply India with the more humble professors of the arts of cookery and music. Ethnological inquirers have been baffled in their attempts to determine, with anything like certainty, the origin of this very remarkable class of fiddlers and cooks; but judging by the result of previous investigations, the problem is apparently one that would baffle the ingenuity and learning of a Darwin. They are genuine hybrids of the true sable hue, looking as if they had been covered with a coat of tar wash. In many cases, the dark lustre of their skins could be appropriately compared only to the polished blackness of a life-guardsman's boot.

This model crew likewise boasted the possession of a superior piper, whose renown was in all their mouths. Very probably, in other circumstances, we might have been disposed to dispense with the strains with which, with a liberality we were scarcely sufficiently grateful for, he was at all seasons ready to entertain us. We thought it right to encourage his musical abilities, particularly for one reason. The Andamanese would no doubt be able to appreciate the melody he produced from his favourite instrument, and we anticipated wonders from the war-dance with which we intended to gratify the natives on the celebration of our *fête* of fraternization with that interesting race of cannibals. But poor Sandy, like so many of his countrymen, even in these days of rampant teetotalism, was a thirsty soul. He dearly loved a drop of something stronger than either water or tea, and unfortunately he was inclined to be unreasonable in the frequency with which he repeated the doses that he considered necessary for his constitution—absolutely necessary in so trying a climate, and especially when engaged in an expedition in which all might find it requisite to be able to screw their courage up to the sticking point. We were not sorry that ere long we were deprived of the ear-piercing strains of our enthusiastic piper, although we regretted the cause that condemned him to silence. It was found necessary, after repeated warnings had been of no avail in restraining him in the gratification of his favourite appetite, to deprive him of his liberty, with the hope that the stocks would have some moral influence upon a character which was thrice armed at all points against every description of rational argument—at least, on this particular question. His vagaries became so extravagant, and his conduct so obstreperous, that we were compelled to resign ourselves to the loss of his assistance in the exercise of that civilizing and softening influence in which music has always been represented as playing no inconsiderable part. It was destined that the rude manners were not to be softened, nor the savage soul soothed to rest, by any strains that the bagpipe could produce.

The first part of our long and slow voyage at length came to a termination, and we found ourselves at the port of Moulmein. The view of this place from the sea is very pleasing and agreeable. Nothing could be prettier or more picturesque than the scenery which we now looked upon for the first time. After the unchanging monotony of the sea, the beautiful and romantic view on which we now gazed with feelings of more than usual delight, called forth expressions of the warmest admiration. The sparkling river, its waters smooth and bright as a mirror, glowing beneath the dazzling rays of the sun, winding its tortuous way among hills of an unusual aspect, and of strangely varied form, presented a striking contrast to the dead level of that alluvial plain which extends around Calcutta. The busy aspect of the port gave life and variety to the exquisite natural scenery, which was further enlivened by the peculiar appearance of its native population, who, although all accounts agree in representing them as lazy and indolent, incapable of being roused to exertion by any ordinary motive, are certainly a light-hearted and laughter-loving people.

As the large steamer in which we had come so far was not fitted for the intricate navigation of the Andaman coasts, we were here to be transferred to the little war-steamer *Pluto*, which had been placed at our service by Government. As she was of light draught, she was admirably suited for experimental navigation in the shallow seas around islands, and among the dangerous reefs with which their coasts are often fringed. She was ordered not only to carry us to our destination, but also to return with us to Calcutta, when the object for which the expedition had been undertaken was accomplished.

As she had not made her appearance by the time we arrived at Moulmein, we determined that, while we were waiting for her, our time should not be lost in idleness or frivolity, but turned to some useful purpose. We therefore employed our enforced leisure, in the first place, in making preparatory trials of our photographic instruments and materials. We had ample opportunity, in the course of our peregrinations, for testing the great value to travellers of this modern discovery, by which the most beautiful features of natural scenery, and the most delicate workmanship of human skill, can be reproduced with the nicest fidelity and accuracy. We were accompanied by a photographic artist of great talent, Monsieur Mallitte, who had previously enjoyed the benefit of considerable experience in that department of the art in which his services were chiefly required on this expedition. We considered ourselves truly fortunate in having secured the services of one who was not only an artist of undoubted ability, but whom, during the long hours at sea that might have passed tediously without his society, we found to be at all times a most pleasant and entertaining companion. I ought, perhaps, to state that this gentleman was specially in my own employment, and that it was entirely as a volunteer that he formed part of our expedition. With all that spirit and love of adventure which characterize the lively nation to which he belongs, he followed us in all our wanderings; and when we thought that any of our expeditions might be attended with danger, he would accompany us in spite of all remonstrances, never for a moment considering that his civilian occupation ought to exempt him from the obligation of showing himself at all times a trusty and faithful comrade. He lost, however, no opportunity of labouring diligently in his own special department; and through his unwearied application we were enabled to carry back an invaluable collection of photographic pictures of the country and people—the rich and varied scenes of nature, and striking groups illustrative of the life and customs of the natives of the Andaman Islands.

During the period of our detention at Moulmein, the gallant Commissioner of the Province, Colonel Albert Fytche, showed great interest in the object on which we were engaged, and rendered us invaluable services, in return for which we can only express our sincere gratitude. He not only entertained us right royally—for in what part of the world, whether it be within the torrid zone or amid the snows and frosts of Lapland, are not good dinners given and received among English gentlemen, as the most perfect exponents of interest and good-will?—but he rendered us every assistance in his power in preparing our plan of proceedings, and afforded us facilities, which, but for his interest and kindness, we should not have enjoyed for conducting our investigations to a successful issue. Twelve Burmese convicts—men who, from their previous habits, were accustomed to find their way in the dense and tangled forests of these regions—were selected and placed at our service for the purpose of preceding us as pioneers, and cutting a path through the thick growth of underwood that, according to the information we had received, and as we afterwards found to our cost, rendered the Andaman forests totally impervious to the most persevering traveller without such assistance.

From the local arsenal we obtained a boring-rod, the working powers of which we had not a few opportunities of testing. In islands like the Andamans, where there is nothing that even in appearance approaches what we should call a river, where not even running rills of any magnitude have been discovered, it may be imagined that an instrument so necessary in the search for fresh water, was appreciated as one of the most appropriate and valuable gifts that could have fallen into our hands.

While we were detained here, we had an opportunity of examining, in a collection of savage implements of destruction, certain arrows which possess the reputation of carrying almost certain death to any unfortunate whom they may pierce. Being labelled as poisoned, and preserved with great care, they are regarded with that amount of awe which instruments so formidable are calculated to inspire. Some experiments were performed for the purpose of discovering, if possible, the nature of the poisonous substance by which they were rendered so deadly. Selecting a few lively, vigorous, and healthy fowls, we could not help feeling something like remorse at the thought that we were going to sacrifice their useful lives for the purpose of gratifying what was, on our part, in a great measure, a matter of curiosity—though no doubt useful too. Our expectations as to the result, however, were not realised. The poison of such deadly repute produced no effect on the bodies of these winged and feathered bipeds; or, at any rate, so far as we could detect, no effect more mischievous than that of increasing their already ample and accommodating appetites. In truth, these arrows, which had been previously regarded with a shudder by all who passed them, were now discovered, by an easy and simple experiment, to be entirely innocuous; rather an amusing illustration of the manner in which fear and ignorance magnify dangers which a slight examination may discover to have no real existence. We have every reason to believe that many of the alarming anthropological characteristics ascribed to the Andamanese may be discovered to be equally mythical.

In the meantime, we employed our enforced leisure in submitting our arms and ammunition to a careful examination. We did not know what might be before us, and thinking it the part of wisdom to be prepared for the worst, we set about putting everything in fighting trim without any further delay. Our naval guard were drilled assiduously, until they became *au fait* at the most necessary military manœuvres; so that, if circumstances rendered it advisable, they might be prepared to act as marines on shore. We were proceeding to the Andamans with no hostile intentions; we had no desire to meet with enemies in the natives, but we had received such ideas of their warlike character and fierce disposition, that we considered it imperative, both for the sake of our own safety, and for the success of the expedition, that we should be prepared to repel aggression. There is no disputing the axiom of which we have heard so much in these recent days, that the enjoyment of peace is best secured by readiness for war.

In a part of the world so near to the Andamans, we had buoyed ourselves up with the hope of obtaining some further information, on which we might unhesitatingly rely, regarding the land and people. Although we applied ourselves, with the most praiseworthy industry, to gleaning as many useful particulars as we might find of practicable avail, our harvest of knowledge was really very small. We met, indeed, with one gentleman, who had landed on the islands, and spent some time among the natives. When he was informed of our desire to collect as much preliminary information as we could, he made us acquainted with the result of his experience, which we found to be totally different from all that we had learned from other Andamanese travellers. So far from being the savage, merciless, and hostile race that others have described them to be, he seems to have found in them all that is attractive and winning—all that banishes fear and inspires confidence—an obliging, amiable, hospitable, and altogether interesting race, who therefore must have been most unjustly maligned by all who had previously given the world any description of them. He had come across such wild animals as tigers, but no wild men; he had seen deer browsing on the hill-sides. He had wandered along the shores of a lake which he described as being of a zig-zag form, and he had been a witness of many other interesting objects, the existence of which the account of no other visitor or traveller had led us to expect; and we therefore could not avoid expressing a wish that he would favour us with his guidance in the examination of islands which seemed associated in his memory with so many pleasing recollections. Perhaps it was a wise prudence that led him to decline the offer. We also learned that he was the author of a pamphlet intended to enlighten the world by a more faithful representation of the Andamans and their inhabitants than any that had yet appeared. I procured it, and read it carefully through from beginning to end. The impression its statements produced on my mind may be gathered from the fact that, if I had seen the name of the immortal Munchausen on the title-page, I should have been in no degree surprised. The knowledge subsequently acquired by myself, from personal experience, enables me to say with confidence that no dependence can be placed upon the information, if it can be so called, which this little pamphlet professes to communicate.

The opinions of an amiable old lady, whose acquaintance we had the pleasure of making, ran in quite an opposite direction from those of the gentleman just alluded to. When we had any opportunity of enjoying her society, her manner was such as to show us she evidently considered myself, assistants, and crew, as doomed beings. A glance of unaffected pity shone in her mild eye whenever it happened to fall upon any one of us. She expressed her unqualified belief in all that had been ever said or written regarding the anthropological disposition of the Mincopies; and when, on our departure, she took a solemn and affecting leave of us, she ventured to hint at what, in her conviction, would be our certain and unavoidable fate. What else could be the result of such an ill-omened voyage? All who had ever ventured to these islands of evil repute—and, among the rest, her personal friend, Dr. Helfer—had never returned to tell the story of their sufferings, but had doubtless formed the savoury meal of some savage epicure.

We had been delayed waiting for the *Pluto* longer than I had at first anticipated; and although I had no reason to complain of the manner in which both my companions and myself were treated in our present quarters, yet we were anxious to be once more afloat, that we might the sooner accomplish the task on which we were engaged. When, therefore, it was announced to us that the *Pluto* was ready for sea, and that we could embark when we pleased, there was not one of us who did not receive the news with feelings of considerable satisfaction. All our stores, instruments, &c., having been put on board, and our crew, native and European, with the men to whom had been assigned the duty of acting as guards, having been duly mustered, on the evening of the 8th December we were reported ready for sea.

Although the *Pluto* had been fitted up and victualled with the greatest rapidity, it was no small pleasure to see how perfect were all her arrangements. Everything seemed to be in its proper place, and in a shorter period than an uninitiated landsman could have supposed it possible, every one was able to find the post assigned him—so that, as is invariably the case in ships of the Royal Navy, the duties of all on board were discharged with the regularity of clock-work.

The *Pluto* was only a small vessel, comparatively speaking, but she was well armed—indeed, for a craft of her moderate dimensions, she was heavily armed, and all her warlike arrangements appeared to be very complete and effective—at least there is no doubt they would have proved so, if we had ever had occasion to put their efficiency to the test. In addition to the usual complement of officers, an experienced gunner sailed with us, and, besides the large native crew, we had twelve Europeans. These, with the officer and guard from the *Semiramis*, all fully armed and equipped, furnished us with a tolerably strong party of Europeans for our protection. The reason we were so numerously and effectively guarded was, in the first place, because we did not know what dangers we might have to face; and then it would be a mere truism to add, that in proportion as our feeling of security was more undoubting, with so much the more zeal and energy would we all be able to give our minds to the duties marked out for us.

Nor was this all. The foresight of those to whom had been entrusted the care of fitting out the expedition had still further provided for all our anticipated wants. We were accompanied by a small schooner, which we took in tow, and which was laden with an ample supply of coal, to supply any deficiency that might occur, if our own stock, in case of unexpected detention, or any other cause, should run low. A brig, with a supply of fresh provisions, and a further stock of fuel, was also placed under orders to meet us on our return. She was to be dispatched in time to fall in with us at Interview Island, and there minister to our wants.

On Thursday the 9th of December we set sail for our ultimate destination. We, one and all, bade farewell to our hospitable entertainers with feelings of gratitude which I will not attempt to express. I will only say that the kindness we had received was, in reality, one of the strongest incitements that could have been brought to bear upon us, to stir every man up to the faithful and energetic discharge of his duty; and the fact that such was the case will, I have no doubt, prove a more satisfactory return to those who made so many sacrifices for our comfort than the most expressive words we could commit to paper. There was not one of us who did not feel that the hearty sympathy, the encouraging words, the hopeful farewell of his fellow-countrymen was an ample reward bestowed on him in anticipation of the services by which he was, at least in some measure, to merit such devoted and genuine friendship.

Once fairly started, we all looked forward to the hope of bringing the expedition to a successful issue with feelings of exultation; for all that is new and adventurous calls forth energies that are only too apt to slumber in the routine of our every-day duties. The very appearance of the vessel on which we were embarked was calculated to inspire feelings like those which animated the old discoverers when they started on their voyages in search of new lands; feelings, we say, similar in nature, though doubtless very different in degree. Our steamer, heavy as was her armament, and loaded with all that was necessary for our future operations, cut through the waters "like a thing of life," leaving behind her a long trail of sparkling foam, marking the course she was pursuing, straight as an arrow. Look up at her tall tapering masts, apparently so slender and fragile, yet strong enough to bear her ample sails bellying before the wind. Look along her dark, low, snake-like hull, and observe her graceful lines, her beautiful curve. When one is at sea in such a vessel, always supposing he is not suffering from sea-sickness, that enemy to all enchantment, he cannot wonder that the sailor should regard his ship with feelings almost as warm as the patriot his native land, or the exile his distant home.

Our crew consisted of a strangely mingled collection of human beings. Anyone devoted to the study of ethnology would have had ample means for adding to his store of knowledge in that science, by observing the peculiarities of the various nationalities of whom there were specimens on the deck of the *Pluto*. Limited as was the number of our European crew, among them might be found the self-dependent Anglo-Saxons, active and fiery Celts, fair Norsemen, stout Finlanders, swarthy Italians, and Maltese distinguished by their bronzed faces and their guttural speech. In addition to these, we could boast of one Frenchman and a Hamburgher, with a Portuguese or two as swarthy and as guttural in speech as the Maltese. These constituted the European complement, forming, it must be allowed, with two natives of North and South America, a pretty varied representation of the white branch of the Arian family of the human race. As regarded the dark, or rather the black portion of our crew, Africa supplied us with stokers and pokers, well seasoned for their hot and laborious occupation by the burning sun of their native plains and deserts. China was laid under contribution to supply us with carpenters. We had sailors of various castes from the Malayan peninsula, the ports of Hindostan, and the Malabar coast. Our cooks hailed from Burmah, from which we had also a party of convicts, to whom were to be assigned some of the laborious tasks that we might find necessary on reaching our destination. Last of all, Bengal supplied us with our personal attendants. There was considerable truth in a remark made by one of my companions, that if the earth were overwhelmed by a deluge during our absence, or if the whole race of mankind were swallowed up by an earthquake—we alone being left to show that such a creature as man had once trod the surface of the globe—an ethnological inquirer, endowed with the skill and knowledge of a Cuvier or an Owen, would not find it difficult, with this comprehensive representation of the original stock, to form a pretty accurate conception of the principal tribes, nations, and tongues existing upon the face of the earth at the period of this supposed calamity.

It needed, however, no such catastrophe to enable those who were anxious to increase their knowledge of their kind to derive interest from the appearance and characteristics of our varied crew—such a number of men collected, within a very limited space, from all corners of the earth, all engaged on the same expedition, one not devoid in some measure of peril and uncertainty, and all regarding it in some peculiar point of view most consonant with the habits of their previous life and training. Many of them, indeed, had no idea beyond that of their daily alternations of rest and labour, and seemed to have little or no curiosity as to where they were going, or what was the object of the voyage on which they were engaged.

Most of us who were capable of finding pleasure in such speculations were for some time in no condition to indulge in them. That demon who has no mercy on those who are only casual visitants to his domain had laid us prostrate; and except to a feeling of misery that nothing can alleviate, the mind is a perfect blank while the body is suffering from sea-sickness. While the unpitied sufferers lay groaning upon the deck, with what envy they regarded the unconcerned sailors, leaning upon the gunwale, spinning to each other long yarns of their former adventures at sea; and, alas, sometimes turning the poor landsman's stomach upside down when, with genuine gusto, they turned their quids in their mouths, or surrounded themselves with clouds of tobacco smoke from repeated whiffs at their short black pipes. Some of the old salts were quite unrivalled in their talent for manufacturing long stories, more or less credible, founded on their former experience of life on the ocean wave. They appeared never to be at a loss for striking and marvellous incident, to the recital of which, as was to be expected in these days of the general diffusion of useful knowledge, even the more inexperienced of the younger sailors appeared to listen with a faith that was evidently much shaken by doubts. It was pleasant occasionally, in the calm evenings, when the glorious sun of the East was declining in the heavens, tinging the Western hemisphere with a flood of purple glory, to listen to the dark Maltese seamen, so gay and light-hearted, as they twanged their tiny guitars, while their voices accompanied them with some romantic song chanted to one of the monotonous melodies occasionally heard on the shores of the Mediterranean sea. The Malays and their congeners formed a most remarkable contrast to these happy and thoughtless islanders. There they are, sitting on the deck, in solemn, silent groups, evidently under the influence of that pernicious drug in which they all indulge, and which they manage always to have a supply of. It would be useless to attempt to deprive them of this enjoyment, which they consider a necessary of life. The iron is not more strongly attracted to the magnet than they are to this potent and injurious drug, which steeps their senses in forgetfulness, or rouses them into a state of fury and excitement the contemplation of which is alarming to the onlooker. Their coal-black eyes are fixed and staring, lighting up their dark countenances with an unnatural brilliancy. If they were summoned to the performance of any trifling duty when under the influence of their favourite drug, they went about it in a dreamy, dilatory manner, of which it is hardly possible to convey an adequate impression by any description. One who had never seen them in a similar state before might have imagined that they were walking in their sleep, while their strange movements, as they dragged their limbs languidly after them, could apparently be accounted for only by supposing that they were suffering from an attack of catalepsy. The various Asiatics were generally distinguished by the same peculiar characteristics. They all passed the time in much the same way; their leisure hours being devoted to alternations of sleeping and smoking. Occasionally they joined in conversation with each other; and when their tongues were once thus unloosed, they chattered away in that monkey-like manner which is peculiar to them, accompanying all they said with an abundance of expressive gesticulation.

With this varied crew, obeying the energetic directions of our truly sailor-like captain and officers, the *Pluto* made her way over the waters in a way satisfactory to all. Her mobility, if I may so express myself, was great, and she danced lightly and speedily over the waves. Her draft of water was more than usually light, not more than four feet, I believe. She was also flat-bottomed, and, being without a hold upon the water, she seemed to be perpetually in search of the lowest level of every wave, of every ripple, over which she passed. Owing to her peculiar construction, her decks were occasionally inclined to an angle at which even experienced sailors found it difficult to maintain their upright position. Her yards kissed the white crests of the waves as they coursed along. As for the way in which she rolled from side to side, it was more sudden than agreeable. So rapid were her changes of position, that when we expected the wine glasses to go over on one side, she would suddenly place them in equal peril on the other, and thus keep them in a perplexing state of equilibrium.

Although most people find it rather inconvenient to be confined for any length of time to the narrow limits of a vessel at sea, I cannot say that such was my own experience in the present case. There was much to observe that made the time pass pleasantly enough, apart altogether from the society of those who were accompanying me as the heads of the expedition. I would sometimes sit upon the bridge, and observe, with ever increasing interest and curiosity, the novel scene presented by a ship's company, the elements of which were so varied in complexion and character. The conversation of those who were not otherwise occupied was of the most polyglot description, such as only a Mithridates or an Adelung could comprehend, so numerous were the languages and dialects. So far as my comprehension extended, I found that the subject of their conversation generally was the appearance, character, and manner of the people whom they were soon, in all probability, to be among. They had all heard more or less of the not very attractive representations of the Andamanese that were generally circulated, and they were never tired of indulging in all kinds of speculations as to the adventures they might be involved in among a race of whom they knew so little that was certain. The natives of Hindostan particularly revelled in the wildest imaginings about those unknown and terrible islanders. Their pictures were all of the most monstrous and terror-inspiring description; and no artist but a Chinese one, familiar with the most grotesque delineations of hippogriphs, and of all kinds of monsters possible and impossible, could reproduce faithfully the pictures painted by their excited fancy. It is perhaps scarcely credible, but it is nevertheless true, that the least exaggerated and outrageous notions prevalent respecting the Mincopies represented them as a nondescript kind of men, with horses' heads and lions' tails. That they had an unlimited capacity for human flesh was an article of faith which no one ventured to dispute, and if anyone had done so he would only have been laughed at for his pains. With them accuracy of knowledge was synonymous with capacity of belief. When to these terror-inspiring representations it is added that they believed these savages to be proof against any bullet, whether of lead or of silver, it will excite no wonder that the prospect of coming into very close communication with them was not particularly relished.

Nor was this feeling of respectful terror confined to the Asiatic portion of our followers. Even our hirsute, weather-stained Europeans, accustomed to wandering adventurous lives, and reckless of danger, fearing nothing in any ordinary human guise, spoke confidentially to each other with bated breath, picturing the Andamanese as a race of cannibals more terrible than any whom previous voyagers had ever dared to visit. Although we would scarcely venture to say that they looked forward to their meeting with them with actual fear, it is certain that the prevalent representations of their man-eating propensities had inspired them with an uncomfortable feeling, which they found it difficult to conceal, disguise it as they chose. As they said to each other, they were ready to meet either man or devil in fair and open fight, but their boldness of heart seemed to fail them at the thought of coming in contact with a hideous race who would entrap them in some treacherous ambuscade, deal death among them with clouds of poisoned arrows, and, finally, in their banquets, feast on their dead bodies.

At midday on the 11th, after a voyage which had so far been as favourable as we could wish, we sighted the uninhabited island of Narcoudan. Seen from the ship at the distance of forty miles, the appearance it presented was that of a bold, lofty hummock projecting abruptly from the sea. A few hours after we had passed it, the high lands lying to the south of Port Cornwallis appeared in sight, at first only faintly descried, but ere long distinctly visible to all on board. As we gradually approached land, and the water became more shallow, orders were given to slacken speed, and we stood in very slowly. Fortunately it was daylight, and the entrance to the port could be made out without any difficulty. We therefore steamed in at half-speed, and at eight o'clock, after making a circuit of the magnificent harbour, anchored off Chatham Island.

The sight of land, after a voyage of considerable length, generally affords pleasure to all travellers, landsmen or seamen. There was so much that was new and beautiful in the natural scenery on which I now looked for the first time, that I regarded it with great delight. Yet, although a very distinct impression of its peculiar and characteristic beauties remains on my mind, I do not feel disposed to attempt any minute or accurate description of it. The pen is not very well adapted to convey a definite impression of natural scenery; and it is seldom that the generalities to which the writer is forced to confine himself produce the same picture in the minds of all who peruse them. He may himself have a very clear impression of what he wishes to describe; but the imagination of his reader is generally satisfied with the fancy pictures of his own mind, the more distinct parts of which may have been suggested by the most salient points of the author's description. The physical characteristics of a country require the aid of the pencil to give definiteness to the language of description, before it is possible to produce in the mind of the reader anything like a correct impression of a landscape he has never seen. Still, although the attempt may be a failure, I must endeavour to give something like a general description of the scenery now spread out before me.

The land presented a series of low undulatory hills, the character, arrangement, and colouring of which formed a spectacle of the most lovely and attractive description. The lower parts of the various eminences were of a dark purple shade, gradually brightening towards the top, which reflected with dazzling brilliancy the golden tints of the morning. The vegetation with which they were profusely covered, was of the usually brilliant and gorgeous character seen only in tropical regions. Every hill, from its summit down to the water's edge, looked like a neglected but beautiful garden, in which nature, left to its own resources, had scattered abroad and vivified the seeds of vegetable life with a prodigality of which our poor sluggish soil, even in the most favoured parts of Europe, is altogether incapable. The shore was indented with numerous bays, in some of which the waters, shaded by the overhanging hills, and the abundant foliage of the trees, presented cool spots on which the eye could rest with a sense of pleasure and relief; while in others they shone with all the brightness of a mirror, flashing back the dazzling rays of the ascending morning sun. The belts of pure white sand, with which the bays were edged, had a silvery radiance that contrasted beautifully with the rich colouring of the vegetation and trees by which they were immediately surmounted. Nor was this the only one of these pleasing contrasts in which nature so often delights, presented to us by the natural picture on which our eyes were turned. Some of the hills were more rugged and torn in their appearance than others, having evidently at some time felt the effects of those shocks that have given so much diversity to the face of the globe. We could descry many of those shattered rifts and clefts that yet bore testimony to the irresistible power of the earthquake. Great boulders of rock were scattered here and there over the plain, smoothed and rounded by the action of water. The face and summit of the wildest cliffs were softened and adorned by patches of rich velvet moss, over which, like glancing lines of crystal, pure rills of fresh water, making music with their soft murmur before they reached the descent over which they fell, precipitated themselves with a loud dash, throwing glistening showers of spray around in all directions.

The beautiful bay or harbour in which we had cast anchor being land-locked, and protected from the winds, was as calm and peaceful as an inland lake; to which, indeed, in appearance, it bore no slight resemblance. The green surface of the sea surrounding our vessel was not ruffled by a single ripple; or if one could be heard now and then breaking like soft music on the shore, it only made the stillness more impressive by contrast with the perfect peace that followed. The scene altogether was at once novel and beautiful, and we all felt its influence more or less. In the perfect silence of nature we seem to hold more immediate communion with it; and it is then, if at any time, that she whispers in our ear those higher thoughts, those richer fancies, that find their natural expression in the language of poetry.

None of us could perceive even the slightest sign of any form of animal life on the island. The sailors, generally not much impressed with the beauty and variety of natural scenery, were anxious to know at once the worst of those formidable natives of whom they had heard and carried with them such remarkable stories. Even the unusual silence of land and sea, the solemn stillness, unbroken by a single sound of life, the universal repose by which they were surrounded, produced upon their minds an impression of solemnity and awe which at first they were unable to shake off, and in which, indeed, there was not one of us who did not to some extent share. A feeling of relief was produced by the sight of a few beautiful pigeons, which, with a couple of kingfishers, with plumage of the most lively and brilliant description, constituted all that we had yet seen of life.

The highest elevation in sight was that known as Saddle Hill. Its prominent crest rose high above the altitude of the numerous lowly neighbours by which it was surrounded on all sides. In comparison with them, it would have been no misapplication of terms to call it a mountain. Its summit appeared shrouded in a great hood of clouds, whose bright fleecy forms, floating in the transparent atmosphere, seemed to be attracted to it, enveloping it in a gauzy veil of clouds, and sometimes hiding it altogether from our sight. Occasionally a few would clear away, leaving an opening, through which we could discover, unveiled in all its beauty, the tree-covered summit. The mountain altogether, when visible in its complete elevation, presented an appearance at once picturesque and grand. In some places we could observe that its sides were exceedingly abrupt; precipices, resembling walls of rock, butted frowningly over the profound abyss that lay beneath them, presenting a spectacle dark, gloomy, and sombre, unrelieved even by the slightest trace of the luxuriant vegetation of which we saw so much all around. Many of the valleys even exhibited no signs of fertility, the surface being stony, covered with masses of rock, and shut in by crags, which threw a dark shadow over the ground beneath—thus adding to the severe and yet picturesque grandeur of the scene, which seemed to harmonize more with the reported savage character of the natives than the enchanting variety of land and sea by which our vessel was immediately surrounded.

But however pleasing it may be to behold natural scenery, this was not the object for which we had come. We were engaged on a mission of practical importance, which required for its successful completion all the time at our disposal, and all the energies of which we were capable; and it was therefore necessary that we should without loss of time commence our labours. The plan of operations which we considered it best to pursue had already been determined, as we had fully discussed and considered the question during the period of our stay at Moulmein.

Our first care was that we should be able to discharge our duties with security, for, making all allowance for the exaggerated views prevalent among our followers regarding the savage character of the inhabitants of the Andamans, it was a well-known and established fact that they were a subtle, crafty, and merciless race, as the testimony of all preceding visitors represented them to be. Although their arms and discipline were far inferior to ours, they had the advantage of greatly superior numbers on their side, and they were familiarly acquainted with all the hiding-places of the country. The forests particularly were dark, intricate, and impervious to light; they could conceal themselves in any part of them without our knowledge, and, obeying their treacherous instincts, they might at any time rush unexpectedly out of their concealment, and, before we could take any step for our safety, surround us on all sides. So swift, silent, and unexpected were they in their movements, that we often found them, by sad experience, to be in our immediate neighbourhood when we thought that they were at a safe distance. We shall have an opportunity, hereafter, of narrating some of the treacherous attacks to which we were exposed.

Again, it was not long before our men began to suffer

much from illness and general depression. The climate had a very unfavourable influence upon their health; and many parts of the land being the constant abode of malaria in its most concentrated and deadly form, several of them were necessarily laid aside from utter prostration or constant fever—a state of things in which it would be impossible to take the many precautions necessary against the enemies of all kinds that were waiting ready to assail us. Quinine was used as a remedy against the subtle, depressing, and deadly influence of the malaria. It was issued with the coffee distributed at daybreak, in which a certain proportion of it was mixed. No man was ever permitted to land without having first swallowed this simple mixture, which we considered an excellent febriguge, and a certain quantity of biscuit with it. It was our invariable custom to muster the men on deck immediately after this light and wholesome morning meal, to pass them, as it were, in review, informing ourselves carefully as to the health and strength of each man, and then examining with equal minuteness the condition of his musket, and the quantity of ammunition with which he was provided. The most urgent orders had been frequently given that no man, however hard-pressed, should fire at any time without the order of his superior officers. To men who have not passed through a regular course of military discipline, such an order seems to be utterly unreasonable, as we soon found out in the course of our experience. It was only with the aid of constant supervision, and the maintenance of the most unswerving authority, that obedience to a command which the safety of the men themselves rendered necessary, could be secured. Indeed, we were all so thoroughly convinced of the reasonableness and importance of such an order, and, at the same time, of the difficulty with which its observation could be maintained, that our opinion was, that on such irregular expeditions as that on which we were engaged, none but steady, well-trained, carefully-disciplined soldiers should be employed.

The measures we took to ensure security in the examination and survey of the islands were such as prudence dictated. There were several of our men whom we had discovered to be at once courageous and trustworthy—adventurous and yet cautious—and from these we selected an advance and rear guard, with flanking parties, each of which, when told off, was placed under the command of one of the Commission. An effective system for the communication of orders, when any of the parties were at too great a distance to hear distinctly the loudest human voice, was adopted. The clear and piercing note of the boatswain's whistle was audible at a great distance in those solitudes where the silence of nature is so seldom disturbed by the sound of human voices, and never by the loud pervading murmur proceeding from the varied operations of human industry. An intelligible code of sounds having been agreed upon, and those who were expected to obey them having been instructed in their meaning, the system was soon found to be practically successful, and there were none of those irritating delays that frequently render the communication and execution of orders so dilatory and uncertain. At the same time, while any party was engaged on land, a careful look-out was kept up from the tops of the steamer, and signals were hoisted when there seemed the slightest reason to expect the appearance of any of the savage bands, indicating also the direction from which their approach was apprehended. The boats in which we landed were always left, during the period of our inland journeys, in the charge of steady and intelligent men belonging to the ship's crew, with orders that they should remain constantly at a sufficient distance from the shore to give themselves an extensive outlook over the country, so far at least as the thick jungle permitted, so that they might not be attacked unawares by savages, who, with the instinctive cunning of all uncivilized tribes, were always planning to effect by secret stratagem what they were unable to accomplish by open force. The two cutters and the gig were the boats usually in requisition when we landed.

As an indispensable means for bringing the object of our expedition to a successful issue, I thought it advisable to become thoroughly acquainted with the general appearance and features of the locality in which our operations were to be carried on. There was one thing also I was particularly anxious we should be able fully to account for. Chatham Island, as we have already mentioned, had been previously visited for the purpose of establishing a convict settlement there; but the settlers had suffered so much during their residence on the island, that they were compelled to abandon it in the year 1796. The unhealthiness of the climate had been found to be extreme, and I therefore thought it a matter of great importance to discover, without delay, from what cause this fatal insalubrity proceeded, what it was that poisoned the atmosphere and produced those exhalations that were so deadly to all who breathed them. I proposed, therefore, in the first place, to sail completely round the island, making a general and accurate, if not minute, survey of those natural peculiarities that affect more or less the salubrity of different localities.

The idea was one for which I had good reason to congratulate myself, as it was not long before a discovery was made which was quite sufficient to account for the ill-health of settlers unaccustomed to the climate, and who, in those days, when the laws of health and sickness were not so clearly ascertained and observed as they have been since, had taken no precautions to guard against an evil which they neither knew nor apprehended.

This was the existence of an extensive salt marsh, which bounded a considerable portion of the island in the direction of the prevailing winds. It was very shallow, and the bottom was left uncovered twice in the course of every twenty-four hours. The deep belts of mangrove by which it was fringed were so dense that even the powerful rays of a tropical sun were unable to penetrate beneath them. Here was the origin of disease and death for which we sought, and which it was well for ourselves we had so soon discovered, or who can tell how fatal might have been its consequences? Such a dark, muddy, festering mass of vegetable compound was sufficient to impregnate the atmosphere far and wide with the seeds of disease, infirmity, and death. The smell that proceeded from it, when slightly disturbed, or with every footfall, was sickening and oppressive beyond all power of expression. The application of some of those means by which modern agricultural industry is promoted would transform this dark, dank, and decaying mould, the result of the rotting and disintegration of the rank growth of ages, into a material of almost inexhaustible fertility. Turned, cultivated, and exposed to the purifying influence of sun and air, the deadly and pestiferous vapours would be exhausted, and a fertile and productive soil would reward the pains and labour bestowed in transforming this field of death into a land of corn and wine for the support of those whom it as yet only prostrates with disease. Is it too much to hope that so beneficial a project, a prospect so encouraging, may yet be realized? Dismal swamps have ere now been transformed into corn-producing fields by the application of human ingenuity and labour, and what reason can be given why the same advantageous change should not be effected here?

This point cleared up to our entire satisfaction—as far at least as the explanation of past evil effects was concerned—our next object was to ascertain, what was of infinite importance to us, what provision of fresh water we could depend on securing during our stay. We scoured all parts of the country lying within convenient distance of our floating home; and, in the course of our peregrinations, discovered several rills and streams which seemed to promise an abundant supply. The water we found to be as pure as could be desired; clear and limpid as crystal. In estimating the quantity that could be obtained in our neighbourhood, we came to the conclusion that a daily supply of five hundred tons could be depended on.

The forests on Chatham Island are of considerable extent—the growth of centuries; and had probably only once before resounded with the stroke of the woodman's axe. The individual trees were large and lofty, their branches covered with dense masses of rich green foliage. But such was their number, and so closely were they packed together, that it was impossible at once to form a correct idea of their gigantic dimensions. They appeared to be really dwarfed from absolute want of elbow-room. Besides, they were in a great measure hidden from view by the immense growth of parasites which twined about them, cramping and confining them in their efforts to strike out their branches, which got tangled and involved among the overwhelming mass of foliage which clung to them. The great trunks were festooned with flowers and plants, which circled about them in endless forms, in all the unstudied grace and rich profusion of nature. Among these was the air-plant, the beauty and elegance of which, as it clasped the noble old forest trees, and threw its leaves and branches in graceful festoons from one to the other, would be described more faithfully by the pencil than by the pen. Unfortunately it was not in flower at the time, which we had reason to regret, as its flowers are said to be more than usually beautiful. Orchids of rare beauty, many of which were doubtless of novel form and character, grew in abundance; and if time had been at our disposal, we might have added to our botanical knowledge and resources by the collection of numerous specimens. But we had unfortunately no leisure for an occupation so amusing and pleasing. The variety of creepers was endless—from the slender, delicate, twining tendrils of the convolvulus, to the boa constrictors of the forests, the dimensions of which struck us with astonishment, many that we saw being fully as thick as the body of a full-grown man. The trunks and branches of the great forest trees were so completely interlaced, entwined, and bound round with these, that several tall and ample stems were seen so firmly grasped in their hold, that even when severed from their roots, they were still maintained in their original erect position by the supporting grasp of their parasites.

The mangroves, with their long hanging branches falling to the earth, and again taking root, grew in an almost impenetrable line of forest along the shore, even projecting far into the water. At high tide, we penetrated their shady recesses, and found ourselves protected from the dazzling rays of a burning sun by the thick foliage, forming beautiful arches, beneath the shade of which we felt as though we were housed in some fairy bower of the most delightful evergreens. At low tide, their gnarled roots were seen spreading to an endless distance along the ground, and so closely and intricately interlaced together, that anyone could walk securely upon them, the footing they afforded was so close and firm. We frequently saw the savage natives, whose feet were accustomed to such a flooring, passing along it with a swiftness and security that rendered our attempts to follow them, with any hope of overtaking them in their swift career, utterly fruitless. It would have required considerable time and practice before any of our men, several of whom were no indifferent proficients in gymnastic exercises, and who could ascend and descend the rigging like monkeys, could have acquired facility in preserving their equilibrium on a path so slippery and uncertain. Any rash attempt to overtake the swiftly gliding savage soon ended in the discomfiture of the rash adventurer, whose fall—happily doing no injury to himself—raised a peal of laughter at his expense among his amused comrades.

After such a good morning's work, into the spirit of which our company had entered with all necessary enthusiasm, there was not one whose appetite was not quickened for the healthy enjoyment of an abundant breakfast, for which purpose we returned on board. As the men were not yet accustomed to the peculiar work required of them, and were fatigued by making their way through the jungle, they were allowed a couple of hours' rest, that they might be prepared for a long pull in the course of the day.

At two o'clock we landed on Chatham Island, in the vicinity of the spot where our instructions gave us to understand the old settlement had been established. Here we discovered some of the first native huts that had yet come under our observation; and miserable apologies for human dwellings they were, being merely small open sheds, the roofs of which were formed of dried leaves of the wild palm, supported on four small central posts. The earthen floor was covered nearly a foot deep with the shells of oysters, muscles, and other molluscæ, which were also scattered about in profusion on the open space by which these primitive habitations were surrounded.

Our course led us along the sandy beach. It was pleasant to remain within the influence of the inspiring sea-breeze, which, in comparison with the sultry atmosphere of the valleys of the interior, or the mephitic exhalations from the deadly marsh already described, seemed to be laden with the very essence of health and strength. The sparkling silvery sea-sand, which had rarely been trod by any civilised race of men, was crisp and firm beneath our feet. As we wended our way along, enjoying our work in a way that made it seem like play, our attention was attracted by a small group of cocoa-nut palm trees, evidently planted by the old settlers, for none were found elsewhere in the vicinity of this great harbour.

The hill, on the summit of which was built the settlement that owed its foundation to the enterprising and intrepid Blair, was now before us. We were anxious to ascend to the slope on which we might still find its remains, but the eminence was so thickly covered with the luxuriant vegetation of the island, that the task appeared to be one attended with no inconsiderable difficulty. Our Burmese convicts, however—a patient, quiet, uncomplaining lot, to whom all the more laborious tasks were assigned—were set to work; and though it was not executed without considerable difficulty, we had the pleasure of seeing a path cut out by which we could easily ascend. As we made our way up the hill, we soon came upon the vestiges of which we were in search, even the most familiar objects of which excited our lively interest, as testifying to the former presence of those who were once engaged on a mission of the same nature as that which had brought us to this solitary island. Broken bricks, tiles, and stone that had been used in building, were lying about in every direction, all so thickly covered with the vegetation that had grown during the intervening years, that they appeared imbedded in the soil, and it was not until we had stumbled over them in our onward progress, as we frequently did, that in some cases we became aware of their presence, or were able to ascertain what they were. Although the elevation was by no means considerable, not more, I believe, than one hundred and fifty feet, yet from the numerous trifling difficulties that constantly impeded us in our ascent, and from the necessity under which we were of clearing our way before us, the day was far advanced before we had completed our upward progress, and when we at length stood upon the summit of the hill, the sun was fast declining below the horizon.

The scene upon which we looked from the summit was one well calculated to fix the gaze of all who delight in new varieties of natural scenery. All around the hill, as far as the eye could see, extended what literally ap-

REMAINS OF THE OLD SETTLEMENT, PORT CORNWALLIS, CHATHAM ISLAND.

peared to be an ocean of vegetation, gently swaying and undulating before the light breeze of the evening. The rich crimson of the tropical sunset contrasted with the endless shades of silvan green that distinguished the spontaneous vegetable growth of successive years. The remarkable profusion of trees and plants, the closeness with which the various parasites were laced and interlaced together, may be gathered from the fact that not only our light Burmese followers, but also several of our more robust English, or, at any rate, European nautical companions, walked, without the assistance of their hands, as in climbing, almost to the top of several of the loftiest trees, the path that they took being over the twining trunks of the creepers, unexampled for their prodigious size. To the very verge of the horizon this astonishing exuberance of vegetation extended. All that we heard was the gentle rustling of innumerable leaves, slightly moved by the gentle breeze of evening; all that we saw was this ocean of green, in which not even an opening the size of a man's hand could be discovered after the longest, closest, and most searching observation.

The day was now nearly at an end, and we were almost exhausted by our labours. Not only the declining sun, now on the verge of the horizon, but our own sensations admonished us that it was ample time to repair our exhausted energies. There is nothing like the faithful discharge of duty, especially in the open air—labour accomplished with zeal, good-will, and energy—to stimulate a man's appetite; and our stomachs told us, with as unerring exactness as the chronometer, that it was time to return to the ship for a late dinner. The appetite we had acquired enabled us all to enjoy the good things provided, and the process of digestion was assisted by agreeable conversation on all we had seen, heard, and done during our excursion. After having considered and determined on our plan of action for the following day, we all retired for the night to our hammocks—a nautical term by which we may be excused for designating our comfortable berths on board the *Pluto*.

CHAPTER III.

Notes and Reports—A Night Scene—Discovery of Native Huts—Search for the Cemetery of the Former Settlers—Stragglers—A False Alarm—Enduring Brickwork—Restless Spirits—Restraints of discipline—A Survivor of the *Prince*—Insalubrity of the Neighbourhood of Port Cornwallis—Discovery of the cause—Craggy Island—Our First Sight of the Natives—Their Astonishment on perceiving us—Preparations for Landing—Our Unfriendly Reception—A Defiant Chief—A Party of Native Women—Their Helpless Terror—Their Ungraceful Appearance—A Mincopie Matron—Bellicose Pantomime—Jealous Fury of the Male Savages—A Native Canoe—An Unsuccessful Linguistic Attempt—Landing on Craggy Island—Interior of a Native Hut—An Unexpected Attack—Bad Firing—An Unfortunate Accident—The Evening *Dolce far niente*—Opinions regarding the "Scrimmage"—Useful Admonition to the Crew—Saddle Hill Photographed by Mons. Mallitte—Departure of the *Pluto* greeted with Yells of Triumph—Obstinate Enmity of the Savages—Unsuccessful Issue of our First Attempt to hold intercourse with them.

Dr. Playfair, Lieutenant Heathcoate, and myself, made each our independent observations, taking note even of the most minute circumstance that might afterwards prove useful, either for knowledge or for application in some form. To secure the utmost accuracy, the memory was not trusted with a load of facts, not to be noted down perhaps until they had got hopelessly jumbled together, but everything was faithfully recorded the very day it occurred, when the impression was vivid, and before error, that creeps in so subtly with delay, had time to distort our simple narrative of facts. And not only so, but each evening all the notes were placed in my hands; the part of the official report having reference to the day was compiled from them, after we three had met in solemn conclave for their discussion, finally giving them the stamp of our united approval. This was the routine of every day—the task from which nothing was allowed to divert our minds; and in whatever circumstances we might be placed, the day's work was not considered as accomplished until the day's report was fairly disposed of. It was our most anxious wish to ensure the utmost exactness and truth of description, and therefore not a word was entered in the record for the perfect accuracy of which all could not vouch, if called upon to do so. From the detailed journal of each successive day, thus made to account for its own transactions, the present general account of our visit to the Andamans, and of our daily operations, was extracted, abridged, or compiled.

The men of our party also, of all tribes, tongues, and nations, had their own serious confabulations, into which they seemed to enter with quite as much earnestness as we thought it necessary to display in what we considered our more important consultations. But so it is;

each class forms its world for itself, and enjoys its own special subjects of interest and amusement. It was pleasant to look on the various groups of hearty, willing, hard-working fellows, enjoying the pipe of friendship, and spinning interminable yarns, more devoutly believed in the more incredible they were, while the cool evening air refreshed them after the heat and toil of the day. As subsequent events proved, one of the subjects they had most earnestly discussed was the propriety of introducing theatricals, and of obtaining facilities for the enjoyment of their recreations. In such plans we all heartily concurred; for experience has proved their beneficial influence in enabling the men to pass pleasantly and happily many hours which, in places where they would probably find little to attract them after the first novelty had worn off, would otherwise hang listlessly and heavily upon their hands. All their projects of this description were subsequently realized, and were enjoyed with all the hearty and almost child-like delight of sailors.

Before midnight all was still and silent on board the *Pluto*, save the regulated pace of the solitary sentinel as he trod the deck. Before retiring to rest, I again came on deck to take a last view of that scene the aspect of which had appeared to me so novel and interesting during the day. The spectacle was one that language would fail in attempting to describe. The beautiful expanse of water all around, the faint murmur of the dark forests on the land, and the stars and constellations shining in the great temple of heaven, formed altogether a picture of solemn grandeur, imposing silence on the reflective mind, and stirring up some feeling of awe and devotion in even the most thoughtless. I looked round on the tranquil night-scene with feelings really too deep for utterance, and then retired for the night, secure in the confidence of that vigilant watch which was never intermitted during the whole period of our stay in the islands.

The next day was Saturday. Almost with the first streaks of dawn the silence that had reigned during the night was broken by the sound of our men preparing for the resumption of their daily labour. A special task had this day been assigned for each of the leaders of the expedition, and, our forces being divided, a fair proportion was assigned to each. Lieutenant Heathcote proceeded in one of the boats to explore a bay on the north side of the great natural harbour in which the steamer lay at anchor. As they were rowing slowly along they came upon a pretty extensive reef composed of very fine coral, from which several specimens were hammered off, and carried away as trophies. He also discovered several native huts, but perceived no signs of the recent presence of any occupants, nor was he able to find in the vicinity even the smallest rill of fresh water, such as is generally found near those localities fixed upon by the natives for either a partial or lengthened sojourn.

The remainder of us landed again on Chatham Island, to the north-east end of which we directed our course. Our photographer accompanied us, having, it is needless to say, a complete set of his apparatus with him. We were anxious to discover, if possible, the burying-place of the former settlement, and anything that might prove of interest as memorials of our predecessors. We found it difficult to make any progress, and toiled painfully and slowly on. It was found absolutely necessary again to have recourse to the labours of our Burmese contingent, for this rank vegetation was on all sides in our way, a natural barrier that only force could remove. Slowly and perseveringly they preceded the party, cutting a passage by which we were enabled to advance, though certainly not with the quickness we all considered desirable. The course we selected led us ere long to a small mound, up which, with the aid of our Burmese pioneers, we laboriously made our way. It was evidently a position in which a flag-staff had been formerly fixed. The slope was strewn with a number of circular bricks, that had doubtless formed part of a column of masonry; and at the base of the same elevation we could ascertain that a small patch of the rank growing grass was of a darker colour—indicating, in all probability, the presence of the dead—than that around it. The view from the top of this mound was precisely the same as that already described in our operations of the preceding day—nothing to be seen within the whole compass of space that the eye could take in but a continuous, uninterrupted sea of dense vegetation, so close in many places as to resemble an enamelled lawn of forest leaves.

With all the pains that had been taken to discipline our men, and to teach them to act with something like military obedience, the end had not been so perfectly attained as we could have desired. Either from the shortness of time, or from the difficulty of getting men, who had been brought together in a rather miscellaneous way, to perform their duty with all the regularity and firmness that are always the best signs of a well-disciplined body, little events were constantly occurring to show how much several of our followers were still wanting in this respect. One of the most striking marks of their deficiency was, that they were easily thrown into a state of alarm, and, to use the language of Scripture, when it so expressively describes the terrors of a guilty conscience, they sometimes fled when no man pursued. The first example of the defective training of our force occurred during the early days of our stay at Chatham Island. Although the most imperative orders had been given for the men never to venture beyond a certain safe distance from the main body, yet we were constantly annoyed by the terrors, real and imaginary, of stragglers, and by our own apprehensions for them during the time of their disappearance. A foolish fellow had, on one occasion, wandered away from his column, and, after struggling with difficulty through the thick tangled stems and roots, without well knowing whither he was going, and becoming more and more confused as he wandered on without being able to recover the trace of his companions, all at once he was brought to a stand-still by the sight of what appeared a large dusky living body slowly and cautiously making its way towards him, stealing onwards, as he thought, in such a stealthy way as to avoid his observation. Perhaps it is not much to the credit of our civilization, but the solitary European, however well armed, often dreads to come in contact even with a single savage of the woods, as our straggler supposed this to be. In the panic of the moment, without the exercise of the slightest caution, he fired his musket upon the advancing body, and then rushed back with all the blindness of fear to the column he ought never to have quitted. The report of the piece in the silent solitude of the forest resembled that of a nine-pounder, and, reverberating like a continued peal of thunder among the surrounding hills, at once excited the apprehension, among our little body, that some danger was menacing us. Every man, without a moment's loss of time, was on the alert—all their arms, grasped with a firm hand, being held ready for instant use, and for some time every one held his breath, nothing being heard but the crashing sound made by the trembling fugitive, as, with more than usual speed, he made his way over the crackling roots and branches in his path. It was a fortunate thing that all firing without orders had been strictly prohibited, for, otherwise, as none knew of the absence of this thoughtless straggler, he might have been received by his alarmed comrades with some well-aimed shots, that would have made shorter work with him than the real or imaginary object of terror from which he fled. However, the advanced guard were steady old men-of-war's men, who stood silently to their arms until the breathless, hatless, shoeless, and speechless fugitive, with hair dishevelled, and a wild scared look, burst like a bomb into their midst. The alarm spread even to the steamer, for, on hearing the shot, the party left on board hoisted the caution signal at the fore, while we all waited with bated breath, and fingers on our triggers, ready to give any corporeal enemy that might have the audacity to show himself a warm reception. But the spirit of valour had been evoked to no purpose, and although the straggler told some wonderful story of what had driven him to seek safety in flight, no appearance was put in. The only sound of living thing we heard was the cooing of a colony of wood-pigeons, perceived by none of us till that moment. It is true we also heard a short, low muffled sound, something resembling that with which the monkeys of Ceylon cŏmmunicate with each other; but no human voice was heard, and nothing at all formidable made its appearance. It was, we have every reason to believe, one of those stupid, unreasoning panics to which an ignorant man is likely to yield in such circumstances, when his own terrors create for him the alarming object before which he takes his flight, putting all the energy and life he has in his heels.

The panic excited in our main body by the escapade of this foolish fellow subsided as quickly as it arose, and sloping their arms over their shoulders, they smiled at the causeless alarm that had excited almost as much terror in some of them as the first sight of the foot-mark on the sand in the mind of Crusoe on his solitary island. The articles of dress the trembling runaway had left behind in his precipitate flight were recovered for him by some of his less timorous comrades, who did not know whether to laugh or be angry at him as, on receiving back his hat and shoes, he restored each to its right place.

We now descended the hill for the purpose of selecting a position from which the remains of Blair's abandoned settlement could be photographed. The preparations for this took up a great deal of time, the masses of old masonry being held so tenaciously in the grasp of the strong creepers, and so profusely covered with vegetation, that before we could expose to view these interesting ruins—for so they appeared to us—the labour and delay were such as to call into requisition all the patience we possessed. The work had been done as solidly and effectively as if the settlement had been intended for a much longer existence than was actually its lot. The brickwork was firm and secure, as perfect as it was on the day when it came fresh from the hands of the builders, several of the arches being still unbroken. Monsieur Mallitte included as much in his picture as the aperture of his lens permitted. Strangely, however, not a single particle of the stonework, to which allusion is made by Colonel Symes, could be discovered, although we made a diligent search for it, and, with the usual amount of labour and difficulty, displaced a great quantity of the obtrusive vegetation that concealed everything from our sight.

Leaving the hill, we made our way to the shore, and wandered along the sandy beach. Coming to the small rivulet from whose clear and transparent waters the old colonists were abundantly supplied, we forded it, not without some difficulty—for we were compelled to clamber over the rough masses of sandstone with which its bed was encumbered. From its bank we discovered a way by which the peaceful colony of beautiful pigeons that had been disturbed by the fire of the thoughtless straggler before mentioned could be reached. They were, however, as may be anticipated, very difficult to approach. Unaccustomed to the unusual sounds by which their privacy was disturbed, they were very wild and wary, and took flight the moment they perceived any movement among our party. We managed, however, to shoot a number of them, which we carried off, to add to the variety of the supply in our larder.

We discovered frequently in our rambles that the men of our guard were not disposed to be quite as amenable to discipline as we considered necessary. There was a considerable spice of untamed savage nature in some of them; and everything in the form of restraint, however necessary, was an unbearable burden to them. Their ideal of liberty was licentiousness, and in their uncontrolled vivacity they were equally ready at all times for a frolic or a fight. Such a crew formed a strange outgrowth of modern civilization, a sort of varnished savages. Ignorant of the power of combined action, to which they had been all their lives unaccustomed, we found the task of subduing them into patterns of discipline not quite so easy as we probably at first imagined; and as most of them had what they called some "dodges" of their own, we had good reason to fear that not the least laborious part of the duties before us would be to keep them subject to the reins of discipline it was considered imperative to impose upon them. Many of them were wild adventurons seamen, who had led roving and unsettled lives in all parts of the globe. Excitement and danger were the elements of the atmosphere in which they lived; and as they were utterly reckless of their lives and persons, it was with difficulty they could be induced to exercise even ordinary caution when they were threatened with the most imminent perils. The officer who commanded them was a man according to their own hearts; he was the most daring of their number, and always in front when there was the least chance of an encounter of any kind. His life had been a very adventurous one, and the experience of danger had not taught him to fear or avoid it. He was on board the *Prince*, at Balaclava, in that terrible storm of November which so soon followed the battle of Inkerman, and was the sole survivor of that lamentable calamity. When the unfortunate vessel went down, he was washed by the tempestuous sea on to a ledge of rock, from which perilous position he was with great difficulty rescued by means of ropes let down from the overhanging heights. Such was the spirit of adventure by which this fearless man was animated, one might well imagine that on that night of dark and ominous memory he had imbibed the very spirit of the Black Sea tempest.

The previous attempt at settlement on this island, and on this particular part of it, had not been persevered in; and it required no unusual discernment to discover the cause of the temporary failure. If there was nothing more than the unusual insalubrity of the locality, arising from the salt marsh by which it was fringed, the settlement could not be considered a desirable one so long as such a source of malaria was allowed to exist. The British Government, or its representatives in India, have never considered it necessary to endanger the lives of criminals, and therefore came to the conclusion that the transportation of offenders to a locality so fatal to health would be a step that no argument could justify. This was a result much to be regretted in some points of view, for there were circumstances that rendered Port Cornwallis better adapted for the purpose than any other; and if such means of prevention and cure as those with which we are now familiar had been then taken, there would have been no necessity for abandoning it. Although we afterwards came ourselves to the decision that it was the locality best adapted for a convict establishment, still we considered it desirable to extend the sphere of our researches, in order, if possible, to succeed in the discovery of one which might offer superior recommendations.

We therefore lost no time in returning to the boats, which were waiting for us at a short distance from the shore; and being taken on board, we rowed to the ships, and breakfasted about noon.

The anchor being raised and the steam up, we steered along the coast, taking a southward direction. We were anxious, however, before leaving this part of the island, again to land, our purpose being to ascend, if practicable, the Saddle Hill, with the view of studying its geological peculiarities, and of collecting specimens of its botanical productions. We therefore continued to coast along the island at a moderate speed, keeping as near to the shore as due consideration for our safety permitted.

About 3 P.M., as we were following the course already indicated, a small islet, Craggy Island, was discovered, the coasts of which, on drawing near to it, we perceived to be very rocky, and its general appearance picturesque and pleasing in the extreme. When we came to what seemed a suitable spot, we formed the determination of anchoring under its lee. We sailed round it, however, in the first place, with the view of obtaining a better idea of its general appearance, and had just returned to the spot which the Captain judged a suitable one for anchoring in, when our attention was attracted by a sight that it had not yet been our fortune, on any part of the larger island, to obtain, namely, that of a group of natives. As, strangely enough, probably from their position, and the interest of the occupation in which they were engaged, their attention had not yet been attracted to us, we had an opportunity of taking a leisurely observation of them. They were stationed on the edge of a bold reef of rock, looking down towards the water, and from their gestures we concluded that the occupation by which they were so absorbed as not to observe our approach, was that of fishing. A glance at them through the glass was sufficient to satisfy us that our supposition was correct. It also enabled us to discover what our naked eyes had not yet remarked, another group of savages on a sandy part of the beach. A canoe was observed at a short distance from them, lying, as it appeared to us, high and dry upon the shore.

When we first perceived this band of natives from the steamer, we had slackened our speed so much as scarcely to move at all. Our object in this was not only to have a leisurely opportunity for examining them, but also that they might not be disturbed by the noise of the steam and paddles, which fortunately had not yet attracted their attention. We next determined to approach considerably nearer to the shore, probably within a few hundred yards, and to drop anchor at a convenient place and depth. An object so large and prominent as the steamer, accompanied in its progress by the loud noise of the engines and the constant plash of the paddle wheels, could not long escape observation; and, of course, we had no wish it should, but the reverse. As we drew towards the reef already mentioned, the native party stationed on it were observed all at once to make a sudden start, and to stand transfixed with unspeakable astonishment and awe. It is not too much to say that they seemed to be completely paralysed by our sudden appearance on their coast. If we had dropped from the clouds, or risen from the sea, their wonder and admiration could not have been more excessive. They appeared all at once to have been struck dumb—their wondering gaze fixed in one direction, and on one sole object. What was it? what was in it? what was to come out of it? and how was it to affect them?—were thoughts that no doubt simultaneously occurred to their agitated minds at the sight of this puffing, smoking sea-monster.

Their torpor was of short duration, for the shouts of the crew, however unintelligible to them, were sufficient to convince them that the monster ship, the fire-vessel, that had excited their wonder, contained human beings, and was under the direction of human will and hands. They would start, and gaze, and look in amazement at each other, as the loud rattling noise made by the fast unrolling anchor chain, and the more unaccountable sound caused by the escaping steam, as in clouds of dense white vapour it issued shrieking from the steam-pipe, at once appalled their hearts, and excited their curiosity. When they had at length succeeded in shaking off the torpor produced by this unknown and mysterious object of terror, their conversation and gestures became animated beyond all power of description.

Nor was the feeling among the seamen and others on board the steamer much less intense than it was among the savages on land. The moment the latter were seen, the excitement became intense. The romantic stories by which they had amused their leisure hours were recalled to mind, and all the circumstances of terror with which they were rife were greatly exaggerated by the active imagination of the more ignorant and timid. As the savages, regaining confidence, raised a shout that sounded in our ears like one of defiance, the influence of discipline was not sufficiently powerful to prevent some of the younger and more excitable of our crew from hurling back their challenge from the ship's side, where we were all assembled, having left our various occupations to gratify those feelings of curiosity which all entertained.

In the meantime, my two friends, the captain of the *Pluto*, and myself, held a short consultation, in order to determine in what manner we should approach and greet the natives, so that, if possible, we might obtain their confidence, and banish all fear and suspicion from their minds. What other method could be adopted than that generally found available with savages?—namely, to endeavour to hold intercourse with them by friendly signs, and to load them with such trifling presents as they most value, and which they would regard as the best evidences of our good-will. On the command being given, our usual order was soon restored, and dead silence succeeded the first burst of excitement that had followed the discovery we had made. The crews of the two cutters were piped to duty; the men appeared with their loaded arms, which were carefully and quietly stowed away in the boats; and in a marvellously short space of time, all were reported ready for proceeding to shore. Our men were carefully cautioned as to their conduct with the natives; that they should abstain from any action calculated to provoke their anger, or to excite their suspicion; that no liberty should be taken with their females; and that they themselves should be as patient, long-suffering, gentle, and kind as possible in all their dealings with them. By such a course of conduct they could not fail ultimately to win their good-will and confidence, and thus they would promote their own security, and forward the object of the expedition.

The two crews now fell into their places, went down the ladders in regular order, one by one, and took their places in the boats, their oars raised upwards. The regularity and discipline of the crew of a man-of-war's boat always forms a spectacle at once pleasing and impressive. There was an alacrity in their movements, an expression of cheerfulness on their countenances, and a general air of determination, which showed that the extravagant fables regarding the prowess and cruelty of the savages, even supposing they did in some measure give them credit, had in no way daunted their courage or excited any fears as to the result, now that they were to be brought, it might be, into violent collision with them. The steady old coxswain, who had seen no end of service, and had passed through many a stirring adventure, raising his hand to his eyes to shade them from the rays of the setting sun, calmly surveyed the menacing group of Mincopies, and then, turning round, exclaimed, with something like an audible stage whisper, meant for all to hear, though not immediately directed to all, "Well, I'm blowed if they're not mere naked savages after all!" to which the men, leaning on their oars, grinned that silent but expressive response in the affirmative, which sailors have acquired the habit of. Such of the natives of India as accompanied us, as well as those that remained on board the steamer, still showed symptoms of being under the influence of the imaginary fears their own terror had created; and if they did not see the lions' heads and horses' tails, it was because they cowered with fear behind the bulwarks. Such, at least, was their own explanation.

The savages, meanwhile, were carefully watching all our proceedings—no movement, however trifling, escaping their observation, or failing to be interpreted in some way intelligible to themselves, and generally not favourable to us or to our designs. Their predominant feelings appeared to be wonder and curiosity; they were either too cunning and cautious to show any signs of terror, or they really experienced no such sensation. As our men descended the ladders one by one, and took their proper positions, the natives closely observed all their proceedings, their excitement evidently increasing; and when at last the two boats were pushed off from the steamer's side, the oars flashing in the rays of the setting sun, as they rose in perfect harmony of movement from the water, a sharp instantaneous shout, or rather yell, that seemed to express one concentrated feeling of defiance and enmity, burst from the dusky throats of all the fighting-men assembled on the beach.

A peculiar natural phenomenon rendered the scene still more striking and impressive as the interval between the two parties, the savage and the civilized, was gradually diminished by the onward motion of the boats. The spray, as it rose in clouds from the breakers dashing on the shore, reflecting the rays of the declining sun, magnified considerably the slight figures of the natives, making massive and formidable giants of men who were in reality little more than sable dwarfs. As the cutters neared the part of the shore where they had stationed themselves, and they clearly perceived that we were making preparations to land, their excitement was such that they appeared as if they had suddenly become frantic. They seemed to lose that restraint and self-control which it is the pride of the savage to exhibit in time of danger, and jumped and yelled like so many demons let loose from the bottomless pit, or as if there had been a Bedlam in that locality, and they the most unmanageable of its frantic inmates. Their manner was that of men determined and formidable in the midst of all their excitement They brandished their bows in our direction, they menaced us with their arrows, said by common report—so often a liar—to be poisoned, exhibiting, by every possible contortion of savage pantomime, their hostile determination. To use a common vulgar expression of some of the seamen, they seemed to have made their minds up to "chaw us all up."

One man, who stood prominently out from the others, and who seemed to direct their movements, was, to the best of our judgment, their chief. The spear which he flourished incessantly was terminated by a bright, flat, pointed head, which gleamed with flashes of light, as, circling rapidly in the air, it reflected the rays of the sun. Sometimes he would hold it aloft, poising it in his uplifted hand, as if with the intention of hurling it with unerring and deadly aim at the first who dared to approach the shore of his native island. At length, in a paroxysm of well-acted fury, he dashed boldly into the water, boiling and seething around him as it broke in great billows on the beach, and on the rocks by which it was defended, and fixing an arrow in his bow he shot it off in the direction of the steamer, as if that were the arch-enemy that had provoked his bellicose fury. This was an impotent act of blind rage, that rather depreciated the noble savage in our estimation. The ridiculous was so closely associated with the sublime, that a hearty laugh greeted his absurd display of courage, which reminded us of some of those laughable acts of tragi-comedy that are occasionally exhibited on the stage. The contagion of our mirth spread from one boat to the other, and from both to the steamer, until we all joined simultaneously in one hearty laugh, which undoubtedly excited the astonishment and ire of the gentleman in black, who had intended to strike us dumb with terror and amaze by the above formidable representation of his prowess. The very echoes in the surrounding hills were awakened by the rollicking hilarity of our men; and, to the chieftain's vexation, his native rocks joined with the hostile stranger in turning his over-hasty valour into ridicule.

But meanwhile what was doing on the sandy beach, where the other party of natives were collected? There was evidently some performance of a very different description in the course of enactment there, the nature of which, when we became aware of it, fully accounted for the remarkable heroic antics of the warrior on the reef. A timid knot of frightened females, as destitute of any respectable patch of clothing as their male protectors, ran to and fro in helpless, hopeless alarm. They evidently did not know what to do, as, with those significant gestures in which untutored savages so often indulge, they expressed more plainly and impressively than they could have done by language—even if it were intelligible to us—the anxiety and terror by which they were possessed. They wrung their hands, threw themselves on the beach, seemed to look towards us with gestures of supplication and prayers for mercy; and then, covering their faces with their hands, tried to shut out the untoward object which had filled them with such feelings of dismay. Some of them, perceiving the light canoe which had been drawn up upon the beach, drew the notice of their companions to it, and made an attempt to get it down to the water's edge; but, with their utmost exertions, they could not succeed in accomplishing this object. Although savages do not hesitate to put their women to any kind of labour they have the strength to perform, and which can be imposed upon them, they had evidently had no experience in such work as this, for nothing could be more awkward than their movements, and, so to speak, more unbusiness-like than their entire proceedings. Although their failure was no doubt a very serious matter, as it appeared to them, to us it was amusing in the extreme—for nothing could be more absurd than the manner in which, in their alarm and confusion, they rolled themselves about on the sand, forming altogether as ludicrous a spectacle as it is possible to imagine. Their appearance, too, was by no means attractive; and this made us less restrained in the expression of our mirth, for if there had been anything like beauty among them, even though black, it might have induced us to look upon them with greater interest and respect. But the distinct sight we had of them through our powerful glasses showed that they were not merely plain and unattractive, but absolutely hideous—and far from pleasant objects to look upon. Their complexions were as black as soot could make those of our Ethiopian minstrels at home. Their small dwarfish figures were hard and angular, and their general contour the very reverse of graceful. Indeed, they were far inferior in this respect to the men, whose mode of life in all probability favoured a more complete and graceful development of the corporeal frame. It is true, tastes often differ very much; but in this case the harmony of opinion was remarkable, and no one had a flattering word for the ladies of the Andamans—about as uninviting specimens of the black portion of the fair sex as it had ever been our lot to look upon.

Their heads were perhaps the best part about them. They were certainly small, bullet-like appendages, but they were not otherwise ill-formed. The fact that they were entirely destitute of that natural ornament which has a graceful appearance even when the phrenological development is far from being what the professors of Spurzheim's "mental science" call beautiful, namely, an abundant head of hair, or even any hair at all, did not at all tend to make their other defects less perceptible. The red ochre with which their bald occiputs were daubed was no doubt meant as an ornament, but we cannot recommend it as an article of the toilette, for it only rendered their appearance more repulsive. Around the waist, and resting on the hips, were slung small wicker baskets, in which were deposited whatever they had been successful enough to procure while fishing, an occupation in which they might have been engaged when the unexpected appearance of our dreadful fire-ship struck them with admiration and wonder. Our attention was particularly attracted by the appearance of one of them, a stout, matronly-looking dame, perhaps beyond middle age, and her visage wrinkled so as to be absolutely hideous, who wore two of those useful ornaments which look for all the world like the foundations of those well-shaped cradles on which modern female civilization hangs the petticoat which the belles of Craggy Island have not had the ingenuity to invent for themselves. We do not profess to be very profoundly versed in the æsthetics of dress, and therefore leave it to those who have devoted their whole attention to a subject of so much importance—particularly to *the* sex—to determine whether the light wicker-work fish-baskets thus worn be not the real original crinoline, the birth-place of which is still a matter of doubt to many profound inquirers. If it has come so far, we need not wonder that it has taken firm root as one of our standard female institutions, and is found impervious to the most merciless attacks of masculine criticism, the poisoned shafts of which rattle against an armour they cannot penetrate, and fall to the ground without the infliction of the slightest injury.

But we are digressing too much, and have almost forgotten where we were. The crews were in their places, and inspired by the words "Give way, lads!" all the oars kept dipping simultaneously in the water, and impelled by their powerful and well-timed strokes, the boats glided swiftly along, and were soon close to the beach, on the soft shining, silvery sand of which we landed, at the distance of only a few feet from the stranded canoe. The poor Andamanese women were now wringing their hands with ten-fold desperation; and at last, under the influence of their panic, fairly fled, taking refuge in the thick jungle with which the greater part of the island—which is of very inconsiderable extent, probably not more than fifty yards in breadth—was covered.

Our appearance so close to the women on shore was regarded with amazement and anger—judging by their gestures—by the party of warriors on the reef. Their gesticulations became every moment more and more violent. In their excitement, which had evidently risen to boiling point, they shouted fiercely to us, they brandished their weapons, they menaced us with their bows and arrows. Nothing could be more expressive than their pantomime, which seemed to be the very language of nature, describing, in a form which admitted of no ambiguity, the feelings with which they regarded us. That we had directed our course in the first place to the part of the beach where the women were collected, evidently gave them a very poor opinion of our courage. Why did we not come at once to them, fight them like men, and leave the poor frightened women alone?

Although we had not the same facility and natural grace in expressing our sentiments by pantomimic gestures, an acquirement in which the calm reflecting Englishman is always inferior to the impulsive savage, we did our best to signify, as eloquently as we could, in our stiff way, that we had no hostile purpose, and that, só far as their not very tempting ladies were concerned, our intentions were free from all reproach. Everything was done to allay the storm of wrath that had been excited, and to avert their savage hostility, by showing that our most anxious desire was to conciliate them by acts of kindness and good-will. To convince them how scrupulously we wished to respect their females, and also to prevent any of our inconsiderate young sailors from causing mischief by following the less repulsive of them with amorous intentions, sentries were posted under the charge of an officer, with the strictest orders that none of our men should be allowed to direct their steps in the direction of that part of the jungle where the Mincopie women had taken refuge. This was done in such a way as to make our purpose as intelligible as possible to the angry and jealous party of men on the reef. Their canoe also was preserved from injury, and while we were standing beside it a number of such articles as are generally found to be attractive to savages—looking-glasses flashing in the sun, beads of the most dazzling and brilliant colours, and other articles of finery—were held up before them, turned in all directions, so as to attract notice and excite their cupidity, and then deposited in it. At the same time we availed ourselves of the opportunity of observing the manner in which it was constructed. It seemed to have been scooped out of the trunk of a single large tree, and was long, narrow, and gracefully shaped. It contained a small outrigger for the purpose of steadying it when out at sea. A large torch, formed chiefly of some kind of resin, several small and slender-shaped paddles, and one or two baskets, filled with a quantity of different kinds of shell-fish, were also found in it. The sand around the canoe was disturbed by the restless movements in which the women had indulged on perceiving our approach, and the contents of the small baskets which they wear on the hips were lying about in all directions, having been abandoned in their alarm wherever they had fallen. The print of their footsteps, for the most part small and symmetrical, could be traced to the jungle, as they scattered themselves in hasty flight the moment our approach was observed. Within the wood all was perfectly still and hushed, not a single subdued cry or whisper indicating where the timorous fugitives had concealed themselves, or whether they were still in our vicinity. Our men grumbled a little, though in all good-humour, at not being allowed to go after the savage beauties, to have a look at them. Their only consolation was to admire themselves, with many jokes and jests, in the looking-glasses, which they considered it unnecessary to leave behind in the boat, regarding them as so many useful articles thrown away, as they could not see to what use the Mincopie women, without that head adornment which is the greatest ornament of their sex, could put them.

Returning to our boat, we re-embarked with the intention of approaching more nearly, and endeavouring to reconcile the angry party on the reef. The breakers were rolling rather high, and prevented us getting so close to them as we desired. As they saw us advancing in their direction, they lost none of their former defiant courage, but still continued loudly to menace us, defying us to come on and meet them. No fear, no hesitation was perceptible in any of them. Their implacable hostility was expressed with the same energy as ever in all their attitudes and gestures. Our endeavours to appease them, by showing that we had no hostile intent, that we desired only amicable intercourse, produced no effect on these obstinate savages—for we cannot have failed in making our kind and pacific intentions intelligible to them. Standing up in the stern sheets of our respective cutters, we held out our hands, waved white handkerchiefs, exhibited numerous dazzling strings of beads, unfolded pieces of cotton cloth for their acceptance, and made use of every gesture we could imagine fitted to express amity, peace, and good-will. We shouted as loud as we could, to be heard over the incessant roar of the breakers as they dashed upon the rock, the word *padoo*, which we had found in Colebrooke's vocabulary, where it is represented as meaning *friend;* but it failed in producing the desired effect, and drew from the excited and angry natives only yells of fierce derision. The nearer we drew to the shore their manifestations of hostility became more decided; and all our endeavours to avert their fury only seemed to render them more implacable in their determination to resist all our attempts to conciliate their friendship. Showers of arrows were discharged at us, but as they fell short of the boats, no one was injured by them.

Finding the savages in this impracticable mood, all our amicable advances contemptuously rejected by them, we at last saw how useless it was to persevere in so thankless a task, and determined, in the meantime, to leave them to their own councils. Accordingly we pulled away quietly along the shore, taking a southward direction, looking out as we proceeded for a convenient landing place. We also hoped that in the interim their angry passions might have time to cool down, and that our proceedings would show them we had no desire for anything but friendly communication. As we proceeded along the coast of the island, a few of the party continued to watch us closely, following us at a safe distance. After thus dogging our progress for perhaps more than half a mile, they suddenly, as if in obedience to some previously concerted plan, discontinued their pursuit, and disappeared among the dense woods that extended down close to the beach.

After rowing along about a couple of miles, in search of a sandy part of the shore, where it would be convenient to land, we at length discovered a place that seemed suited for our purpose, a shelving beach covered with shingle. As it was a lea shore, and there was a considerable breeze, the north-east monsoon, which blows fresh at sunset, great care had to be exercised in the management of the boats in running in towards the shore. The usual precautions were observed on landing. A small party was left with the boats, to look after them. The men were all well armed. They were reminded of the crafty, cunning dispositions of the natives, who would do all they could to catch us in some ambush; and they were therefore exhorted, for their own sakes, to attend as closely as possible to the rules of discipline already urged. They were accordingly formed in order, and marched up the shore. As we had good reason for supposing that our friends of the reef were not far off, and there could be little doubt were watching, though unseen, every step we took, we were well on our guard, and kept up a constant outlook for them.

Almost immediately opposite the place where we had landed, we discovered a tolerably large square hut. It was well thatched, and prettily embowered under the wide-spreading shady branches of the acacia tree. The eaves of this primitive abode were remarkably low—so much so, that, before we could enter it, we were obliged to stoop almost to the ground. Having crept in, however, in the interior it was found high enough to enable the tallest of us to stand upright under its thatched roof. There was no one within, although there were signs that it must have been previously occupied, probably at no remote period. It was adorned with the not very inviting ornaments usually found in the dwellings of the natives. The floor was strewed with numerous fish bones, and the skulls of pigs and turtle were suspended from the roof. Nothing was disturbed. Everything was allowed to remain as we found it, only a small looking-glass and a few strings of beads being left behind for the owner, or for any of the natives who might enter the hut, to show that our feelings were only friendly, and with the hope of being able thus gradually to conciliate the implacable dispositions of these obstinate savages.

On leaving, we proceeded on our course along the beach, Mr. Cotgrove being in front, in charge of our advanced guard. We were allowed to continue our journey for a short time in perfect peace, observing the natural features of the place, remarking the unusual scenery, collecting botanical specimens, or noting the geological conformation of the island. We had not, however, advanced more than a quarter of a mile, when our peaceable observations were disturbed—it cannot be said in an unexpected, but, at any rate, in a very disagreeable way. On turning a sharp angle of projecting rock, our ears were saluted by a formidable yell, that rung sharply from the jungle, and almost before we could turn round to look for our enemy, a shower of long arrows fell among us. In a moment our men faced sharply round, and fired a close volley into the midst of the tall trees, from which it was plain the arrows had been discharged. This was contrary to imperative orders, and though, perhaps, in the circumstances, it need excite no surprise, it showed they were not yet broken in to that order so essential to men acting together in a body. For some little time similar *contretemps* occurred, all fortunately harmless in their results; but ultimately the end desired was gained—they learned to restrain their impatience and wait for orders, and the strict discipline which they were at first inclined to regard as so unwelcome a yoke, they learned ere long to consider as the best means of safety and protection for themselves, and as rendering them most formidable to the bands of savages who attacked them. I observed, also, that, in firing, our men raised their firelocks too high, and discharged their contents among the branches of the trees. Consequently none of the savages were injured, and they had no reason to regard our weapons as in any way more formidable than their own bows and arrows. Without leaving one wounded man behind, they gradually slipped away among the trees, and that evening we neither saw any more of them, nor experienced any further annoyance from their hostility.

Our men, however, were of a different opinion from ourselves as to the result of their fire. They did not seem, for a moment, to imagine that so close a volley, even though their weapons were discharged at random among the trees, could have been fired with no other expenditure than that of powder and lead. One of them accordingly came up to me, and, touching his hat, said, "Please, sir, may we bring in the bodies? Three of them are lying dead under the trees." As at first I did not know but there might be some truth in this assertion, the required permission was given without hesitation, and a party set off on this voluntary labour. We followed them, smiling, hoping the result would be to teach them a useful and necessary lesson. On coming to the spot which they had indicated as that where the bodies were, they perceived none; but, believing they were there, began turning over the leaves thickly scattered on the ground with their carbines. In this way the place was thoroughly searched, but all in vain. To their inexpressible disappointment, not a drop of blood was to be seen! The dusky warriors had not only left behind no body, but not even so much as an arm or leg was discovered, which could be displayed as a trophy of their first contest with the Andaman natives. We smiled quietly at their discomfiture, which had something of a comical character in it. "Well, lads, where are the dead bodies?" we inquired. "What has become of the wounded men?" "Why, sir," answered one of the sailors, the spokesman for the rest, "they have run away." The men could not be convinced their fire had been so ineffective. Several of them maintained they had covered their men, and that they could not have escaped their assured aim; while others asserted, with no less pertinacity, that they had seen those who had fallen wounded get up again, and scamper off through the forest. If there was no evidence that any of the savages were slain, there was plenty that many of them had escaped; for the prints of their feet were visible all over the sandy soil along which they had scoured in their secure and, as it appeared, precipitate flight.

The sun having now set, and the dark shades of night

gathering rapidly round us, we made up our minds that it was high time to find our way back to the *Pluto*. As we by no means felt sure of not being taken by surprise, we omitted no precaution to guard against it, and, keeping a good outlook on all sides, we returned in safety to the beach, where our boats were waiting for us. Here an unfortunate accident, that was the cause of much inconvenience and pain, occurred to myself. The men had all embarked, leaving me the last to enter the boat; and as, with the aid of a strong arm and one foot pressed against its side, I endeavoured to lift myself up with a spring, the cutter moved slightly on the crest of a wave, my foot slipped, and I fell with my whole weight on the prow, as the boat bounded back to the shingle. I was struck on the right side of the chest, a blow so severe, that for a moment I felt as if the breath were completely knocked out of my body. Assistance was immediately at hand. A couple of stalwart and willing men jumped out, and, lifting me carefully up, soon deposited my unfortunate person safely in the boat. We then started without any further delay for the steamer, and after a good pull of nearly an hour, guided through the darkness, which was now complete, by the lights which it exposed, we were deposited safely on deck, and, exhausted by the day's labours, were well prepared for the generous fare provided for us.

The last serious portion of the day's work was, as we had previously determined, to draw up notes of the events that had occurred within the last twenty-four hours, and to embody, in the form of a report, those observations which we considered to be permanently useful, so far as regarded the special object of our expedition. This task accomplished, we could throw the burden off our minds for a while, and enjoy the pleasures of agreeable intercourse with well-informed companions, whose instructive, spirited, and witty conversation never failed to make the night hours, before retiring to rest, pass away agreeably, only with greater speed than we desired. This evening our exploring party and the officers of the ship adjourned to the bridge, whence, while discussing our adventures and prospects, or idly smoking our well-flavoured cigars, we contemplated a scene the strange contrasts of which could not but suggest themselves to a reflective mind. The mirror-like expanse of the surrounding bay, reflecting the silvery rays of a refulgent moon—the silent, unceasing ripple of the waters as they gently laved the distant shore—and the deep repose in which all seemed to be hushed beyond that dark outline which marked the existence of land—how pleasing, how soothing a sight was it, in contrast with the restless, furious, implacable passions of the people who called that land and bay their own, who had no hospitable reception for the stranger that came among them, but, indulging in that hostile disposition excited by suspicion, distrust, the desire of plunder and the thirst for blood, transformed a scene in which there should have been the abodes of peace and plenty into a field of contention, strife, and bloodshed, when civilized men came among them to offer them a share in the benefits they themselves enjoyed, and to instruct them in the truths by which their own minds were enlightened. But, alas! as is the case with uninstructed human nature everywhere, they loved darkness rather than light; and in the perverse folly of their abject minds, would understand none of the signs by which amity and good-will were offered, and could not be induced to receive from the hands of their fellow-men the grasp of friendship which we were desirous of exchanging with them. Our first experience of the natives was so far a complete confirmation of the statements that represented them as constituting one of the most obstinate and irreclaimable tribes of savages to be found in the dark places of the earth.

The men of our crew, too, were scattered in animated groups about the deck below us, discussing eagerly the events of the day. The "scrimmage" gave rise to a variety of hostile opinions, which were expressed with such ardour and noise, and such an abundance of very intelligible gestures, that we sometimes almost feared lest the martial valour which had been displayed in the afternoon against the natives might now be exhibited by the partisans of different opinions among themselves. Their ineffective fire was the great subject of comment. It was improbable, almost incredible, that their united volley had made no victim, and rather than allow that so much powder had been expended without dyeing the soil with blood, without being followed by the sacrifice of some lives, they were disposed to accept any of those absurd exaggerations by which sailors, in their unintelligent simplicity, are always ready to explain what they cannot understand. There was not one who was not ready to maintain that he had marked his man, that his ball must have struck him, and if no trace of blood had been discovered, or no wounded or dead body was left behind, it was because, like all savages, their hides were ball-proof, and the shot that would have penetrated a European and laid him low, must have rebounded like a ball from their hardened carcases. The explanation might not stand the test of a very searching examination; but as it seemed to explain what they were resolved otherwise not to comprehend, it was thankfully accepted, in want of a better, as a satisfactory solution of a difficulty that was nearly setting them all at angry variance with each other. Their credit, as respectable shots, which some of the crew claimed the right of being considered, was thus saved among their companions, who might otherwise have made them the mark for jeers which are never endured so patiently by the person who must bear them as the one who inflicts them thinks they ought to be.

The effect of the unfortunate injury I had received was such as to prevent me enjoying that repose which would have been more than usually grateful to my wearied frame after the various adventures of the day, and their accompanying excitement. I passed a long, restless, and troubled night; every attempt to turn in my hard, narrow couch being attended with the most agonising pain in the side. Indeed, my suffering was so great as to render this simple feat almost impracticable. The discomfort arising from being obliged to lie constantly in one position was so great, that I at last determined to get up and wander about the deck of the now silent vessel. Fortunately the weather was so favourable as to render this agreeable, so far as I could enjoy it with my constant feeling of uneasiness and pain. The night was truly beautiful—the atmosphere bright, clear, translucent, such as an Eastern night only can display. The heavens were now spangled with hosts of stars, the refulgency of which was such as we are not accustomed to see in our home climate. The outline of the vessel, with its tapering masts and various cordage, was faintly shadowed on the smooth surface of the bay, while on the reef at a little distance the white surface of the breakers dashing against the rocks could be perceived, marking with a white line of foam the boundary of sea and land. After spending a considerable time on deck, I returned to my berth, and managed to get through a night of pain and suffering in the best way I could, submitting, with as much patience as I could muster, to what I knew was in the meantime irremediable.

At daybreak, a more careful examination of my side was made by Dr. Playfair, in whose ability and discrimination I had so much confidence that I would have readily committed even my life into his hands. His opinion was that I must have fractured a rib or two, an inconvenience rather more serious than I had bargained for at the very outset almost. On the other hand, as there was no displacement, and only very trifling pain when the chest was touched, a tight bandage was all the treatment considered necessary; and I had, therefore, the gratification of inferring that my case was not a very serious one, and that, with a little patience and submission to the doctor's orders, I should be able again to move about with all my usual ease and activity.

Next morning, after coffee and quinine, which were always distributed before any work, however important it might be considered, was engaged in, the men were mustered on deck for the purpose of receiving some useful admonition. The impropriety they had been guilty of, in so hastily firing off their pieces without waiting for orders, was urged; and they were exhorted to keep in mind that when everyone acts as he thinks proper, obeying only the impulse of his own blind passion or hasty judgment, there can be no such thing as that discipline which men, both soldiers and sailors, must observe, if they would act harmoniously together, and bring the common object which they have set before themselves to a successful issue. Regard to their own safety, which was essential to the success of the expedition, should counsel them to act at all times with prudence, or who could tell to what dangers they might expose themselves, at a time when it was least desirable? An earnest hope was expressed that the incident which had just occurred would prove a useful lesson, and teach them the necessity of at all times preserving their *sang froid*, in order that they might be able to act with deliberation and caution. The admonition appeared to produce a good effect, and they all promised better behaviour for the future; they would rigidly follow the instructions given them, and henceforth they would take care there should be no occasion to find fault with them.

The morning being favourable, the boats were again got ready to take the landing parties ashore. Having taken their places, they started off in the direction of the beach, where they landed about seven o'clock, without any interruption. A strict look-out was kept up for any natives who might be waiting for us, or preparing an ambuscade for our reception, but none were visible; and no unexpected flight of arrows, no terror-inspiring yell, disturbed the men as they disembarked, and were drawn up on shore. As it was a beautiful morning, and the atmosphere as favourable as it could be for such a purpose, Mons. Mallitte took a photographic view of the Saddle Hill, which, from its summit to its base, was clearly visible, without intervening cloud or obscuring mist. It had also been determined to march to it, and to attempt the ascent of its rugged sides; but although it seemed at first that there could be no difficulty in carrying such a purpose into effect, it turned out that it would prove a matter of considerable labour and time, and that, therefore, for that day at least, the proposed attempt must be abandoned. We ascertained, in the first place, that the base was a considerable distance inland; and that even to get so far would severely tax our energies, as impenetrable forests of gigantic trees, laced together by a net-work of jungle which would have to be cut through by our pioneers, intervened between us and the hill. Then we were enabled to see by our glasses that its sides were intersected by several deep ravines, which would make the ascent a matter of greater difficulty than we had anticipated, or had made preparations for. Seeing that the attempt, therefore, would occupy much more time than we could at present devote to it, it was for the moment abandoned, in the hope that a more favourable opportunity might occur ere long. At eleven o'clock we returned to the shore; got into the boats, and returned to the ship.

During the time we had been ashore, no trace of the savages had been seen. Had they been warned off from our vicinity by the reception we had given them the previous day, when it was seen their hostility could not be disarmed by kindness?—or were they watching our movements from some safe hiding-place among the thick and obscure recesses of the jungle? It is impossible to say, but at all events they made no sign. The canoe also had disappeared from the beach, and the shore looked like that of some deserted or uninhabited island. Meantime, as we were all now on board, the *Pluto* was getting up her steam, and no sooner did she begin to move than the well-known yell of the savages was heard, and they were seen issuing from the thick underwood, and spreading along the shore. Our departure seemed to be regarded by them as a sort of triumph, at least so we judged by the shouts they sent after the departing vessel. Their undiminished hostility was manifested by shaking their fists at us. The gestures in which they indulged were anything but courteous, and were evidently meant to express that the principal feeling with which they regarded us was one of contempt. Such was the encouraging farewell with which we set sail from this part of the island.

Thus ended the first essay we had made to conciliate these obstinate and self-willed savages. However, we were not to be discouraged by our failure, thorough as it was, and we buoyed ourselves up with the hope that our future relations would be more amicable, and that in any succeeding interviews in which the natives might be persuaded to take part, our persevering determination to act as friends, if they would only allow us, would overcome the suspicions which had rendered them so hostile, and induce them to venture on friendly and confidential intercourse with us.

CHAPTER IV.

Our Progress along the Coast—Gigantic Trees—The *Ficus Religiosa*—Exploration of the North-West side of the Bay—Our Burmese Pioneers—Mangrove Swamps—The Reverberation of Sound—Navigation of the Upper Strait—Effects of our Progress through the Fetid Water—Our Return to the *Pluto*—Barren Island—A Sailor in Hot Water—Monsieur Mallitte Photographs the Cone—Ascent of the Cone—Dr. Liebig's Account of the Island—The Slopes towards the Sea—Masses of Lava—A Stream of Hot Water—Dr. Liebig's Ascent of the Cone—The Cracks and Fissures in its Side—The Crater—Strata of Tufaceous Formation—Preceding Accounts of the Island—Probability of Sulphur near the Surface—Proposal to work the Cone—Account of Captain Blair's Settlement—His Survey of the Coast—Clearing and Cultivation of Chatham Island—Condition of the Settlers—A Storm off Cape Negris—Progress of the New Colony—Account of a Large Cave—Glutinous Birds' Nests—Fortification of the Settlement—Determination to Abandon the Settlement—Major Kyd's Report—Minute for the Abolition of the Settlement.

I HAD not been able to go ashore myself on the last occasion with the boats. The accident I had unfortunately met with had completely laid me up; and my broken ribs were the cause of great pain and uneasiness to me. Not only was I unable to take any part in the expeditions of the crew during the day, but I could obtain no rest at night, and altogether had a most uncomfortable time of it. When an attempt was made on the previous day to mount the Saddle Hill, Lieutenant Heathcote availed himself of the opportunity to take an accurate measurement of it, and ascertained its exact height.

The steamer now proceeded at a moderate speed along the shore. As there were no coral reefs to endanger the ship, none of that thick growth of mangrove, spreading even into the sea, to impede our progress, we kept close in by the beach, which was composed of fine soft silvery sand. We left this part of the island because we considered it unnecessary to attempt any further investigations in the neighbourhood. The dark, dismal, tidal marsh could not have failed to affect the health of our crew by the abominable exhalations proceeding from it, and which, when borne in our direction by the wind, might carry with them disease and death to our best men. Such unnecessary exposure would probably have ended in the complete frustration of the object for which the expedition was undertaken.

As the steamer proceeded along, we were so near the coast that its most minute indentations, and the general appearance of the land, could be distinctly surveyed. At one place that seemed to admit of our easy approach, we proceeded towards the shore with part of the crew, and landed without interference, no natives apparently being in the neighbourhood. The trees that grew near the beach were of the usual gigantic dimensions; among them were several specimens of the *Ficus Religiosa*, while the universally useful bamboo grew in profusion all along the coast. The sight was refreshed in numerous places by the sight of beautiful pools of fresh water, clear, cool, and sweet, the diamond sparkle of which pleased the eye, while the ample draughts of it, in which we indulged, refreshed our wearied frames, rather exhausted by wandering so much while on shore during the heat of the day. The unusual dimensions of the trees on every side continued to strike us with amazement, because it was not one here and another there that presented trunks of such ample dimensions, and branches shooting at such an altitude, but because such monsters of the vegetable world were general, and could be seen wherever the eye chose to direct its gaze. One was selected very much at random for measurement. One of our Burmese convicts—first-rate climbers, who can ascend the most gigantic trees like monkeys—was sent up to the top with a chain, and, its measurement being taken, it was found to be seventy-six feet in girth, its mighty stem, which looked like the mast of a great ship, being supported by the smaller trees around, which propped it up as buttresses. In the course of our rather desultory rambles, we picked up a snake of considerable dimensions. Its soft, shining, slimy body was of a beautiful green colour, and it was perfectly innocuous, or we should not have handled it as we did.

At two p.m. Dr. Playfair and Lieutenant Heathcote proceeded to explore the land on the north-west side of

BURMESE PIONEERS.

the bay. It was a great disappointment to me that I was still unable to accompany them, but the pain in my shoulder was too troublesome, excruciating even, and it was so stiff that I could make hardly any use of my arm, and therefore would have been of very little service to my companions if I had gone with them. Captain Baker and I, therefore, amused ourselves with coral gathering; but the spot we selected for the purpose was not very favourable, and we procured very little to reward all the trouble to which we put ourselves. In the evening we again returned to the *Pluto*, on the decks of which we could have lingered far into the night, so enthusiastic was the admiration with which we regarded the clear starlight evenings of this truly beautiful climate. The nights were generally very bright, and often, also, extremely cold. The fall of dew was found to be very abundant, and there was great evaporation in the bay.

Proceeding ashore at the usual hour next morning, our proceedings were much the same as on the two preceding days, and productive of no results of any importance. Our Burmese convicts were kept constantly employed as pioneers—strange pioneers of civilization, if they should ever turn out to have been so—and by persevering labour they succeeded in cutting a way for us through the jungle; but their exertions and our own explorations could effect no good purpose here. The locality at which we were now landed had many disadvantages. The mangrove swamps were found to extend along the coast in every direction. There were none of those immense forest trees from which timber could be obtained; and such sparkling, inviting pools of fresh water as we had seen on landing the previous day, had quite disappeared.

One evening, when the *Pluto* was lying at anchor in Horseshoe Bay, we tried a sort of simple experiment on the effects of sound in the dead silence of night in that tropical climate. One of our guns was loaded and fired. The result astonished us beyond measure, by the striking phenomenon presented both to eye and ear. The flash, for a moment, lighted up the whole scene with an effulgence that displayed every object clearly and distinctly, as if it had been evoked from the womb of mystery by some magician's wand, the jaws of darkness almost instantaneously again devouring it up. The report was terrific—an overwhelming volume of sound bursting at once upon the ear, and almost deafening us, as it were with the roar of a thousand cannons discharged at the same signal. The echo was decidedly the grandest any of us had ever listened to, having something of the imposing magnificence of the thunderclap bursting from the black charged cloud above our heads. It seemed to roll from side to side of the bay in mighty reverberations. Fourteen times we distinctly heard it, diminishing in volume each time, as if it were endeavouring to escape by the narrow entrance to the bay, and at last dying away in what sounded almost like a grand hushed murmur.

It was also in this locality that, on looking over the side of the ship, we witnessed for the first time a phenomenon of singular beauty, such as can be seen only in tropical climes. I refer to the magnificent illumination of the coral banks, on which we gazed while looking over the side of the ship, and which, it is no exaggeration to say, transcended in lustre and beauty all I had ever seen described in the most alluring of fairy tales. It was a sight of brilliance far surpassing anything the most active and gifted imagination could conceive, and which an ordinary pen, therefore, must inevitably fail to describe in anything like terms adequately expressive.

At no place on this part of the coast, although we examined it with as great minuteness as possible, as the *Pluto* slowly steamed along the shore, could we perceive any locality that seemed at all suitable for a convict settlement. We therefore determined to remove to another quarter, and steered in the direction of the Upper Strait, with the view of ascertaining if, even with the light draught of our cutter, there was no passage through between the two dissevered sides of the island. On preparing to enter it, we found that even at high tide there was a bar of sand to be crossed, on which the water was very shallow, only a few feet at the most. As the possibility of navigating this strait was a point the determination of which was of some importance, we made all the necessary preparations to undertake it at daybreak. In order to protect our crew against the fatal influence of the pestiferous *miasmata* they must of necessity inhale—at any rate, in the latter part of our progress—they were fortified with quinine in larger doses than usual in their coffee. And we had reason to congratulate ourselves that this precaution had been taken; for none but those who have actually passed through the strait can form any idea of the disgusting task we had to perform. As the cutter was the lightest boat in the ship, we embarked in it, and set off with the resolution of getting through the disagreeable operation with as much speed as was consistent with its complete accomplishment.

Neither officers nor crew, knowing the importance of the task in which they were engaged, showed any hesitation in performing what they regarded as a duty, although fully aware of the danger they encountered—a danger which is generally regarded with more aversion by the minds of men than that of meeting any foe face to face in the field of combat. We also took with us an extra supply of excellent strong grog, not for the purpose of inspiring our men with resolution to accomplish a disagreeable voyage, but to prevent, as far as possible, the evil effects many, if not all of them, must doubtless experience before they had sailed through the strait, if it should turn out that that could be accomplished. The water through which they had to pass was known in many places to be in such a putrid state, and the exhalations arising from it, especially when disturbed by the touch of the oars and the progress of the boat, so nauseous, that attacks of sickness were the least disagreeable effects to be anticipated. Lieutenant Heathcote, who accompanied us closely, observed the conformation and windings of the passage as we made our way slowly onwards, and the accurate chart in which he has so distinctly delineated this abode of malaria, cannot but be of unspeakable service to future navigators who may make an attempt to find their way from end to end of the Upper Strait.

We made considerable progress at first, and were able to get over sixteen miles of our way, being obliged in the latter part to make the best progress we could through the fetid mangrove swamps, the stench of which was so abominable, that it is almost fortunate we have no language in which adequately to describe it, for a faithful representation might produce the same effect upon others that it had upon ourselves. We were all deadly sick, officers as well as men, and the former were glad to take a good draught of the men's grog, to stay the very disagreeable stomachic sensation from which they were suffering. As we advanced, the putrid, fetid, nauseous water, if it can be so termed with any propriety, became thicker and thicker, more pervaded with deadly decaying matter of vegetable origin, until at length it appeared to be nothing but a thick mixture of mud and water, the foulest in appearance it is possible to imagine. The prospect was so disagreeable, that we were obliged to turn back, and it was with considerable difficulty we got the boat round. The progress that we made through the terraceous compost was necessarily slow, and every step forward was made with the greatest difficulty, nothing but persevering labour carrying our boat gradually through it.

The tide by this time had risen considerably higher, and it was with inexpressible pleasure we saw the water rising above the mass of vegetable mud, until, at its full height, it presented something like its usual appearance. As it slowly rose around us, the spirits and activity of all rose with it; and the depressing sickness being thrown off, the men pulled cheerily along. About the same time a gentle breeze sprang up, which we all inhaled with unspeakable delight, the coolness it imparted to our fevered frames producing a most pleasing sensation. We hailed the sight of the *Pluto,* and the open expanse of water in which she was lying at anchor, with the feelings of men delivered from a purgatory. I could not help thinking that if Dante had known, in his day, of such a fetid marsh as that we had attempted to make our way through, he would have introduced it into some part of his *Divina Commedia,* where he describes, in such horror-inspiring language, the sufferings of vice. To us it was like paradise again to tread the deck of our clean, well-ordered steamer, which we reached about an hour after sunset, after a day's labour that had thoroughly exhausted all who had taken any part in it.

Upon myself the effect was as bad as on any of my companions. The nauseous exhalations I had inhaled had temporarily so enfeebled me, that I was compelled to betake myself, at a comparatively early hour, to my couch for the night. My companions, and the crew of the boat, all suffering in some degree from the same cause, sought relief from their disagreeable sensations in the way they thought most likely to benefit themselves; and the dispiriting effects of the Stygian pool through which they had passed remained upon them till they had eaten and slept them off; for, happily, we had no reason, either then or afterwards, to believe that the poisonous vapours had effected such a lodgment in the constitution of any of them as seriously to affect their health.

The next place we proposed to visit was Barren Island. The steam was accordingly got up late in the night; and at midnight we set off across the open sea, in order that we might reach it at an early hour in the morning.

Barren Island presents a very extraordinary aspect. Its general appearance, as seen from the sea, is very beautiful, while there is something bold in its general contour, surmounted as it is by the tall grey cone in the centre, from which volumes of dark smoke were rising into the clear morning atmosphere. Altogether, the eye of man could not rest upon a spectacle at once more singular and lovely. We steamed round the island, keeping close to the shore, and fathoming in every direction, with the hope of finding a spot where we could conveniently anchor. But our persevering search, and our repeated use of the line, were unrewarded with the success we desired. Not the smallest indication of good anchoring ground could be discovered. In the immediate neighbourhood of the shore, the water was found to be very deep. Even at the depth of three or four hundred fathoms no bottom could be felt. Captain Campbell himself afterwards gave orders for the renewal of the attempt, and at a considerably greater depth, the lead met the resistance of a solid substratum.

In these circumstances we were obliged to disembark, and get to shore the best way we could. In the rolling agitated sea, in which the vessel rose and sank, we got into the boats with difficulty, taking with us all those traps of various kinds we might find it necessary to use, particularly our photographic apparatus, to which the singular and beautiful aspects of the lovely little island would give ample employment. Nor did we forget to provide ourselves with an ample breakfast, for we had previously felt the enfeebling and fatiguing effects of those long-continued rambles, which soon exhaust a fasting body. As we drew near to the wharf, when we were about ten yards from the shore, one of the crew was sent into the sea with a rope to fasten the boat. Immediately on jumping into the water, which was breaking in great billows upon the shore, he roared out that it was boiling hot, a sailor's exaggeration, as we supposed, from which we at least presumed that he felt it comfortably warm. The boat being secured, we all got on shore without the slightest additional difficulty; but I can scarcely give expression to the sensation of surprise we experienced when, on touching the water close to the beach, we found that the exclamation we had regarded as an absurd exaggeration was, as near as it could be, a literal fact. The water was really too hot to be agreeable—a phenomenon the cause of which we felt at once curious to discover. The investigation was not one that taxed either our patience or our ingenuity, for close to the shore a natural boiling spring was discovered, the waters of which were so extremely hot that they rendered the sea in their immediate neighbourhood warm enough to roast crabs in their shells. We could, not, therefore, feel much surprise at the exclamation of the sailor on first touching, even at a distance of ten feet from the shore, the heated water.

We had no sooner landed, than Monsieur Mallitte, struck by the remarkable appearance of the great smoking cone in the centre, made preparations to take a photograph of it; and the skill and correctness with which the appearance of that wonderful natural object was rendered, showing exactly the fine dark silvery surface, was rewarded with the warmest appreciation by all who witnessed the perfect picture his superior photographic manipulation produced.

As the burning cone was the great object of interest in the island, we could not think of leaving without making an attempt to mount its steep ascent. Several of us, therefore, made up our minds to make our way to its summit. We started with a fair amount of resolution, but the difficulties proved greater than I had anticipated. Playfair, myself, and the good dog Neptune, were among the adventurous party; but we were satisfied with making about ten yards over the soft warm ashes, which yielded beneath our feet, and rendered the toil of the ascent greater than we had a mind to encounter, especially as I was still suffering from the effects of my accident, which rendered me less disposed for any exertion than I might otherwise have been. Fortunately there were others not so easily daunted, and whose ambition could be satisfied only by bringing their adventure to a successful issue, and being able to assert that they had stood upon the summit of the cone of Barren Island. Cotgrove, ever animated by the spirit of enterprise, and the daring filibuster Walker, mounted step by step, the difficulties increasing as they ascended, and at last stood breathless upon the summit, enveloped in the irritating blue smoke that ascended from its crater. Walker, probably with a laudable scientific desire to settle the degree of heat proceeding from one of the smoking fissures, sat down upon it, and exhibited the result of his experiment in his charred and smoking trousers, the heat being sufficiently strong to set them on fire. Cotgrove brought down with him a beautiful piece of crystallized virgin sulphur, which he had picked up on the summit; but he gave it as his opinion that there was scarcely any to be found fit for working at less than the depth of one hundred feet. Walker gathered a lump almost as big as himself, rolled over with it, and when he again appeared among us, he looked like a living piece of brimstone himself. Our poor dog Neptune, who judged by appearances, and thought things were really what they resembled, licked him, like Squeers, with much apparent satisfaction. We also discovered that his unmentionables were still burning in some places, and we poured a bucket of cold water over him, with such effect that it made him yell with a vengeance. We also made some examinations of a nature interesting only to geologists, and, from certain appearances that came under our observation, we drew the conclusion that the sea had never flowed round the cone.

As Barren Island is very interesting in a geological point of view, no apology is necessary for the introduction of the following minute account of its appearance and structure, for which I am indebted to Dr. Liebig, a man whose scientific abilities eminently fitted him for the accurate examination of so remarkable a locality:—

Barren Island is a volcanic island, situated in lat. 12° 17′ N., and in long. 93° 54′ E. Its smallest distance from the Andaman Archipelago is in a straight line only thirty-six miles east. The distance from the nearest point of the mainland, near Tavoy, is about two hundred and seventy miles, W.S.W. It lies not far out of the straight course between Port Blair and Amherst, about sixty-three miles from the former, and three hundred and thirty from the latter place. We approached the island on the morning of the 19th March, 1858, coming from the north-east, and steamed round it by south, keeping close to the shore, until the ship was opposite the entrance of the crater, bearing about west and by north from the centre of the island, where she hove to, and we landed.

It is stated in former accounts, that all round the island the lead finds no bottom at one hundred and fifty fathoms, only a quarter of a mile distant from the shore. Captain Campbell found, however, ground at that distance on one side of the island, its centre bearing north-east at a depth varying from four-and-a-half to fourteen fathoms.

Nearing the island from the north, and passing round to the south-east of it, it looks from a distance like an oval-topped hill; but coming closer, the sides of the mountain are discovered to belong to a steep circular elevation, sending out spurs towards the sea, and enclosing a central valley. The sides of the enclosing circle being lower in the direction of the spectator, the upper circumference of this valley is seen in the shape of an oval ring, formed by the crest of the surrounding ridge. In the middle of this ring, the upper part of a regular cone is visible, from the apex of which small white vapour-like clouds emanate. It is also distinguished from the surrounding darker masses by its grey colour, and some large white marks on it, like fields of snow. An entrance is not discernible.

The slopes towards the sea are generally covered with shrubby vegetation, presenting, however, some bare patches towards the upper edge. Small trees grow about the base, where large rounded stones are washed by the sea.

Turning now to the south and south-west, the enclosing wall is higher than the cone and the crest of the opposite ridge, and both therefore disappear from the view. On this side the vegetation down the spurs to the sea may be called rich, and consists of different forest trees of moderate height, interspersed with graceful palms; and where the descent is rocky, the rocks are frequently covered with ferns.

Passing to the westward of the centre of the island, and continuing the survey towards the northern end, one of the first turns discovers a large gap in the circular wall, extending quite down to the base of the island, through which the interior of the valley, with the cone in the middle, opens at once into full view.

The sides of this gap or fissure in the circular wall form a regular cut or short transverse valley through it, opening towards the sea into a small bay, and on the other side into the circular valley, to which it is the only way of access. Opposite this entrance, in the centre of the valley, rises the cone of grey ashes, and surrounding its base the bottom of the valley is filled with black masses of cold lava, which are continued like a congealed stream through the gap, breaking off abruptly when they arrive near the water's edge. At its termination, the stream is about ten or fifteen feet high, and its breadth seems less than farther up. It looks like a black perpendicular wall, drawn across the entrance and facing the sea.

This lava consists of a black basalt mass (matrix) throughout which are disseminated innumerable semi-transparent little crystals of a variety of common felspar (orthoclase), and also many bright green granules of olivine. The lower part of its thickness is homogeneous, with a smooth fracture; but from the upper surface to a depth of several feet it is cleft in all directions, whereby the upper part is divided into rough blocks, possessing a spongy texture, as well as countless sharp edges and corners.

The older lava, composing the rocks on the side of the valley, and also the strata of the surrounding ridge, is slightly different from this. The colour of its principal mass is a reddish grey, felspar and olivine crystals are imbedded in it in the same proportions as before, and, in addition, small pieces of black angite of the granular kind, with conchoidal fracture. From underneath the black lava, where it terminates near the sea, issues a broad but thin sheet of hot water, mixing with the sea water between the pebbles of the beach. The thermometer I had with me was not graduated high enough to measure its temperature, its highest mark being 104° F. (40° C.) The water, where escaping from the rock, must have been nearly at the boiling point, judging from the heat felt when the hands were dipped into it, or when the hot stones were touched. When bathing, we found the sea-water warm for many yards from the entrance of the hot spring, and to a depth of more than eight feet. It is not impossible that a jet of hot steam or water may emerge from the rocks below the level of the sea. The hot water tasted quite fresh, and not saline, as might have been expected, showing that it could not have been long in contact with the rocks.

We ascended to the base of the cone, passing along the sloping sides of the transverse valley, through dry grass and brushwood, or over sandy ridges, so long as the solidified stream of lava in the middle left us room to do so. At last we had to ascend the rugged surface of the black lava itself, and cross the circular valley, which has about the same breadth as the transverse valley (not quite one-eighth of a mile), until we arrived at the base, about half a mile from the sea. The cone rises from the lava accumulated in the circular valley, and its base is about fifty feet higher than the level of the sea, at a rough estimate. It is quite round and smooth, and the inclination of its sides is forty degrees. No vegetation of any kind was visible along its surface. We turned to the left, and went up from the north side, where the appearance of a ravine, some way up, only two or three feet deep and very narrow, with some tufts of grass growing along it, promised an easier ascent for a part of the way, and where a rocky shoulder, at about two-thirds of the height, would offer a place to rest. Our ascent commenced at about half-past two p.m., and was certainly the most fatiguing expedition many of us remember ever to have undertaken. The sky was almost cloudless, and the heat consequently was great. The lower third and more of the slope consisted of a powder of ashes, into which we sunk ankle-deep, and we often fell a step back for two gained. A little higher, stones loosening when the foot stepped on them, and rolling down in long lumps, were dangerous to any one following.

Arrived at the rocks mentioned, their nature, and the manner in which the side of the cone bulged out in their neighbourhood, showed that they marked the point from whence an effusion of lava of the same kind as we had seen below, had taken place from the side of the cone, not reaching the mouth of the tube at the apex. The last third of the way from the rocks upwards offered a firmer footing, the ashes being cemented by sulphate of lime (gypsum), which, where it was present, formed the white patches we had already observed from a great distance when approaching the island. The ground now became very hot, not, however, intolerably so, until about thirty feet from the apex a few rocks again offered a convenient seat, not affected by the heat of the ground. There the Aneroid barometer, and the temperature of the air, were observed in the shade of an umbrella.

About half-way between these rocks and the highest point, cracks and fissures commenced to intersect the ground, widening higher up to the breadth of several inches, where clouds of hot watery vapour issued from them. They were filled with sulphur, often accompanied with beautifully crystallised white needles of gypsum, and a sulphurous smell also accompanied the vapour (sulphurous acid). This smell was, however, not very strong, and did not prevent us from penetrating the clouds, when we discovered that what had appeared from below as the summit was in fact the edge of a small crater, about 90 or 100 feet wide, and 50 or 60 deep. At that depth it had a solid floor of decomposed lava or tufa and volcanic sand. Its walls were made up of rocks, in appearance like those of the older lava, and they were highest on the north and south sides. Towards the west the crater opened with a similar cleft to that which had permitted us to enter the island. The vapours rose principally from the northern and southern quarters of the edge, where the fissures were largest and longest, running both parallel and across the edge. The rocks where the sulphurous vapours issued from between them, were covered with reddish and white crusts, indicating the beginning of decomposition of their substance. From the top, the horizon, and more or less of the sea, were visible in all directions, with the exception of the quarter between south and west. The inner slope of the circular elevations enclosing the valley, had no spurs, but was like a plain wall, falling off with a steep descent all round towards the centre. It had a uniform brownish colour, appertaining either to the surface of larger masses of the rock itself, or being derived from the dry grass and smaller shrubs covering the slope. There were no trees or brushwood visible to correspond to the richer vegetation on the external circumference. Horizontal parallel lines, traceable throughout the circle, and rising somewhat like the borders of receding steps, indicated the thickness and strike of the different sheets of lava and tufa which, super-imposed upon one another, formed the substance of the circular elevation. A very good transverse section of it had already attracted my attention, where the left side of the transverse valley debouches into the sea. Several strata of tufaceous formation, alternating with older rock-like lava, could be seen there rising from the rocky beach. One of the most remarkable amongst these was a stratum of rounded stones, like large pebbles, cemented by tufa, exactly like those of the present beach, but at a considerable elevation (about 20 feet) above the high water mark, showing that the submarine base of the island must have been raised since those pebbles had been washed by the sea. All these strata dipped outwards from the centre of the island, parallel with the external slope of the encircling wall. It is interesting to observe that this slope continues under the sea level on three sides of the island at least, at the same inclination as above water, which averages about 35°. This is shown by the soundings, which exceed 150 fathoms at a distance of a quarter of a mile from the shore.

Judging from what we saw, as I have here attempted to describe it, I should conclude that the circular valley and its walls constitute the crater of a huge volcanic cone of submarine basis, which had been the vent for fluid masses of rock, when such eruptions took place on a larger scale than in more recent times. The smaller cone in the centre of the old crater, corresponding in its size to the diminished forces of volcanic action, is of recent origin, and represents those smaller cones of still active volcanoes which are usually distinguished as cones of eruption, from the original ones, also called the cones of elevation.

We have it on record that, about sixty years ago, the crater of the little cone was throwing out showers of red-hot stones of several tons weight, and enormous volumes of smoke (Captain Blair's account, Asiatic Researches, 1795), and but for the isolated position of the volcano preventing its more frequent observation, we should doubtless be able to fix the date of the eruption that left the stream of lava behind, which is now filling the valley and its outlet into the sea. Since that time it has entered the period of decline of volcanic activity, without, however, leaving us the assurance that it will not some day revive again.

From barometrical observations, I deduced the height of the cone by Gauss's formula, allowing for the time of the day and the influence of the hot ground near the summit, to be about nine hundred and eighty feet, from the level of the sea to the northern edge of the crater. This height is confirmed by a trigonometrical measurement of Lieutenant Heathcote, I.N., to whom I am indebted for the communication of his results. He visited the island about four months earlier than we did, when he found the height of the cone nine hundred and seventy-five feet above the level of the sea, and the diameter of the island 2970 yards, 1·68 miles north and south.

The few notes I could glean respecting the history of the island, are derived from the island itself, from the records of the Asiatic Society, and from Horsburgh. We found on a rock in the transverse valley the inscription, "Galathea, 1846," showing that since then no alteration has taken place. The same conclusion can be extended farther back to the year 1831 or 1832, judging from an account communicated to the Asiatic Society (Asiatic Society's Journal, April 1832) by Dr. J. Adam, whose informant landed in the month of March, and reached the base of the cone. By this explicit account, the descriptions of the island in "Lyell"* dated 1843, and in Humboldt's *Cosmos*, both apparently derived from the same source, must be rectified. The narrator states (in "Lyell,") that the sea filled the circular valley round the cone.

* Lyell's *Principles of Geology*.

Horsburgh states that, in 1803, the volcano was observed to explode regularly every ten minutes, projecting each time a column of black smoke, perpendicularly, to a great height, "and in the night a fire of considerable size continued to burn on the east side of the crater, which was then in view."

The oldest account on record is that of Captain Blair, already quoted, taken from his report of the survey of the Andaman Islands. He must have visited the island about 1790, as far as I am able to conclude from the publication in the researches, and the date of his chart of the Andamans, which is 1790. He approached nearly to the base of the cone, which he describes as the lowest part of the island, very little higher than the level of the sea, but he does not mention the black stream of lava. The acclivity of the cone he states to be 32° 17′, and its height 1,800 feet nearly, which, he says, is also the elevation of the other parts of the island. On the other hand, he remarks that the cone is visible in clear weather at a distance of twelve leagues, which would require a height of not more than from 900 to 1,000 feet. I think, therefore, that Captain Blair could have taken no accurate measurements, contenting himself with a rough estimate. If it could be proved otherwise, the island would have subsided eight hundred and twenty feet since he visited it.

From the description in some of these accounts, it would appear that the high vegetation which we found on the external slope of the island is of quite recent origin.

Mr. Adam's authority (1831) states as follows:

"The summits to the north-east were completely smooth; and covered with ashes; those to the south-west, although partly covered with ashes, also have a good many small shrubs over them, with dry and parched grass growing on the surface."

He conjectures from this that the eruptions would take place only in the south-west monsoon, or rainy season, at which time the south-west wind would blow the dust and ashes on the hills in the opposite direction, or north-east; such a conjecture is hardly admissible on the ground given, it being easier to account for the vegetation on the south-western slope, by its angle of descent being much smaller than that of the north-eastern slope.

The sulphur on the top of the cone occurs in such quantity in the cracks and fissures, often lining them to the thickness of more than half an inch, that the question naturally arises, whether the sulphur could not be worked with advantage.

Although in the immediate neighbourhood of the crater, where the fissures are numerous, the ground seems to be completely penetrated with sulphur; this is not so evident in other parts, only a few feet lower, where the surface is unbroken. There are, however, some reasons which seem to promise that a search might be successful. In eruptive cones, like that of Barren Island, there is always a central tube, or passage, connecting the vent in the crater with the heart of volcanic action in the interior. In this tube the sulphur, generally in combination with hydrogen, rises in company with the watery vapour, and is partly deposited in the fissures and interstices of the earth near the vent, the remainder escaping through the apertures.

If in the present case we admit the sensible heat of the ground of the upper third of the cone to be principally due to the condensation of steam—a process of which we have abundant evidence in the stream of hot water rushing out from underneath the cold lava—it is not improbable that the whole of the upper part of the interior of the cone is intersected with spaces and fissures filled with steam and sulphurous vapour, these being sufficiently near the surface to permit the heat to penetrate. It is, therefore, not unlikely that at a moderate depth we should find sulphur saturating the volcanic sand that covers the outside of the cone.

I only speak of the outside, as we may conclude, from the evidence we have in the rocks of lava in the crater, and those bulging out on the side, that the structure of the cone is supported by solid rock nearly to its summit, the ashes covering it only superficially.

From what has been said above, the probability of sulphur being found near the surface, disposed in such a way as to allow of its being profitably exhausted, will depend on the following conditions:

First, that the communication of the central canal, through which the vapours rise, with its outlets, be effected not through a few large, but through many and smaller passages distributed throughout the thickness of the upper part of the cone.

Second, that some of these passages communicate with the loose cover of ashes and stones which envelopes the rocky support of the cone.

Although I have mentioned some facts which seem to indicate the existence of such favourable conditions, and which are moreover strengthened by an observation by Captain Campbell, who saw vapour issuing, and sulphur being deposited near a rocky shoulder about two-thirds of the height, on the eastern descent of the cone, still their presence can only be ascertained satisfactorily by experimental digging.

The Solfatara at Pozzuoli, near Naples, is a similar instance of the production of sulphur. It is a crater in which exhalations of watery vapour, sulphurous acid, and hydrochloric acid take place, and where sulphur is also deposited. The sulphur is gained there by distilling it out of the sand of the crater, to a depth of ten metres, or thirty-two feet; it becomes too hot lower down—and returning the sand, which, after twenty-five or thirty years, is again charged with sulphur. The permanency of the volcano of Barren Island, as a source of sulphur, would depend on the rapidity with which the sulphur would be replaced, after the sand had been once exhausted. The time required for this is not necessarily fixed to periods of twenty-five or thirty years. In Iceland, at a similar spot, the sulphur is renewed every two or three years.

If a preliminary experiment should make it appear advantageous to work the cone regularly, the material about the apex, after being exhausted of the sulphur that is present, could, by blasting and other operations, be disposed in such a way as to direct the jets of vapour in the most convenient manner through uncharged portions of ground. If the sulphur should aggregate in periods of not too long duration, it would be possible to carry on the work of filling up new ground on one side, and taking away saturated earth on the other at the same time—so that, after working round the whole circumference, the earth that had been first put on would be ready to be taken away.

If the periods should prove too long to allow the work permanently to be carried on, an interval of time might be allowed to pass before resuming operations.

Water for the labourers could always be obtained from the warm spring at the entrance of the island.

The distilling or melting of sulphur, to separate it from adherent earth, is a matter of comparatively little expense or trouble. If the sulphur be abundant, it might be effected, as in Sicily, by using a part of it as fuel. It is not necessary to do it on the spot; it might be done at any place where bricks and fuel are cheap.

It is impossible to predict certain and lasting success to an undertaking of this kind, all depending on the quantity of sulphur present, and the rapidity with which it will be replaced.

The situation of Barren Island offers every facility for a preliminary trial. The near proximity of the Andamans insures a supply of convict labour, timber, bricks, and lime. All the wood and iron-work required for facilitating the transport of loads, up and down the hill, could be made on the Andamans.

At sunset we returned to the boat, and on reaching the steamer, into which we managed to ascend without encountering any particular danger, though she still continued to roll heavily, we at once steered again in the direction of Chatham Island.

After we had examined the islands in all directions, sailing round their shores, and taking into consideration the peculiarities of the various localities, we remained firmly established in the opinion we had formed, that Old Harbour was by far the best spot that could have been selected for a convict settlement. Captain Blair, we can entertain no doubt, saw unanswerable reasons for preferring it to all others; and he was a man far too cautious, sagacious, and humane, to undertake such a duty without accomplishing it in the manner best fitted to fulfil the purpose for which he had been charged with it. No subsequent plan, the result of imperfect knowledge and experience, should ever have been allowed to supersede his. His clear judgment and practical sense eminently fitted him for the organization of such schemes; and if he had been permitted by those in power to carry out the eminently wise and judicious plans he had conceived, and submitted to those to whose decision the matter was left, there is every reason to believe that, in the eighty years that have intervened since, a great and beneficial change would have been effected; and in all human probability the Andamans would ere many years have been what Penang at this moment is.

Immediately on our return from the expedition to Barren Island, we again landed, and explored, with the greatest minuteness, the locality of Blair's settlement. Although the labour we had to encounter, in consequence of the unexampled vegetable growth, was extreme, not a nook or cranny of the place was left unexamined; and our conclusion was, as we have already intimated, that this was the only place which fulfilled all the conditions considered requisite for a penal settlement. Here was abundance of wood, for building and other purposes; stone in any quantity could be procured; and, what is of infinite importance in these islands, there were three sources from which, at all seasons, an abundant supply of pure, limpid drinking water could be obtained for the use of settlers and prisoners.

In order that the grounds on which we came to this conclusion may be perfectly understood, we consider that our purpose will be best answered by giving here a more complete account of the operations of Blair and his companions than it was possible to include in the hasty and incomplete notices of former discoveries in the introductory chapter. Besides, the history of his operations must ever form the main subject of interest in every account of the Andamans; and the plans that he conceived for the establishment of a convict settlement in the island were so carefully elaborated, that, as I have already stated, the best thing we could propose to the Government authorities at Calcutta was, in many respects, to do over again what he had already done, to commence again old plans that had been abandoned, and to avail ourselves of all the suggestions that could be derived from the arrangements of the previous settlement, to build up and establish a new one. This account, which will be found to contain many interesting particulars, has been drawn up from various trustworthy sources, as well as from the reports of Captain Blair himself, which were stamped with the full approval of the Governor-General. When the reader is made fully acquainted with the operations of Blair and his party, he will be in a better condition to understand the allusions which we are compelled so often to make to the past, as well as the suggestions we proposed for plans to be realized in the future.

Captain Blair arrived at the harbour where he was to establish the settlement, on the 28th September, 1789. The spot he chose for his residence was Mark Island, now called Chatham Island, which is also the head-quarters of the present colony. He had taken from Bengal a numerous staff of artificers, with provisions for six months. His first act was to raise a redoubt on the east end of the island, in which the guns of the *Ranger* were mounted; and when this had so far progressed as to allow of his detaching some of his men, he sent the *Ranger* to Carmishac, to collect and bring over a variety of useful plants, such as cocoa-nuts, yams, potatoes, &c., and also to procure stock. In this they were completely successful, and the *Ranger* returned with an abundant supply of fruits and vegetables, hogs and fowls, and a good assortment of plants. Very shortly after Blair and his party had first landed on the island, and while they were engaged in the clearing of the jungle near the east end, for the redoubt, a body of the natives came over from the opposite shore of the harbour, and landed near them. Every mode of driving them away, short of actual conflict, was resorted to, but without avail, for the natives boldly began to plunder one of the boats, and it then became necessary to use force. In the skirmish, one of the sepoys was wounded; and in their flight two of the natives were taken. The first, a lad of sixteen, was captured by the Jolly Boat, after he had eluded it for a considerable time by his dexterity in swimming and diving; and after having received a pistol-ball through the cartilage of his nose, which also destroyed one of his eyes, he had the gallantry to shoot an arrow, while swimming, at his pursuers. These prisoners were treated with the utmost kindness, and every endeavour was made to gain a knowledge of their language. The settlers were fully employed in the cultivation of the land, which soon began to recompense their labour. A convenient watering-place for ships was cleared, and a reservoir constructed, and sheds for stores were erected within the redoubt. On the 19th December, Commodore Cornwallis, with H.M. ships *Perseverance* and *Ariel*, arrived at the settlement, and found it "fully equal to what it had been represented." The Commodore also visited Prince of Wales Island, which he was "decidedly of opinion cannot be used as a refitting port for a squadron of ships of war, but he was highly satisfied with the newly-discovered harbour in the Andamans."

Additions were gradually made to the number of settlers from Calcutta, and the natives became for the time less troublesome; and Blair was led to express an opinion favourable to their ultimate usefulness. This impression was unfortunately soon dispelled. Among the most useful members of the community were four fishermen from Bengal, who plied their avocation very successfully about the reefs and inlets of the harbour, and supplied the settlement with excellent fish. These men were missing one evening, and three days afterwards the bodies of two of them were found dreadfully mutilated, and bearing "evident marks of inhuman barbarity having been exercised in putting them to death," by the savages.

Blair, leaving his subordinate, Lieutenant Wales, in charge of Port Cornwallis, occupied himself with the survey of the east coast of the Andamans; and, on the 13th April, 1790, reported that a harbour on the north-east of the island, from which the name first given to it was North East Harbour, was "deserving the attention of the Governor-General." In November of the same year, this new harbour was visited by Commodore Cornwallis, the Commodore-in-Chief of His Majesty's ships in the East Indies, who formed a very favourable opinion of it, and directed Lieutenant Blair to make a particular survey of it. This was executed during March, 1791, and, on receipt of it, the Commodore thus wrote to his brother, the Governor-General: "I think North East Harbour vastly superior for a fleet of men-of-war to Port Cornwallis; the latter, I consider, too confined and liable to accidents, as well as being more subject—from being surrounded with high hills—to sudden and violent squalls. They are alike in respect to fresh water, the runs being occasioned by the rains, and in regard to defence. The island * is not near a gunshot from the farthest shore, which I tried by throwing shot across when working out. And though the island is small, there is a great deal dry at the lowest tides—I should apprehend, full sufficient for batteries." † He recommended the removal of the establishment from Chatham Island to this harbour, and offered to assist in the operation.

The whole of the settlers continued busily employed in clearing and cultivating Chatham Island, the greater portion of which was, by August, 1790, planted with vegetables and fruit trees, which served to supply His Majesty's ships on three occasional visits, as well as the whole of the colonists. The higher parts of the islands were at the same time sown with grass. Provisions were imported as required from Prince of Wales Island or Calcutta. The timber cut down in the clearing was prepared, and applied to the use for which it was best adapted. A portion fit for shipbuilding, or for masts, was sent to Calcutta as specimens, part of the same being used in the construction of a large boat, intended to be

* This appears to refer to North East Harbour.

† Letter to Governor-General, dated 30th June, 1791.

employed occasionally in carrying a despatch A wood of a deep red colour, which gave promise of furnishing a good dye, was collected in such a quantity as might serve to test its market price in China, and despatched to its destination. At the same time the buildings were progressing, and the whole of the settlers, numbering, in August, 1790, one hundred and nineteen working men, were housed. The number of store-houses was increased, and another building was constructed which served as a temporary hospital for invalids from the men-of-war. The settlement continued free from sickness, except that the old men began to miss some few articles of particular nourishment to which they had been accustomed, and without which they were unable to sustain the hardships incidental to a new colony. These were speedily forwarded back to Calcutta. The natives still continued to give trouble both from their direct and open animosity, and from their treachery. An attack on the settlement, for which a number of the natives had collected, was anticipated by the capture of three of their large canoes, which they had left unguarded; and while H. M.'s ship *Vestal* was refreshing in the harbour, an occurrence took place which affords a striking example of the duplicity of the native character. Sir R. Strachan, the captain of the *Vestal*, had accompanied Dr. Blair in his visit to a portion of the harbour, at some distance from the settlement, when they were joined by two young natives, who voluntarily accompanied them back to Chatham Island. "Their youth and apparent innocence," says Blair, "prevented my entertaining the least unfavourable suspicion of them;" however, they decamped during the night, and took away with them one of the boats, which had been inspected and found all secure at half-past one in the morning. Some days afterwards, fragments of this boat were found near the place where these youths had first shown themselves. Besides the work of all description going forward at Chatham Island, a party were engaged cutting an avenue, "extending, in a southerly direction, from the top of Phœnix Bay" to the head of that next it. This avenue was intended to serve as a line of demarcation for the natives, while the clearing of the peninsula to the west of it was proceeded with, this having been selected "on account of its situation, soil, and being well watered, as the best place for immediate improvement and cultivation." In December, 1790, the guns had to be removed from the redoubt and replaced on board the *Ranger*, it being necessary to despatch that vessel to Penang, to reinforce that settlement, which was infested and threatened by piratical prahus of the neighbouring Malay tribes; but the power of attack possessed by the natives had now been well ascertained, and artillery was no longer thought necessary as a defence against them. The next considerable work undertaken was the construction of a wharf, and this was completed in February, 1791, in time to facilitate the landing of 500 tons of naval stores, imported at that time for the use of His Majesty's ships, the whole of which,* employed in

* *Perseverance*, *Vestal*, *Ariel*, *Atalanta*, *Crown*.

the Bay of Bengal, now paid constant visits to the great Andamans.

The settlers had not hitherto been allowed to have their families with them at Chatham Island, although this had been recommended by Blair; but sanction was at last given, in July, 1791, that those settlers who had visited Calcutta, on their private affairs, should be allowed and induced to take their families to the new colony. Any fresh artificers and labourers who were engaged for the settlement had the same option, and generally availed themselves of it. The settlement still continued healthy, and the natives no longer continued their annoyances, but occasionally visited Chatham Island for the purpose of begging a few scraps of iron, or a little food. In September, 1791, Blair was informed of the intention of Government to remove the establishment which he had fostered with such care to North East Harbour; and although this did not actually take place till more than a twelvemonth afterwards, it effectually stopped all progress at Chatham Island. No work was now undertaken but what was absolutely necessary, nor anything of a permanent character. Another garden at the south-east corner of the island was, however, cleared and cultivated, it being desirable to increase the supply of vegetables. The decked boat, built on the island by Blair, and named the *Leeboard*, was sent to assist the *Ranger* or *Viper* (one or other vessel being constantly attached to the settlement), in the survey of various dangers in the neighbourhood of the Andamans, and was found very useful, and, in November, was sent to Calcutta with a despatch, and to bring a a supply of stores. She was further occasionally of essential service in running over to Penang when the stock of rice at the colony ran short. In March, 1792, Blair reports "that the settlement has been so healthy as to have suffered no injury from the (temporary) absence of the surgeon," who had been to Calcutta on leave; and "the natives have been perfectly inoffensive for a long time, and are becoming every day more familiar—they seem now convinced that our intentions towards them are pacific." No opportunity had been lost to assure them of the friendly feelings of the settlers towards them, and to give them confidence in their intercourse with the strangers to whom they were in the habit of showing so great antipathy. On one occasion, when the *Ranger* was about to proceed to the southern Nicobar, one of the natives was induced to go in the vessel; and as he was allowed to bring back to the settlement as many cocoa-nuts as he pleased, the trip was not without profit to him and to his friends. Acts of friendship such as this were not without their good effect, which was evident in the improved demeanour of the aborigines.

On the 16th October, Blair was officially informed of the intention of the Government to remove the settlement at the Andamans to North East Harbour; and, on the 5th of November following, the Governor-General recorded a minute on the subject, detailing the method of the transfer, and the object of the new settlement. The original intention was to establish a naval arsenal at this port, in accordance with the recommendation of the Commodore; and, with a view to the erection of the necessary buildings and fortifications for such an object, Captain Alexander Kyd, of the corps of engineers, was nominated superintendent, and was to be assisted by a subaltern officer of the same corps; the settlement was to be garrisoned by one or two companies of sepoys. Four vessels were to be fitted out for the conveyance of artificers, stores, &c., to the new settlement; and the whole were to be under the orders of Blair, until he was relieved by Captain Kyd. The Governor-General at the same time expressed the satisfaction of himself and his council at the conduct of Blair, and declared that "his attention and abilities in the management of our first settlement at the Andamans claim our warm approbation." He was granted (5th November, 1792) an allowance of 150 rupees a month, over and above his surveyor's allowance, for the time he was in charge of the settlement. Kyd had 1000 rupees a month, besides the pay and all the emoluments of a Captain of Engineers.

Blair, who was at that time in Calcutta, whither he had taken two of the Andamans, had the four vessels above alluded to placed under his orders; and on the 12th November received his sailing instructions. In these instructions it was ordered that the new settlement should take the name which had hitherto been applied to the first, and should be called Port Cornwallis. Blair was to lay the foundation of this new settlement, in precisely the same manner as he had commenced the old. He must begin the clearing of Chatham Island; erect temporary buildings for the shelter of provisions, &c.; lay out a garden, and prepare it for the reception of fruit trees, &c.; dig a well, and, if necessary, build a redoubt. The transfer of the stores, plants, stock, &c., from the old to the new harbour was to be carried on as rapidly as possible; and he was led to expect the early arrival of the Commodore with some of the King's ships to assist in these arrangements. On the arrival of Captain Kyd, the charge of the settlement was to be transferred to him, and Blair was then to finish the survey of the Andamans ("if time should admit"), and ascertain the relative position of the Southern Nicobars with Acheen Island. The Commodore was at the same time informed of the orders given to Blair, who was also directed to attend carefully to all orders from the Commodore.

Blair left Calcutta in the *Union*, with the *Juno*, *Cornwallis*, and *Seahorse*, on the 4th December, 1792. These vessels, as has been before mentioned, carried artificers, a variety of stores and materials, and settlers, to the number of 360, with six months provisions for the whole.

On the passage to Port Cornwallis, off Cape Negris, a violent storm was experienced, in which the ships parted company. The *Union* arrived at the new settlement on the 30th November, and found there Lieutenant Wales in the *Ranger*, who, in accordance with instructions previously given him by Blair, had already commenced the operation of clearing a site for store-houses, and had also prepared a convenient watering-place for ships. Commodore Cornwallis arrived at the settlement in the *Minerva* on the 1st of December, in time to take shelter from a gale of wind which raged with so much violence during the 2nd, that the *Ranger*, riding in four and a half fathoms near the head of the harbour, had the sea breaking entirely over her, and, after losing an anchor, was driven on to a mud bank with only seven feet water, though the vessel was at the time drawing fourteen feet. The *Union* lost two anchors, and was driven on to the same bank, and the Commodore's ship, the *Minerva*, lost an anchor. From Blair's description of this hurricane, it appears to have been of the nature of a cyclone; and storms of this description are well known to have occurred more recently, at this season of the year, in these parts. The centre of this cyclone must have passed only a short distance to the south of Port Cornwallis, as at Old Harbour, when Lieutenant Roper in the *Viper* was making the last arrangement for the removal of the old colony, though a strong south-west wind was experienced at the time of the hurricane, it was not such as to cause any damage; while the *Seahorse* and *Cornwallis*, which, at the same time, were about 160 miles from the settlement,* had fine weather. The *Juno* is supposed to have been exposed to the full fury of this hurricane, for on the evening of the 1st, a vessel—most probably the *Juno*—fired a gun off the mouth of the harbour, which was answered, and the vessel stood to sea for the night, as

* Probably to the north-east.

it was then too dark to enter the port. The *Juno* has not since been heard of, and there is reason to fear that she must have foundered when the cyclone was at its height on the afternoon of the 2nd, as no trace of her has been found. On board this ill-fated vessel, besides the crew, were about ninety settlers, and she carried a large proportion of the provisions for the settlement.

The works of the new colony made rapid progress, and on the 31st December, Blair reported that a space 600 yards long by 100 broad, from the north-west to the north-east point of Chatham Island, had been entirely cleared of the trees and the thick entangled underwood. A double line of dry, comfortable huts had been built, an abundant supply of water secured by wells and tanks, three bungalows erected, a smithy and a pottery kiln were in operation, and a temporary store-house was half-finished. Besides this, a space of about two acres had been cleared on Pitt Island as a kitchen garden and nursery, which was pretty well stocked with fruit-trees from Calcutta and Old Harbour, and in which several kinds of vegetables already began to appear from the seed. A daily supply of excellent fish, generally sufficient for all the settlers, was procured by the fishermen belonging to the settlement, and turtle was occasionally brought from Diamond Island, and cocoa-nuts from the Cocoa Islands. The natives were occasionally seen on the reefs, but they offered no molestation, and showed no inclination for intercourse.

Major Kyd arrived at the settlement on the 5th of March, 1793. Up to the end of that month, the whole of the settlers, with the Europeans and the natives of India, continued generally healthy, with the exception of sores arising from injuries received while clearing the jungle, which, from the scorbutic habit which many of these people had already acquired from the privation of all vegetable diet, proved very difficult to cure. Water was found in abundance—sufficient to water the largest fleets. The soil of Chatham Island appeared to be rich, and far more promising for cultivation than that of the Old Harbour; and, writes Kyd, "from a first view of things, I cannot help entertaining the most sanguine hopes that there are few of the fruits or grains of Hindostan that will not be produced here in great abundance." Application was at once made for an increased supply of artificers and labourers; two hundred convicts were also sent for.

The vessels attached to the settlement were constantly employed bringing turtle from Diamond Island, rice and live stock from Acheen and the coast of Pedi, and cocoa-nuts from Car, Nicobar, &c. Fruit-trees were also imported from the neighbouring continent, and from Sumatra. Building and clearing the land went on vigorously; a cocoa-nut plantation was formed, a granary erected, and cover for the whole settlement provided before the commencement of the rainy season. One hundred and thirteen sepoys and settlers were sent from Calcutta to reinforce the settlement early in May, 1793; seventy-two labourers were despatched at the end of the same month. About this time Blair returned to Bombay, carrying a highly recommendatory letter from the Governor-General in Council to the Governor of Bombay. He had previously submitted to the Council a general chart of the Andamans, and also a full report on the subject, with a tabular statement of astronomical observations, which are to be found in proceedings of the Council of 31st May, 1793. He does not consider the chart complete, for he says, "from the very abrupt inequalities of the depth in several places, it is probable that there may be dangers yet undiscovered." In his report, which is chiefly hydrographical, he gives an interesting description of one of the large caves which are to be found in some parts of these islands, inhabited by innumerable flocks of small swallows, which build the edible birds' nest so much valued by the Chinese as a delicacy and restorative.

"The principal cave is situated at the south point of Strait Island (in Diligent Strait), which is rocky, but not exceeding forty feet in height. The entrance, which is washed by the tide, is an irregular aperture, of about six feet wide, and the same height. On advancing thirty or forty feet, the height diminishes to four feet, and the breadth increases to twenty. Here it is rather dark, and very warm, and the top and sides of the cave are covered with nests; an astonishing number of birds twittering and on the wing, whisking past the ears and eyes. This, contrasting with the melancholy noise of the waves resounding through the gloomy cavern, formed a very uncommon and interesting scene. The birds are probably induced to choose this situation from the caves being inaccessible either to snakes or quadrupeds, and probably defensible against birds of prey. The nests in general are in form the quarter of a sphere, of two and a half inches diameter; one of the sections being firmly fixed to the rock, the other section leaves the nest open above.

"The substance is glutinous; those most in estimation are white and semi-transparent. It has been doubted, and various conjectures have been formed, of what the nests are composed. In smaller and more accessible caves I have observed a mucilage exuding from the rock, moistened by exhalations from the sea, which washes the lower part of these caves. This mucilage, on being dried, had both the texture, colour, and taste of the nest; and what removed all my doubts of this being the substance, was seeing the birds in immense numbers resorting to a cave very productive of the mucilage in the month of January, which is the season in which the birds build their nests. It may now be presumed that the nests are neither of animal nor vegetable, but of a mineral substance."

On the 13th June, 1793, news arrived at the settlement of the war with France, and Major Kyd at once set the whole of the establishment to work, to place it in a state capable of defence against privateers, or any small armed force of the enemy which, for the sake of plunder and destruction, might be induced to visit the colony. An opportune arrival of fresh labourers from Bengal materially assisted in carrying out this object. A hill on Chatham Island was chosen as the site of a work which should command the whole of the cleared space; it was itself defended in the rear by an impenetrable jungle, was steep in ascent in front, and would admit of arrangements being made for the reception of a considerable body of men. "The north-front of the work (the most likely to be attacked) was to have two demi-bastions, and a gun placed in the face of each demi-bastion would command the whole of the valley on each side that is cleared of wood, and might prevent or intimidate an enemy from landing in boats to burn the buildings. The north and the east fronts, as being likely to be exposed to the fire of hostile ships, were to have good ditches, and the earthen parapet was to be fourteen feet thick. The approach to this stronghold was to be defended by abattis and felled timber, the only clear road to it being open in its whole length to the guns of the redoubt, by which it could be completely swept. The vessels in the harbour were also to be moored in such a position as to be protected by the redoubt, and a retreat was provided for the women and children. Kyd having made these arrangements, and set the work forward, went up to Calcutta, to procure the necessary armament, reinforcements, and supplies, leaving the other officers of the settlement to carry out his plans. He at once applied for six twelve-pounders on garrison carriages, and two brass six-pounders, field-pieces, with a proportionate quantity of ammunition and stores; the sepoy detachment to be increased to two full companies, a detachment of European artillery to be ordered in readiness, and a further number of labourers to be sent in the next vessels. He also advised the arming of the vessels attached to the settlement, and that they should bear a proportion of European seamen; and the commanders of these vessels were granted commissions by the Governor-General in Council, "corresponding, as far as possible, with those issued to commanders, &c., of country ships since the beginning of the war."

Major Kyd's recommendations met the entire approval of Government, and the reinforcements he requested were granted, but were not despatched until the end of the year.

On the 14th May, 1794, the Council of the Governor-General report that "the situation of Port Cornwallis has of late proved very unfavourable to the health of the settlers, but we entertain hopes that the place will become more salubrious in proportion as it is cleared."

In April, 1794, the Fort Adjutant at Calcutta was entrusted with the supervision of all matters connected with the establishment at the Andamans in Calcutta—such as the payment of the families of the settlers which remain in Bengal, the procuring artificers and other workmen for the settlement, and the charge of those proceeding to Calcutta for their health or otherwise; at the same time, Major Kyd, the superintendent, was granted an allowance of twenty rupees per diem, in addition to his staff allowance of 1000 rupees per month, with the pay and full privileges of his rank. This extra allowance was given him to meet the extraordinary expenses to which his position rendered him liable.

Major Kyd was then ordered to Penang in the following July and August, to examine the condition of the fortifications there, and report upon the defensibility of the island. He was also to compare the relative value of the positions—Prince of Wales' Island and Port Cornwallis; and "generally to inquire into all important points for the improvement of the island, and for rendering it productive and valuable to the East India Company." In July, 1794, the Government of Bombay sent five European convicts to Port Cornwallis, but the superintendent, considering the settlement not yet in a state to receive them, and being evidently disinclined to the idea of the transportation of Europeans to the Andamans, declined to receive them, and they were returned to Bombay. The Governor-General approved of this proceeding, and directed that no European should be so transported. On the 22nd of November, 1794, fifty more native convicts arrived at the settlement from Bengal; fifty deaths occurred during the rains of 1795.

The minute of the Board, dated the 8th February, 1796, resolving on the abolition of the settlement at Port Cornwallis, is thus recorded:

"Considering the great sickness and mortality of the settlement formed at the Andamans, which, it is feared, is likely to continue, and the great expense and embarrassment to Government in maintaining it, and in conveying to it supplies at the present period, it appears to the Governor-General in council, both with a view to humanity and economy, prudent to withdraw it. He observes that if, at the termination of the present war, it should be thought expedient to carry on the plan with vigour, it could be renewed with very little disadvantage, no permanent or valuable buildings having yet been erected, and there being few stores of value to remove. The expediency of withdrawing the settlement admitted, no time should be lost, so that it may be done before the change of the monsoon. The Board further observes that if it be conceived that this temporary removal from the Andamans could invalidate our claim to those islands, were any foreign nation in the meantime to settle there (a circumstance, however, which is highly improbable), the objection may be obviated by keeping a small vessel at Port Cornwallis, to be relieved every six months. Resolved, therefore, that the marine board be instructed to take immediate measures for the removal of the convicts to Prince of Wales' Island, and for bringing back the stores and settlers of Bengal; that they be further instructed to make provision for keeping a small vessel at Port Cornwallis, to be relieved every six months."

The minute for the abolition of the settlement was recorded in consequence of the receipt of reports from the Andamans, of the death of Mr. Reddich, the surgeon; of Lieutenant Ramsay having left the settlement for Prince of Wales' Island, on account of extreme ill-health; and that the settlement still continued so exceedingly unhealthy, there having been no fewer than fifty deaths during the last rains; and that this long continuance of the fatal effects of this baneful climate has so dispirited every class of men, that they are all solicitous to leave it;" and this notwithstanding that "every comfort and relief the hospital patients could derive from fresh provisions and nourishing diet, had been liberally distributed to them." The settlement at this time numbered 270 convicts and 550 free men and women and children, including the detachment of European artillery and the sepoy guard. The convicts, and such of the provisions and stores as might be useful, were to be conveyed to Prince of Wales' Island; and the colonists, with their property, were to be brought back to Bengal. The necessary arrangements for the conveyance of these people were completed in Calcutta early in March, when Major Kyd left for the Andamans. The convicts and those settlers who wished to go to Penang, were at once despatched there by the vessel prepared for the purpose, and by another which happened to touch at Port Cornwallis, on her voyage to Prince of Wales' Island from Pegu. The rest of the settlers arrived in Bengal early in May, and the settlement was finally abandoned.

Major Kyd, in his report of the comparative advantages of Port Cornwallis and Prince of Wales' Island, dated 4th March, 1795, speaks thus of the climate of Port Cornwallis: "It appears that in the whole year, four months only can be counted of fair weather, viz., December, January, February, and March, though part of the months of April and November may perhaps not be improperly added to this. During this period the weather is dry, the air clear and pure, and, for a situation between the tropics, temperate. Towards the end of March, and throughout the month of April, Fahrenheit's thermometer is seldom below 83° in the shade, from eight in the morning till sunset—during the middle of the day, considerably above 90°, and sometimes as high as 98°. About the middle of April, the rains begin to fall; but it would seem, from an interval of dry weather experienced in the first part of the month of May, that the actual change of the monsoon is not to be considered strictly to take place before the 15th or 20th of that month, which nearly answers to the period of its commencement on the Malabar coast, on the same parallel of latitude. From this time to the end of November, when it ultimately ceases, it continues to rain with little intermission, and often with the greatest violence, attended with constant hard wind and violent squalls. There are, however, some short intervals of fair weather, when the climate is uncommonly pleasant and temperate. It seems to have the whole force of the south-west monsoon, even to a degree more violent than on the Malabar coast, or any other part of India, and to participate, also, in some part of the north-east monsoon experienced on the Coromandel coast, in the same parallel of latitude. Hence there is a fall of water exceeding what is known in any other part of the habitable globe—the greatest fall at Senegal being only 115 inches. In the year 1793 above one hundred inches, and during 1794 no less than 125 inches were measured, which is about double the quantity that falls in Bengal during a season of the greatest abundance. During August, 1795, the settlement was somewhat more healthy."

CHAPTER V.

Resources of the Island—A Long Pull—A Proposal—The Story of a Sailor—The Temperance Ship—The Recollections of Seamen—Favourite Officers—History of David Barclay, the Glasgow Boy—His Early Life—An Unexpected Calamity—The Keeper of a Light-house—A Venerable Benedict—"The Lower Female Orphan Asylum"—Candidates for Matrimony—The Matrimonial Parade—Selection of a Wife—David's Choice—The Bride at her Home—The Birth of a Son—A Melancholy Calamity—David's Funeral—The Arab Boatswain—His Native Airs—The Creole's Report—A Charge in the Dark—The False Alarm—The Filibuster's Somersault—Our Return to the Boat—Rutland Island—Mementoes of Former Storms—Christmas Amusements—The Sunderland Long-Boat—An Unexpected Attack—Bravery of the Author's Jemidur—On a Coral Reef—Arrival at Port Campbell—A Discussion with my Colleagues—Determination to return to Calcutta.

We were all inclined to concur in the opinion of Blair, and other competent judges, that Old Harbour was still the most suitable locality for a convict settlement. The reason that had formerly led to its abandonment was no doubt a very weighty one; but as we were firmly persuaded that the insalubrity of the climate could be corrected, and perhaps altogether removed, by means which would be productive of great benefit in other respects, particularly by turning an unhealthy marsh into corn-bearing fields, we came unanimously to the determination to recommend the seat of the old settlement to the Indian Government, as still the one best fitted for the purpose they had in view. We did not found our preference only on the statements of our predecessors, but we undertook, as was our duty, a great amount of personal labour. Various investigations had been assigned to Dr. Playfair, Lieutenant Heathcote, and myself. Lieutenant Heathcote made minute inquiries into all that concerned the supply of suitable timber and building materials of every kind. The main object of Dr. Playfair's inquiries was to determine to what extent the island itself could be put under contribution for the supply of provisions to future settlers. The quantity of fish adapted for the food of man he ascertained to be inexhaustible, and the stock of small sweet oysters large enough to replenish the exhausted beds in every part of the world. I myself undertook the examination of those sources from which I considered we could depend on an abundant, unintermittent supply of excellent water during the whole year. The day on which I sallied forth to accomplish this duty was one of overpowering heat. I selected several of the crew to accompany me, some of them men of considerable natural intelligence; for even though they may be uninstructed, I have often found—as who has not?—that the experience of observing men frequently enables them to make useful suggestions.

As I had a pull of eight hours before me, with no company but that of my crew, the time hung heavily upon my hands, and the atmosphere was so oppressive that I felt disposed to fall into a state of inactivity—I may almost say lethargy. Fortunately a good idea occurred to me, by which I might at least find amusement for hours I might otherwise have lost in sleep. I requested such of the boat's crew as had anything remarkable to tell—and there were among them some who had led adventurous lives—to narrate to me the incidents of their respective careers. At first, as I anticipated, they were rather taken aback by the proposal, even though I explained to them that I had no desire to pry into every secret of their lives, but merely to listen to the narrative of some of those more remarkable incidents which might have happened to them, forming, as it were, distinguishing epochs in their existence. One of them at last summoned courage to speak, and demanded if he might be allowed to ask a question, the settlement of which rather puzzled himself and his companions. On my answering in the affirmative, and assuring him that he was perfectly welcome to do so, he said to me: "Sir, will you kindly explain to us why, on the Sunday, in the *Semiramis*, the good and pious Dr. Mullens said that bread was the only staff of life?" I told them that they were mistaken, and that Dr. Mullens had not said anything of the kind—because we are told, in the Acts of the Apostles, that all the four-footed and wild beasts, and creeping things, and fowls of the air were sent for the food of man, and in the feeding of the multitude by our Saviour, the loaves and fishes were also destined for the food of the human family; likewise, the fruits of the earth were bestowed, that man might live by the sweat of his brow—that it was by the application of the noble science of agriculture that the earth was made to yield all its riches for the nourishment of man. They thanked me for the information, and as if the sound of my voice, and my willing answer, had inspired them with the necessary courage, some of them expressed their readiness to give me the story of their lives. The one who first spoke was in some respects a remarkable-looking man for one in his position as a common sailor. He was evidently superior to his comrades, both in natural and acquired intelligence, and his whole manner indicated that his habits had been formed in a somewhat superior intellectual sphere. He was, for a seaman engaged in the active duties of his calling, a remarkably pale, sickly, delicate-looking man, and, as I afterwards learned, the son of a Boston physician, who had bestowed on him an education fitting him for a better sphere of life than that in which I found him.

"Sir," said he, scarcely at first mustering courage to look me direct in the face, "my history is in many respects a very miserable one. The confession I have to make is very humbling—I am a wretched and most depraved drunkard. The first ship I sailed in, I may say unhappily, for so it turned out to me, was a temperance ship, with these words, 'Glory to God in the highest, peace on earth and good-will to men' inscribed on a flag she bore. The crew were regularly piped to prayers, and when they were collected together, all hands were earnestly enjoined to practise temperance and sobriety. No swearing or oaths were allowed, and for every transgression of that rule there was a fine of one dollar, even if it were only for a single word of swearing. Unfortunately for me, I had acquired this bad propensity—the impulse that led me to utter blasphemies was almost uncontrollable, and the consequence was, I often got into dreadful disgrace. I wonder the righteous judgment of heaven never struck me down in my dreadful impiety. The ship was really a most desirable one for a sailor to be aboard. The food was abundant in quantity, and in quality it was wholesome and nourishing. Our supply of tea and coffee, both articles which sailors enjoy very much at sea, was also unlimited. Everything was so well arranged, the duties of each individual of the crew so distinctly marked out, that everyone was able to perform his allotted task without that perpetual noise, bluster, and confusion which are by no means uncommon spectacles on board our merchant ships, and the labour was extremely light. The members of the crew were civil and obliging in their intercourse with each other, and I never met with anything but kindness from my messmates. Still the rules of the ship had to be observed; and there is not uncommonly so much folly mixed up with vice, that, although I saw the consequences of my bad conduct staring me in the face, yet such was my infatuation, that, for the sake of indulging in a vile and senseless practice, which, alas! had become too habitual to me, I actually incurred the forfeiture of six months' wages for swearing. My reformation was abandoned as utterly hopeless, so far as human agency, or the ordinary motives of prudence, good sense, and good feeling are concerned. I was held forth as an example to be avoided by the rest of the crew. I was cruelly punished, but I most justly deserved it, for if ever any one did so, I abandoned myself to vice and folly with my eyes open, the miserable consequences of my misconduct constantly staring me in the face, and pointed out to me in repeated but ineffectual warnings. Henceforth I gave myself up more recklessly than ever to my besetting sin, and became every day a more abandoned drunkard. Even now I cannot break myself of the dreadful habit, for when a man once yields to vice it holds him in its grasp with iron talons. The drunkard's mind is a horrible abyss to himself, the mysteries of which he cannot fathom, so completely is every good feeling, every laudable ambition, mastered and overcome by the love of strong drink. I tell you," said the miserable man, with trembling earnestness, "if you were to place a cask of rum on one of these desolate rocks, with a small supply of strong tobacco, and immediately after depart, leaving me to my fate, I should feel no concern—I would willingly drink, and then die like a beast. Like a beast! No; there is no comparison by which such degradation can be represented—die the drunkard's death!"

This unhappy man, however, I must in justice say,

was not such an abandoned reprobate as his jaundiced mind delighted in representing himself. His vice was great enough, and required no exaggeration to depict the state to which it had reduced a man naturally of fine feelings, and endowed with an intelligence above the average. He was courageous almost to a fault, and months afterwards, during the reign of terror which followed the mutiny, I saw him on the jail guard at Calcutta, like a vigorous and energetic son of Neptune, fearlessly performing a duty which required for its execution men in whose steadiness and bravery the most unlimited trust could be reposed. He smiled when he saw me, and, in reply to my inquiries, informed me that strict discipline, under a good and brave commanding-officer, had made a sober, steady, and trustworthy man of such a roving, unsettled reprobate as he acknowledged himself to have been.

Several of the other salts told me the story of their humble fortunes, and of their personal adventures, but there was a wonderful sameness in them all. They did not seem as if they cared much to dwell on those stories of adventure which would have been of most interest to me, but which they appeared to regard as so much things of course, that they merited no particular allusion. In recalling to mind the various ports they had visited in the course of their chequered existence, what appeared to have produced the greatest impression upon their minds was the quality of the grog they had got at one place or another, the tyrannical behaviour of this or that commander, and the fine qualities of the ship they had last sailed in, which in every case, without exception, was the prettiest, swiftest, and sauciest thing afloat. One of my inquiries was, if the service of the Royal Navy was generally popular among seamen now; to which question their unanimous reply was, that it was very much the reverse. If their likes and dislikes were, in many cases, unaccountable, there was at least one worthy admiral to whom they were all ready on the moment to swear allegiance. Admiral Lyons, they assured me, could at all times command the services of the choicest seamen in the Navy. Sir William Peel was spoken of in terms of equal enthusiasm, and the Arctic commanders seemed generally to be regarded with a very favourable eye. As I became interested by their remarks, my desire to know the state of feeling among sailors increased, and I was anxious to learn not only what they liked, but what they disliked. Hearty, good-natured, and accommodating as sailors almost without exception are, still they availed themselves of the true Englishman's privilege of having a grievance. What, then, did they complain of chiefly? The bitter pill in their lot appeared to be, that on their return after a long and distant cruise, they were not allowed sufficient time to see their friends, or even to spend on shore, engaged in that operation which sailors above all other men know how to get through with unequalled speed and dexterity—namely, spending their money.

Walker, a reckless filibuster, was the last man who told his story; but his adventures are so well known to all who take any interest in piratical histories, that it is needless to repeat it. He said, however, he should much prefer a berth on shore to the restless and exposed life of a sailor. The height of his ambition he declared to be, to have the keeping of a flagstaff entrusted to him. I told him it was a very dangerous occupation, especially in tropical seas, and gave him the particulars of one case with which I happened to be at the time familiar; that, namely, of an old man of ninety years of age, of whom it was reported that, at a distance of one hundred miles, he could distinctly see vessels, only in an inverted position. This nonagenarian was the keeper of a flag-staff at the Mauritius, and after a stirring and adventurous life, in which he had escaped many a danger that menaced him with almost certain death, he was blown away from his station in a tremendous hurricane, and never seen or heard of again.

After I had listened to their various stories, and heard the expression of their opinions upon things pertaining to the sea, I was told it would only be fair if I related to them something interesting in my turn. To this I at once assented, and said I should be glad to narrate to them the story a good and worthy man—of honest David Barclay, the Glasgow boy.

The individual so designated was a native of Glasgow, at least such was the generally received belief, for he was acknowledged neither by father nor mother, and all he remembered of himself was, that he had had the pump in the High Street for his foster-mother, and a broom for his bread-provider. David never asked a copper of any passer-by, yet few neglected to give him one.

He seemed fully to appreciate the benefits of such instruction as he was able to obtain; for without any one to explain to him the value of a good education, or to urge him to apply himself to the acquisition of knowledge in his youth, he was the most regular attendant of the Sunday school, and was acknowledged as the best-behaved boy in it. He also frequently attended an evening school in one of the wynds, where he manifested the same application and diligence in the acquisition of such simple elements of knowledge as were taught him. Such was the daily routine of his life for about six years, when he attracted the attention of an enlightened and benevolent magistrate of that great commercial city, who inquired of him if he would like to go to sea, to which his reply was that he should like it above all things. He was then asked if he had no other name than David, and on his answer in the negative, he was further asked by whom that name had been given to him. The dame in the Sunday school, he said, had conferred it on him, with the observation which he had not forgotten—that it was a good scriptural name, the designation of a great and pious man, and that, if he sought to imitate him in all his worthy actions, there would be no fears of his future lot in life. The kind magistrate then gave the youthful David to understand that every man must have a second name, if not more, to distinguish him from the companions with whom he may be associated in life. You shall be named, therefore, after the ship to which I am about to apprentice you, and remember you are henceforth and for ever David Barclay.

Little David thanked the gentleman heartily for the gift of a name, which he accepted with gratitude; and he was duly apprenticed, in proper legal form, in a ship sailing to Calcutta, for which distant port the poor Glasgow boy embarked, probably with as bright visions of making his fortune, and returning to his native land a wealthy and honoured citizen, as any who had ever sailed under more dignified or favourable auspices. The captain, honest Thomas Duncan, one of the commanders of the well-known house of Finlay & Co., was requested to take him under his special charge, and look well after the boy, a commission which he willingly undertook, and, as long as David remained under his charge, faithfully executed.

The career which the boy entered upon with such promise bid fair to be one of unexampled prosperity. For a time all he undertook in his humble way was carried to a successful issue. But at last a sad calamity occurred to him. One dark and dismal night the ship was overtaken by a hurricane, and driven headlong against a great iceberg. By skilful and daring seamanship she was rescued from her perilous position; but while engaged in the discharge of his duties, which absorbed all his attention, the poor sailor's face was frost-bitten, and the effect it produced on him was so great that the good-looking young man became actually repulsive, even hideous in appearance. Although David was a man of firm and resolute mind, this calamity produced such a change in his disposition that he lost all his former cheerfulness, and formed a resolution which no remonstrances could shake, to retire from the observation and society of his fellow-men. On his arrival in Calcutta, he solicited and obtained the post of keeper of the lighthouse of Balatau, a situation which he regarded as one best suited for a man in his unfortunate circumstances. In this remote position he lived at a distance of thirty miles from any neighbour, nor was he desirous of cultivating the acquaintance of any one with whom he might occasionally come in contact. The only opportunity he had of seeing other human beings was once a month, when supplies of oil and food to replenish his wasted stock were brought to him.

His character had retained the impress of his early education. He was a God-fearing man, regular in the discharge of the offices of piety, and apparently deeply impressed with the supreme importance of spiritual things. Still his mind was harassed by many doubts and fears to which his lonely and solitary position was calculated to give rise. He dreaded, above all, that, should he die suddenly, his servants would abandon him, without taking the trouble of bestowing on him the rites of Christian burial. He therefore determined, even while he was himself living, to take measures by which the safe bestowal of his body after death might be secured. He had a water-tight sepulchre constructed of stone, which could be closed by another large stone, with a ring in the centre, shutting down upon it. He also sent orders to Calcutta for the manufacture of a strong two-inch polished mahogany coffin, provided with a handsome white satin lining, and pillows for his head and feet. Before he paid his servants' wages every month, he made them carry him in procession in his coffin three times round his solitary little kingdom, and put him for five minutes in his last home. Old David lived for many years after, indulging himself in this strange fancy, which he insisted on having performed regularly at the appointed intervals.

But a new idea now took possession of his mind. It occurred to him, at rather a late period of his life, that it was not good for man to live alone; and as he generally lost no time in realizing the idea he had once conceived, he determined to proceed without delay to Calcutta, where he had no doubt he should be able to find a helpmate that would suit him.

Now, there was at that time in that city, and there still is, in a better locality, an institution which was then called "The Lower Female Orphan Asylum," but now bears the name of the honoured Lawrence. It is maintained partly by munificent gifts and bequests, and partly by a donation from the Indian Government. The object of this useful institution is to provide for the maintenance of the deceased female children of British soldiers, until they are either married or provided for in some other way. For the former purpose a selection was made from their number at certain fixed intervals; and at the time of which we speak, the process by which this selection was made was a very peculiar one. As soon as a certain number of the young women had arrived at a marriageable time of life, a declaration was made to that effect by sending a circular notice to the commanding officers of the various regiments and depôts stationed at Fort-William, Burrampore, and Dum Dum, to intimate the fact, and to request them to lay it before the soldiers under their command, in order that candidates for the hands of the fair and youthful dames might be induced to come forward, and that each one might select the partner that most pleased his fancy. Accordingly, on the day fixed for the interesting ceremony, the manager for the month, and the secretary of the institution, assembled the soldiers who came forward as aspirants for the honours and joys of matrimony, examined their credentials, and then accompanied them to what was in reality a sort of matrimonial parade, which took place in the large open square of the school. The girls walked up and down in single file, and the soldiers made each their selection; after which the parties were separated for a month, in order to give them time to reflect on the step they were about to take, and to allow them an opportunity of drawing back if their inclinations should in the meantime change. A second matrimonial parade was then held, and if on inquiry it was found that the various couples still remained of the same mind, the affair was considered so far settled, and they were regarded in common language as engaged. During these strange parades, which, it is needless to say, are now quite discontinued, the most amusing scenes sometimes occurred. There, with his tiger-skin helmet, strutted about the handsome horse artilleryman, in his magnificent uniform, with his boots blackened and polished till he could see to shave in them, and his moustachios oiled and arranged in the most telling manner, the cynosure of all female beholders. Then came the grave and steady foot artilleryman, with fewer trappings, but clean and becoming, as sober and composed as if he were a judge on behalf of others, and not a candidate for himself. Last of all came the poor mud-crusher; and though he might be last served, he, too, generally succeeded in finding a mate, but not until the selection of girls from which his choice could be made had been considerably reduced by the previous appropriation of the more handsome and attractive ones.

This ceremony being concluded, they were all introduced into the chapel, where a priest was waiting ready to make them one—a strange kind of union, which often brought together for life many happy and contented couples, and no doubt also frequently the reverse. When the nuptial ceremony was concluded, and they found themselves tied for better or worse, a modest marriage repast of cakes and ale was provided, which they seemed to enjoy more heartily and unreservedly than the highest in the land their *déjeûners à la fourchette*, &c. They were then allowed to depart, with some assistance to enable them to make their start in life as married people.

It was in this way that our old friend, David Barclay, obtained his bride—one whom he fortunately considered the lily of the flock, as he called her to me—for on that occasion I happened to be the manager for the month. In order that he might not be exposed to an unfavourable contrast with younger and more dashing rivals, a day had been set apart for himself on which he might make his selection. He naturally seemed to entertain a good many doubts as to the success of his matrimonial scheme, fearing that none of the young girls would be persuaded to "take up" with such a battered old hulk as himself. With the view of encouraging him, I replied, "David, faint heart never won fair lady;" on which his only remark was, like that of a man making a decisive venture, and determined either to sink or swim, as the case might be, "Well, sir, all right—here goes for a header, and I hope I shall bring up a mermaid." When the poor old man appeared among the girls, there was a good deal of agitation among them, but not of a kind that augured favourably for the happy realisation of his hopes. The half-castes fairly took fright, and ran away shrieking, which was rather a breach of the discipline observed on the occasion, although one his by no means inviting countenance in a great measure excused. "I told you, sir, it would be so," said David. "Bide a wee, my good fellow," I said, "you haven't caught your mermaid yet; but let us see if I cannot do something to help you in this matter." I accordingly took him inside, where he would be free from the presence of so many witnesses, and brought him a girl who I considered, from her natural kindness and gentleness of disposition, and her cleanly, regular, and cheerful habits, would prove, although a good deal too young, in all other respects the very companion for his solitude that he desired. "Here's your lassie, David," said I, to him. He looked up at her anxiously, as if he would read her character in the glance of her eye or the soft lines of her face; and the perusal being apparently satisfactory, he invited her to sit down beside him, and have a little serious talk. When, finally, after a good deal of circumlocution, he came to the point, and asked the plain question for which the ground had been so tediously and laboriously prepared—Would she marry him?—her reply was, that she thought herself too young to marry anyone. "And besides," she continued, "it would break my heart to separate from my little sister, who is in the school also, and whom I must look after." The heart of good old David softening at this remark, he mustered up courage to take her hand, and say, "My dear, if you will be my good little wife, you need never separate from your sister. I have plenty of money to make you both comfortable; and I will give a sufficient sum to Mr. M'Queen, the secretary of the institution, that you may both have the benefit of a good education a little longer yet; and we will afterwards appoint a time when the knot can be tied, and you will then accompany me to my lighthouse at Balatau."

Such was David's strange wooing. Mr. M'Queen accepted the trust confided to him, and gave the additional education the intended young bride was yet to have, such a direction as he thought would fit her to be the wife of a man in David's peculiar position. In due time the latter was summoned to claim his young companion, who was quite willing to accept the lot in life he offered her. The wedding was celebrated in great style, and was followed by an abundant and sumptuous supper at Kiddupore; after which he carried away his mermaid, as he ever afterwards called his amiable bride, in joy and triumph. David conveyed her in safety to his lonely home, determined to do all he could to make her happy in a place that must appear so desolate to one who had hitherto been accustomed to young and joyous companions of her own age. The scene to which she was taken was entirely novel to her. There was something in this sea-washed beacon, and the solitary existence she led in it, which may have had its attractions to a serious and contemplative mind—for such appears to have been the character of hers, otherwise it would be difficult to account for the strange choice she had made. We have reason to believe that so long as the union lasted, with the constant kindness and attention of old David, and the congenial society of her young sister, she passed her life quite as happily as any one could have anticipated in such peculiar circumstances; and David himself, who had previously felt the loneliness of his situation, although he had voluntarily retired from the society of his fellow-men, now found himself perfectly happy in the company of his young bride, who was not only beautiful, but kind in her manner, and attentive to all his wants.

After some months of marriage, an event occurred which added much to David's happiness, short-lived although it was destined to be. On one dark and stormy night, when the elements were let loose, and the winds raged with more than their usual fury, the billows of the Indian Ocean rose in strength and might, and dashed formidably against the walls of the light-house. David, never forgetful of the call of duty, was at once at his post, and as he sternly watched the commotion with which the great deep, a few hours ago so calm and peaceful, was agitated, he thought not of any danger to himself, but only of those poor mariners whose ships were tossed about at the mercy of the furious storm. While he was praying, with all the earnestness of his heart, for the lives of those who were exposed to danger on such a night, he was unexpectedly disturbed by some commotion in the lower part of the tower, and his heart was penetrated by a piercing cry, which, like that of little Paul Dombey, was heard above the noise caused by the raging of the storm. On making inquiry as to the cause, he learned that his wife, who had been *enceinte* for some time, had unexpectedly, in the very midst of the tempest, given birth to a child, the son of his old age. David, however, ever grim, stern, and, even at such a moment, mindful only of his duty, would not quit his post, although it was to take his first-born in his arms; and it was not until the day had dawned, and the fury of the storm was considerably allayed, that he left his place of watch, and, receiving his infant son, blessed the boy, and hoped that one day he would become, like himself, a good and trustworthy mariner, fearless in danger, and able to battle with the storm; for all David's thoughts, whether light or serious, always took, if I may so say, a professional turn.

As soon as his wife and child were able to bear removal to such a distance, he sent them to Calcutta, both that the former might there have the benefit of better attendance, and that in due time his boy might be baptized. David, who had enjoyed a happiness he had never before experienced in the society of one so good and gentle as his Lily, bitterly felt her absence; but as he knew it was for her benefit, and, as he believed, only temporary, he did his best to bear the time of their separation with patience, buoying himself up with the hope of the unalloyed felicity that would be his portion on their reunion. It was now early summer, and on a certain day he remembered, unfortunately for himself, that it was the day kept as the Queen's birthday, which he thought should be celebrated in his lonely tower as well as on the finest ship of the Royal Navy that ever sailed the ocean. So he determined to hoist his flag, and fire what he called a royal salute from his solitary old gun. Accordingly, at the proper hour, having loaded it, he first of all shouted, "Long live the Queen!" and then applied his lighted match to the touch-hole. The rusty old gun burst with the explosion, and poor David's body was blown away into the jungle, where the mangled remains were afterwards found, both his legs having been taken off by the fatal discharge. Those who were employed under him in the lighthouse, in whose welfare he had ever taken the most lively interest, and whose minds, availing himself of the knowledge he had acquired in his youth, he had ever endeavoured to train and instruct, now showed the respect they entertained for his memory. They collected, with all the reverence due to death, his shattered remains, composed them the best way they could, and covered them with the silken flag of the land he had throughout his long and chequered life so faithfully and devotedly served. One of his subordinates proceeded without delay to Calcutta, to announce his death to the authorities, the news of which was received by all with great regret, for notwithstanding the somewhat morose features of his character and disposition, he had been universally respected. As he had met his death by an accident, an inquest was held on his remains, and a verdict of accidental death returned. On the occasion of his funeral, the chaplain of the regiment then in garrison at the nearest station, came over to conduct the most solemn and awe-inspiring of all the rites of religion, that service with which the dead are committed to their last home; and so profound was the respect in which this worthy man was held, that the band of the regiment also was sent out to give more solemnity to the burial ceremony by accompanying their progress to the grave with the solemn strains of the Dead March in Saul. In obedience to his own previously expressed wishes, his servants, after carrying his body three times round the compound, let it down into the tomb that had been prepared for him, and among all the mourning group, it need hardly be said, there was not one who was ashamed to weep for the good man thus suddenly cut down. A parting volley was fired over his grave, the band played "Rule Britannia," and all was over. A small and modest monument was afterwards raised over the place where all that is mortal of the venerable old sailor reposes;

and there, in that solitary spot, where the murmur of that ocean on which he may be said almost to have lived and died is constantly heard, David awaits the sound of the last trumpet. Who is there that will not join in the prayer with which I conclude this notice of so good a man—Peace be unto him!

But we had other sources of amusement besides telling stories either true or imaginary, and the remainder of the pull was most agreeably diversified by the music of our Arabian boatswain, who possessed a guitar, an instrument of which he appeared to be perfect master. The airs he played were generally of a tender, melancholy, and plaintive cast, and when he accompanied them with his voice, the effect in the midst of the still waters was extremely beautiful. In this way we whiled away the time until it was almost sunset, when we reached the shore and landed, for the purpose of examining the locality, and particularly the watering-place, which was said to be capable of providing a very large and constant supply of good fresh water.

Immediately on landing, the first thing we noticed was a group of cocoa-nut trees, which were said to have been planted by Blair. The moment he saw them, our filibuster, putting his rifle to his shoulder, fired, and by the shot detached a large branch from one of the trees, on which the welcome fruit appeared to grow in great abundance. The men were enjoying their evening repast on the nuts with great gusto, when Thompson, the Creole, who, according to his usual custom, had been straggling to a distance from his companions, who was always ready to take alarm even at his own shadow, whose ever active imagination could transform trees into men, and whom nothing could cure of his perverse habit of exaggeration, came rushing among us as fast as his legs could carry him, saying that among some trees, in the direction of which he pointed his trembling hand, he had seen a great number of lurking savages—how many he could not say exactly—but three hundred at least, and very probably a great many more; for such systematic exaggerators always assume a certain candour of manner, and would have you believe that they are rather moderate than otherwise in their rash estimations. Still, whatever reason we might have to doubt the word of such a fellow, it was necessary to be prepared for all contingencies; so, addressing the men, I said, "Now, my lads, gird up your loins, load your pieces, ram your charges well home, and carry your guns full cock. Williams, go on board the cutter, and ask Captain Baker, with my compliments, to send me Mr. Eales and some of the *Pluto's* crew remaining on board;" for I thought it best to be prepared, in case the fellow's statement should prove true. If it came to a hand-to-hand fight, we could not take too many precautions to avoid a reverse, a thing which, considering the paucity of our numbers, was quite within the bounds of possibility. "Now, then, boys," I continued, "follow old Hawk-eye, and mind the advice I gave you before—don't fire at the heads of the savages—level low—and take care that every one of you covers his man. Then clap on your bayonets, and close with them sharp."

Encouraged by these few rough and ready words, always the best when there is any prospect of real fighting, my lads started off, with a shout of exultation, at a quick pace, proceeding in the direction of the jungle where the savages were said to be concealed. And true enough, after we had advanced about a hundred yards or so in an open part of the jungle, we came upon what appeared to us, in the gradually increasing dusk of the evening, to be a pretty considerable body of natives. "Hurrah!" I shouted; "a cheer for the Queen, and in at them, lads!" With a wild shout of defiance we made a rush into the very centre of a native village, which we had not observed concealed among the trees, from which in the obscurity it was difficult to distinguish the small leaf-covered Andaman huts. But our excitement was now dissipated in a moment, for the enemies we had intended to attack with so much vigour regarded our advance towards them very coolly, not even taking the trouble to stir; and just when we got in among them, determined to scatter them in all directions, our illusion was dispelled, and what we had taken to be a numerous body of savages was discovered to be a group of the charred and wasted stumps of trees, about the height of men, and with small branches remaining, extended like arms. Can anyone imagine such a revulsion of feeling as was immediately caused? We had all, in the firm belief that we had enemies before us, discharged our firearms, and the space around us was filled with smoke and sulphur. On its clearing away, it was with no little dismay we discovered that we had sustained as much, and perhaps even more injury than if we had actually come in contact with a band of natives. Two of our men lay stunned upon the ground, having rushed, with blind, headstrong violence, against the stumps of some trees, by which they had been thrown back with great force, falling heavily on the ground. On raising them, it was at once perceived that they had sustained considerable injury, and were completely insensible. They were immediately removed to a stream of fresh water in the neighbourhood, and, after a quantity of the cold and reviving liquid had been repeatedly dashed upon their heads, they gradually recovered, and were soon restored to consciousness, although some time would have to elapse before they were again fit for duty.

We now heard a sound indicating that the men whose assistance we had begged from the *Pluto* were fast approaching in our direction. Here was the possibility of a new danger. Might it not happen that, as in the obscurity of twilight we had mistaken the trunks of trees for men, so they, in the darkness of night, which was now complete, might mistake their friends for foes?—for if they rushed on with the same blind and undistinguishing zeal and haste that marked our own advance, it would be almost impossible to give them timely warning, in the midst of the confusion and noise, of the serious mistake they were making. So, considering it necessary to take all prudent precautions in order to protect ourselves from such an attack, I gave orders to our men to enter and lie down in the huts, advising them to be on their guard lest they should be struck by any stray

Coolie bullet, as the approaching party made their way into the village. Fortunately, I was aware of one circumstance which, in the midst of all my fears, was calculated to inspire me with confidence that all would end well. The officer at the head of the Coolies was a cool and steady sailor, and seeing everything perfectly quiet all around him, the probability was that he would not suffer any useless expenditure of powder and shot, but direct his party to restrain the impulse of their valour, and preserve their ammunition until they really saw a living enemy before them. It turned out exactly as I expected. Seeing no opponent, he imagined that in all probability we had been ourselves able, without his assistance, to render a good account of the natives; and he and his party therefore advanced quietly until they were challenged by us, and we had given them a true and faithful account of all that had occurred—at which, as may be imagined, both officer and men enjoyed a good hearty laugh.

Immediately afterwards, our friend the filibuster, always anxious to be present where anything in the way of adventure was going on, made his appearance in a way that somewhat astonished all. As we were standing engaged in conversation, with the large hollow stump of a tree immediately in front of us, we were sensible of some large body making, as it were, a somersault over our heads, and alighting in the hollow of the tree, from which, like Harlequin, in a Christmas pantomime, after the execution of some astonishing leap, he immediately reappeared, grinning broadly at us, and making us grin as broadly as himself. With that thoughtlessness which distinguished him, nothing would then satisfy him, but, carrying out the illustration, to have a last blazing scene of triumph—and so he set fire to the old trunk, the last remnant, doubtless, of some veteran of the forest. Being rotten to the core, and as inflammable as tinder, it immediately blazed up, and for about half an hour kept up a bonfire which illumined the forest for some distance round, and enabled us to ascertain, beyond any doubt, that there were no enemies whom we had any reason to fear within some distance of us. Besides, the effect of the blaze was really very grand and beautiful. As the night was now pitch-dark, it lighted up the gloomy recesses of the forest, and revealed to us holes and corners that by daylight had been completely invisible to the naked eye.

The gunner now came up with the guard and plenty of lanterns, in order that we might not miss our way in returning to the beach, and might be able, in the darkness, to see where the boats had been left, and get on board of them. We immediately embarked, and, pulling out for the ship, were very glad when we once more put foot upon her deck. We were all completely done up with fatigue, and being as hungry as a pack of famished tigers, were soon engaged in restoring the exhausted vigour of the inner man, after which we yielded ourselves up to the sweet delight of Nature's best restorer—balmy sleep. So complete indeed was our exhaustion, that we no sooner retired to our berths, than we were all instantaneously in the land of dreams; and no one, I believe, heard the reverberations of the evening gun, as, in the dead stillness of night, it resounded with more than ordinary effect.

The next morning we held a council, to consider the result of the explorations we had made; and after having discussed the capabilities of various localities that seemed more or less fitted for the establishment of a convict settlement, we decided to abide by our former conclusion, that this—Old Harbour—was the place we should recommend to Government. But as we were still desirous to examine other localities in the Andaman Islands, with a view of collecting facts, and making ourselves better acquainted with the character and race of the natives, whose origin was still an enigma to us, we were resolved to continue our researches a little longer, with the hope of rendering them more complete; and we were fortunately able to acquire a considerably larger amount of knowledge than we yet possessed, both with regard to the zoology and botany of the islands, and the manners and customs of their inhabitants, an account of which will be found in one of the following chapters.

Having so far, then, completed our work satisfactorily, we steamed out of the harbour, and directed our course to the southward. Our object was to land at Rutland Island, the bold rocky coasts of which we wished to examine, as well as the interior, on the highest eminence of which there appeared to be a locality admirably fitted for being used as grazing downs for sheep. The island, on approaching, presents a very striking appearance; but there is scarcely any place at which a landing can be easily effected, for, except in the small bay on the coast, there is no appearance of a shore or sandy beach, nothing but bold rocks resisting the fury of the waves ever dashing in foam against the firm barrier they present. On examining the shores of this limited bay, we discovered several fragments of ships that had at some previous period been driven ashore on these coasts, and the fate of whose crews was now to us mere matter of conjecture—a mystery which we should probably never be able to solve, for none of the fragments presented any appearance by which it was possible to ascertain to what ship they had once belonged. Sad mementoes these of the dangers to which those who go down to the sea in ships are constantly exposed in the performance of their hazardous and perilous duties!

It is well known that the storms in the Indian Ocean are often extremely violent, doing a great deal of damage both by sea and land. We saw a striking instance of their effects on this very island, at the southern end of which the largest trees lay scattered for some distance along the ground; even the most gigantic having been uprooted and thrown down by the resistless fury of the hurricane. These signs of devastation extended for several hundred yards inland. Having sailed about for some time without noticing anything interesting enough specially to attract our observation, or perceiving any of the natives, we made our way, towards evening, for Macpherson's Strait, a secure and well-protected haven, where we anchored for the night.

The next morning, being the great festival of Christmas, we were disposed to give the men a holiday and a special treat, a resolution on our part to which they, of course, very readily responded. As we were anxious, when giving a treat, to provide something on a respectable, if not magnificent scale, we subscribed a purse of five hundred rupees for prizes for the best rifle shots. Jumping in sacks and boat-racing were also encouraged in a similar way; and, as a matter of necessity, in the exclusively English sense of that word, the whole affair was to be wound up with a jolly good dinner, the prime constituents of which should be—*cela va sans dire*—roast beef and plum-pudding, not forgetting a good ration of brandy to put life and mettle into their amusements. Their expectations of a long day's pleasure were very vivid, and were no doubt so much the more lively, seeing it was the first day's reprieve from active labour they had been allowed since we sailed from Calcutta. The poor fellows, indeed, had altogether had a very laborious time of it, for in consequence of the extreme stringency of Lord Canning's order, they had been constantly kept at hard work, and some of them were beginning to murmur the old schoolboy proverb, that "all work and no play makes Jack a dull boy." I think I am not wrong in saying that the reality, although their amusements were for a time interrupted, fully came up to their expectations. They were all up by cockcrow, and appeared on deck gaily dressed in their very best, and looking, as men-of-war's-men always do, the very pictures of cleanliness.

They had all been piped to breakfast about a quarter of an hour, when one of them, happening to give a glance over the side of the ship, said he saw something that looked like the long-boat of a Sunderland ship, lying on the beach about half-a-dozen miles off. This set all the men agog, and as my own desire to discover what truth there was in the sailor's statement was as great as that of any of the crew, I sent Mr. Cotgrove in the jolly-boat, accompanied by four able seamen, to proceed immediately to the place indicated, and endeavour to bring her off. The men selected, having doffed the finery they had assumed for the day, and found their way again into their working toggery, got into the boat, and poising their oars like seamen who knew thoroughly how to handle them to the best purpose, they exerted all their strength, and the boat darted away smoothly and quickly on her errand from the ship's side. They continued rowing with all their might and main for about an hour and a half before they reached the object presumed to be the boat of a Sunderland ship—by what sign, known only to sailors, the man professed to know the boat of a Sunderland ship from that of any other port, at such a distance, I am unable to say—and when they did so, they met a very unexpected reception, and one for which, unfortunately, they were totally unprepared. The long-boat turned out to be a native canoe, and her crew a considerable number of the savage islanders, all of whom were armed; while among our men who had gone on this goose chace among the Andamans, nothing more formidable than a clasp-knife or two could be mustered to use in self-defence, if, as from the menacing attitude of the savages seemed very probable, they were attacked. Here was a fix. Their only hope was that they might be observed from the ship; but even if they were, before assistance could be rendered them, it was quite possible, as one said jokingly, they might be killed and eaten.

The natives, on perceiving the approach of the boat and seamen, showed the usual signs of that implacable fury into which they were always so ready to lash themselves. As Mr. Cotgrove, followed by his men, landed, and ventured to approach them, they were received with a shower of arrows; and unfortunately, as it seemed to us, not without effect, for one of the men was observed to fall, apparently seriously injured. The matter now looked very serious, and as certain appearances had raised suspicions on board the ship that all was not right—a suspicion confirmed by the signals afterwards made from the shore—I had the crew assembled, informed them of the situation of Mr. Cotgrove and his followers, and requested those who were not afraid to undertake the risk to come forward as volunteers for a duty in which, as the savages now appeared to be pretty numerous, there might be considerable risk not only to limb but also to life. A sufficient number came forward at a moment's notice, and that excellent officer, Mr. Eales, being set over them as Lieutenant, they were supplied with twelve rounds of ammunition, and immediately set off with vigour to relieve their comrades in distress. I accompanied them myself as a volunteer. It was not long before we reached the scene of action, and our appearance, so ardently longed for by the seamen and Mr.

Cotgrove, soon changed the gloomy aspect of affairs. The man who had disappeared, and who we imagined had been seriously wounded, immediately turned up from his hiding-place; and it was discovered that, in consequence of not wearing shoes, he had injured his foot when walking on the pointed coral rocks, and had taken refuge in the boat, in the bottom of which he had been lying, bleeding like a pig. The shore was completely defended by a natural barrier of these coral reefs, and we had to walk and wade over them with great difficulty, for about fifty yards, before we reached the sandy beach. We immediately formed a crescent, with Mr. Eales on one flank, and myself on the other, and proceeded onwards in the direction of the spot where we had seen the natives. But they must have taken alarm on perceiving the approach of a reinforcement; for, like all savages, they are very sharp-eyed, and the canoe was now nowhere to be seen. For a short time we were in some perplexity as to how they could have disposed of it; but, on considering the features of the locality, we could entertain no doubt that they had succeeded in concealing it in some dark corner of the mangrove forests by which the coast was deeply fringed. Although our eyes wandered searchingly into every nook where it was possible for such an object to be concealed, we could discover no signs of its hiding-place. At last, however, the sharp eyes of my Jemidar spied it out, and immediately on making the desired discovery he exclaimed with exultation, "Coxswain Sahib, there it is!" The sailors, however, though they turned their eyes in the direction indicated, did not stir; and the Jemidar, marvelling at their unaccountable inactivity, exclaimed, in his irrepressible excitement, "You Englishmen, why don't you advance? Why don't you go in, and take the canoe from these naked savages? You ought to be ashamed of yourselves, now that I have shown where it is, and am willing to yield to you the post of honour! Why don't you go in and take it?" The men received this indignant harangue with great patience and good-humour, and, when it was concluded, astonished the angry orator by bursting out into an unrestrainable fit of laughter, which must have been excited rather by the manner than the matter of the address, for, seeing that it was delivered in pure Hindoo, there was not one of them capable of understanding a single word of it. The worthy Jemidar's blood, however, was now boiling, and as no one was stirred up by his inciting speech to make the bold venture, he probably thought example might prove more effective than precept, and rushed forward amid a shower of arrows from the savages, who, for their own safety, had retired to a little distance. Everyone imagined the Indian would return before he had advanced many yards. The brave fellow, however, actually persevered, though he continued to be a mark for the unceasing flight of native arrows, and succeeded in what he had so boldly attempted, carrying off the canoe in the very teeth of the enraged savages, who, it is no exaggeration to say, would gladly have eaten him in their anger, black though he was. The British tars, when they saw what he had accomplished, received him with all honour on his return, giving him a mighty cheer of congratulation for the bold exploit by which he had distinguished himself. Goodwin, the coxswain, patted him patronizingly on the back, saying, as he gave the slight Hindoo rather too many of his kindly but not very gentle taps, "Jemmy, dear, you have a black face, but a brave heart!"

As we had no wish, except in the most extreme cases, to come to deadly quarrel with the natives, I was always anxious that there should be as little firing as possible. In this case we had not found it necessary, though the affair looked threatening at first, to have recourse to our death-bearing weapons; but unfortunately one shot was fired in the direction of the natives—wantonly, as it appeared to me; and from the quantity of blood we afterwards saw on the ground, it must have caused serious injury to some poor wretch. Meanwhile, the canoe was secured, and, under the charge of Mr. Cotgrove, brought back with a flowing sheet to the ship.

Although our Christmas festivities had been for a time interrupted by this occurrence, the men were by no means disposed to renounce them. So we had no sooner returned to the *Pluto* than preparations were made to resume our amusements, and everything being made ready for the games first of all, they were vigorously contested, and went off with as much success as we could possibly desire. There was a keen and eager rivalry among the men to distinguish themselves in the various feats of strength and agility to which sailors are addicted, and every one did his best to win a prize. The races were run with a will, and the running in sacks afforded the usual fun and frolic.

After the unwonted exertions of the day, the Christmas fare was heartily enjoyed, and over their allowance of brandy and water the usual sailors' yarns were spun out to an interminable length, until at a rather late hour even the most eager listeners were forced to take refuge in sleep.

The next morning we steamed out of Jolly Bay, and proceeded in a northern direction. As we wended our way along at a moderate speed, we came upon the entrance of a passage which must have escaped the observation of Blair, for it had not been explored by him. On making our way into it, we found that it was a land-locked harbour of considerable dimensions, but not of the slightest use for practical purposes. By the order of Earl Canning it was afterwards named Port Mouat.

After Lieutenant Heathcote had taken note of its various hydrographical features, we steered out of it, and continued our course northward. We kept in very close to the shore, closer, as it afterwards turned out, than prudence would have dictated, for we had not long left the above natural harbour when we were startled by a rasping sound, that showed we had got into too shallow water, even for a vessel of the light draught of the *Pluto*, and were touching the bottom; and before anything could be done to get the ship out to sea, she struck hard and fast on a coral reef.

The savages, who doubtless had been observing our

progress from the forests on the shore, although we were never aware of their vicinity, soon began to show their dark visages, their coal-black eyes gleaming with satisfaction at the mishap which had befallen us. They had soon collected in considerable numbers, but offered us no molestation, as we proceeded to take the necessary measures for lightening the ship, and getting her off the reef, which they watched with eager curiosity, making all sorts of comments to each other on our proceedings. They were evidently in a state of great glee, probably, if the worst reports are true, contemplating the possibility of enjoying a feast on our remains if the vessel should go to pieces! We were in skilful hands, however, and although our position at first wore a rather desponding appearance, by the continued exertions of the crew, the good ship was at length delivered from her immoveable position, and, as soon as she could float freely, was taken out to a safer distance from the shore, and proceeded on her voyage. If our officers had not been men possessed of good practical seamanship, we might not have got over this difficulty either so easily or so speedily as we did. We reached the destination for which we were bound without any further hindrance, and in the course of the morning entered Port Campbell. This locality presented a more animated appearance than any other place in the Andamans we had yet touched at. As we steamed round the magnificent harbour, we saw on every hand signs that we were in one of the headquarters of the natives. The shores were lined with numerous villages, if these collections of primitive-looking huts, in which the natives house themselves, can be so called. In all directions canoes were drawn up on the beach, or paddling along the coast. As soon as the inhabitants observed our approach, they emerged from their confined huts, and lined the shore, men, women, and children, in considerably greater numbers than we had yet had any opportunity of seeing. Here we had another example of that inconsiderate exaggeration in which sailors are so prone to indulge, a fault of which, apparently, nothing can cure them. They would insist among themselves that the number of huts, and of the savages to whom they belonged, was much more numerous than they actually were. For instance, if a village was composed of thirty huts, they would insist there were at least three hundred. Hence, when we had only their statement of any circumstance in which number was an element, we always found it necessary to make a considerable deduction from their estimation, and might generally go so far as to divide by ten any number they explicitly stated.

We made a complete circuit of the harbour, followed as we proceeded by the watchful and curious eyes of the natives, whose astonishment at the ease with which we managed our large vessel, and turned her in any direction we chose, was unbounded. The afternoon was now considerably advanced, and, as we intended to land, it was fully time to do so, if we did not wish to be caught by the darkness of night. We accordingly came to anchor a little before sunset, and landed at a place not far from the mouth of the harbour. It was a singularly lovely afternoon, and when we had clambered up Colonel Symes' romantic rocks, we looked round upon a scene of the greatest beauty and animation—the waters of the magnificent bay reflecting the rays of the declining sun, and the natives scattered along the beach, some following us at a respectful distance, others continuing to watch the steamer, which was an object on which they were never tired of gazing, and so much the more wonderful because utterly incomprehensible. We sat down to rest ourselves on the summit of the rocks before mentioned, and our Arab boatman, who had accompanied us with his never-failing guitar, favoured us with some of his original music, singing particularly a few of his wild native ditties, the plaintive melody of which produced a kind of pleasing melancholy in the mind of the listener. We felt, in our novel position, in such a state of exquisite happiness, that we remained in the enjoyment of this *dolce far niente* until it gradually became dusk, and we were afraid the darkness would gain upon us. So we returned without any further loss of time to the boats, and rowed out to the *Pluto*.

We weighed anchor at daybreak, and steamed away towards the Middle Strait. On reaching it, we anchored off its mouth, and breakfasted. The tide was low, and we waited until it rose sufficiently to take us over the bar at the entrance of the strait separating the Middle from the South Andaman. As soon as we had sufficient water, we entered and proceeded through it. The strait was, in the greater part of its extent, bounded by very deep patches of stunted mangrove, the growth of that plant being evidently checked by the unusual quantity of fresh water that falls into the strait during the rains. Its effect cannot but be exceedingly prejudicial in a sanitary point of view, as all the land lying in a north-easterly direction must be rendered exceedingly unhealthy. It would be quite possible, however, to reclaim it; and, if properly cultivated, it might form a rich soil for the growth of rice.

On leaving the Middle Strait, we again proceeded in a northern direction, until we reached Interview Island, where we had the happiness of finding the brigs, which, as had been announced to us, were to await our arrival there with a supply of coal. They also brought out a quantity of fresh provisions; but what we valued above all were the letters we received from home, for which we were all anxious, after so long a separation from friends and acquaintances in whom we were deeply interested. We had almost forgotten it was the nineteenth century, and had led such Cook and Vancouver lives in this uncultivated region, that we were now nearly oblivious of the civilised world we had left behind us. The newspapers looked to us as the *Times* would have appeared to Rip Van Winkle. And what events had been taking place in the world since we left, but particularly on the continent of India, in which we were all specially interested! Havelock, the gentle and Christian soldier, at a moment when the world was beginning to pour its honours down at his feet, had resigned his glorious life at the Alum Bagh. Lucknow had been relieved by the unwearying valour and perseverance of our inimitable troops. The 34th Regiment of Native Infantry had mutinied at Dacca and Chittagong, and the deluded wretches had met a fate which, although we could not but regret the necessity that rendered such decided proceedings necessary, they all richly merited. They had been killed to a man. This, as may be supposed, was exciting news to us. Some were so shocked that they could scarcely believe such wholesale slaughter could have been permitted on the earth, however atrocious might have been the deeds that rendered such punishment or vengeance necessary. All business was suspended for a time by the excitement into which we were thrown; and we formed into little groups, to compare notes, and converse about the several items of news our letters contained.

The heat was now so great that it produced considerable effect on all of us, making us very idle and listless. However, we had no longer anything of importance to do, for, after the decision we had come to respecting Old Harbour, the main object of our expedition was accomplished. So we had more time to devote to national, political, or domestic affairs; and in devouring our letters, and discussing public events, we were not sacrificing time which should have been devoted to the public service, but only relieving our own tedium, after the active and often disagreeable operations in which we had been so long engaged. We were now living in a sort of dream-land. Our existence, in fact, was a sort of midsummer night's dream without Titania. There was no one more given up to this aimless life than myself, and I wandered about like one who did not know what to do with himself. My colleagues declared I was homesick, and had made up my mind to return, to which they were rather averse, as they still had some objects for which they wished to remain, and were therefore anxious I should not decide to depart so soon.

There was sufficient reason in their remonstrances. They were desirous to see more of the islands they had been visiting, and to collect some mementoes of them. They had been so long and incessantly engaged in the duties imposed by Government, that they had had no time to look about and collect a few curiosities, which they might exhibit on their return. They maintained that their friends and acquaintances would regard them as Goths if they did not profit by the opportunity they now enjoyed, of increasing their knowledge of a strange race, regarding whose origin and existence so little was known, and of bringing back with them such curiosities as they could manage to pick up, illustrative of the modes of life and the peculiar customs of the Andaman Islanders. As yet they had not even a stick or a feather even to show their acquaintances when they reached home, and people would certainly gape with astonishment when they were informed that, although they had been to so remarkable a place, and had passed so long a time in it, they had brought nothing from it that would satisfy the eager inquiries of those who were ever hunting after the curiosities of foreign or savage lands. This was all very well, and they urged their pleas with great ingenuity and perseverance, but I was obliged to be firm also, for their anxious desire to remain could have been gratified only at the expense of public duty. Their statements, no doubt, were perfectly true, and their arguments sound and valid, but we had not come to the Andamans as persons travelling only for their own pleasure, but with a certain distinct object, which Government had entrusted to us in the belief that, when it was accomplished, we should immediately return and render a faithful report of our proceedings. This was a view of our position from which no representation, no entreaty, however forcibly put, could induce me to deviate. I had myself been anxious to remain, and had asked Lord Canning's permission to do so; but he had taken the same view of the matter as that which I have just expressed, and had refused my petition.

Lord Canning's reply was to the effect, that, in the present unsettled and lamentable position of India and its affairs, the political object of the mission was of paramount importance, and that all personal considerations therefore must be put entirely aside. I was perfectly satisfied with his lordship's explanation, feeling assured that if, with due regard to the interest of the country, he could have listened to my request, he would have done so willingly, and without delay or hesitation. Instead of that I was ordered, so soon as the object of our expedition to the Andamans had been accomplished, to go neither to Rangoon nor to Moulmein, for the purpose of making out a report, but to proceed at once to Calcutta, where, on my arrival, further directions would be given. As I had been refused, so, painful as it was to me, must I in my turn refuse.

So ended the only discussion in which there was anything like a difference with my colleagues. *Ne cede malis* is an injunction that it is ever advisable to keep in mind, as the careful observance of it will save us at all times from many evil and disagreeable consequences. The surmise of my colleagues, I may also add, was fully confirmed when they made their appearance in Calcutta. In the various circles in which they moved, Andaman curiosities were considered as indispensable as letters of introduction, without which they were never considered as welcome guests. Well, what did it matter to them? In affairs of duty, the main thing to regard is that the duty be done.

CHAPTER VI.

Interview Island—Last day of the Year—South Reef Island—Hostile Demonstration of the Natives—A French Volunteer—Preparations for Landing—The Cutters—Attacked by the Mincopies—A Truculent Chief—An Unexpected Volley—The Wounded—Escape of the Mincopies—Examination of the Wounded—Dr. Playfair's Request—A Young Andaman Captive—Coral Reefs—Danger to Ships—Visits to the Smaller Islands of the Groups—Steward's Sound—Sound Island—Deficiency of Water—The Andaman Archipelago—Ross Island—Disappearance of all Vestige of its Former Occupation—The Cinque Islands—The Labyrinth Islands—Landfall Island, or the Cocos—Jack—An Account of Two Andaman Captives—A Strange Freak—The Fishermen at Sand Heads—Arrival in Calcutta—Reception by the Governor-General—Jack's Visit to Lord and Lady Canning—General Curiosity to see him—Jack Photographed—Anecdotes of his Residence in Calcutta—Attacked by Cholera—Sent back to the Andamans.

As we had now fully determined to bring our proceedings in the Andamans to a close, and return to Calcutta with as little delay as possible, there was only one place we were still desirous of visiting, in order to collect some information regarding it, before finally taking our departure. This was Interview Island. We accordingly proceeded from the Middle Strait, where we at this moment were, and still continued our course to the northward, until we arrived at the coasts of the island which was destined to be the scene of the most painful adventure in which we had yet been engaged.

Interview Island, as we gradually approached its coasts, presented a very fine appearance, the rich green of the vegetation with which its gradually ascending slopes were covered, contrasting beautifully with the limpid azure of the sky. Its position is such that, lying parallel to the mainland, or the larger island, and at a short distance from it, at a point where there is a great indentation in the latter, it forms an exceedingly safe and commodious harbour. This natural harbour is very spacious, and so protected from the storms by which the surrounding seas are agitated, and from the violent winds by which they are lashed into fury, that ships can at all times rest secure from danger within the welcome haven which it affords. At both the north and south extremities it is of easy access, and egress can at any time be obtained with equal facility and safety. Once anchored in this commodious haven, the south-west monsoon may blow with all its fury without exciting the anxiour fears of the captain or crews of the vessels reposing calmly on its glassy surface. The vegetable growth with which the island is covered is of the usual dense and luxuriant description seen in all the Andaman group. Its appearance was exceedingly fresh and reviving, doubtless owing to the fact that the island is abundantly watered. It contains such abounding sources of that primal necessary, that ships may there at any time replenish their gradually diminishing store. All round the coast was the usual belt of mangrove, except at the southern end, where it entirely disappears, the land being there of greater elevation, and its general aspect consequently much more salubrious. In all other respects it bears a strong resemblance to the remaining islands on the western shore, its elevation being nowhere very considerable, and the land bearing evident marks of its exposure to the violence of the elements, to which, in the south-west monsoons, it is subjected, and from which the favourably situated harbour already alluded to is, by the interposition of the island, fortunately protected.

Should these islands ever be colonized to any extent, Interview Island may hereafter become, by the labour of its colonists, a valuable settlement. The soil, if cultivated, might doubtless be rendered, in many parts, very productive. From its free exposure to the sea in the greater part of its extent, the atmosphere is more than usually salubrious, and the persevering agricultural settler would not be so much exposed to those mephitic exhalations which quickly render a man incapable of all exertion, but, preserving his vigour of constitution unimpaired, would be able to devote himself unceasingly to those toils by which barren places are soon made to glow with the golden fruits of harvest. In all, then, that regards the health of the settlers, a most important consideration, Interview Island may be favourably recommended as a good field for the labours of the colonist. In many essential respects, however, and particularly regarded as the locality for a convict settlement, it is so inferior to Old Harbour, that it was not considered necessary to devote much time to a minute examination of it. The number of its inhabitants was remarked to be greater than that found in any other part of the Andamans; but, so far as we were able to carry our observations, it appeared to share in the general deficiency of animal life which we had already observed as a characteristic of all the other islands of the group.

The last day of the year was that on which we visited Interview Island. The morning of that day dawned as auspiciously as any other since the expedition had arrived at the islands, but it was destined that, before its close, it should be marked by an event more disastrous than any it had yet been our lot to experience. We had been told, with what appeared all the assurance of perfect knowledge, that the inhabitants of Interview Island were amicably disposed, and would not, as their fellow-countrymen had hitherto done, receive us as enemies, a statement in which we considered ourselves justified in putting entire confidence. We therefore resolved to avail ourselves of the opportunity which we now possessed to hold such intercourse with its native inhabitants as we could prevail upon them to accord to us, for it was our anxious desire to add as much as we could possibly gather to the little stock of knowledge we had already acquired concerning them. It is true, we had obtained considerable information from the statements of those who had previously visited the islands, but our desire was that our knowledge should be founded, as much as possible, on personal experience, and the result of familiar intercourse. We therefore determined, as this was our last opportunity, that *coûte que coûte* we should come into contact with them, and by such means as circumstances might suggest, endeavour to fathom their character a little more profoundly than we had yet been able to do.

Accordingly, after a slight and hasty survey of some parts of the coast, we steamed quickly round Interview Island, which is several miles long, until we came to South Reef Island, where, as we observed several hundred natives on the shore, an eligible opportunity seemed to present itself. We could see, by means of our glasses—for we were still at some distance when we first observed them—that many of them were engaged in fishing, the rest employed in various other occupations, or rambling idly along the shore in little groups, engaged in animated conversation, accompanied with a great deal of expressive gesture. We steamed quickly on, and dropped anchor at a place where the distance between the Reef and the mainland was about two miles. We were anxious, if we could, to have landed before we attracted the observation of the natives, and to appear in their midst before they could make any hostile demonstration, if they were so inclined. But they were too sharp for us, and before we could make the necessary preparations for landing, some of them had perceived us, and communicated the fact of their discovery to the other natives, who were thrown into a state of agitated commotion by our sudden and unexpected appearance. They then lined the shore for some distance, others appearing from time to time to add to their number, already considerable. As was natural, they seemed to watch all our movements and proceedings with the greatest interest and curiosity, as we also did theirs.

As we were making preparations for landing, Monsieur Mallitte, the French photographer, came up to me and expressed his great anxiety to be permitted to accompany us. As I did not appear willing to accede to his request, he pleaded his cause with great earnestness and eloquence, urging me to remember that he was the only Frenchman on board, and that if he remained behind it might be attributed to cowardice—a suggestion intolerable to any Frenchman, civil or military. I had good reason, however, for doubting the propriety of allowing him to go with us. I told him the enterprise in which we were engaged was a very serious one, and that, notwithstanding all we had heard of the pacific disposition of the natives of the island, it was quite possible our landing might not be accomplished without risk, and that the danger might even be so great as to involve the possibility of bloodshed and death, if we should come into violent collison with the inhabitants. Whereever there was such peril I represented to him that none but those who were obeying the dictates of duty had any right to be present, and that therefore I did not feel inclined to accede to the request which he, prompted by the love of adventure, or by a sort of national *amour propre* and rivalry, had made to me. Besides which, I had an impression that when volunteers insisted on taking part in such expeditions, the desire to distinguish themselves, to which, in his case, was added that of reflecting honour on his country, almost always carried them into positions of more than ordinary peril, and, to use a familiar phrase, brought them to grief. Now, as I afterwards reflected, in wishing to persuade him not to accompany us, I had used the very line of argument most calculated to make him persevere in his desire; for how could an ardent, brave, and adventurous Frenchman ever allow any one to say that he had been persuaded to keep away from a scene of danger solely by a prudent fear or caution, or by the wish to save himself from a peril to which others with whom he was associated were exposing themselves? I saw clearly that I had made a very palpable mistake, and as he remained persistent in his desire to form a member of our party for shore, and urged his cause with all the earnest vehemence of a Frenchman who was determined not to give in, I was compelled to yield to his wish, and to suffer him to accompany us.

The cutter by this time had been detached and lowered. The men's arms, having been previously loaded and capped, that we might be ready for any unexpected attack, were stowed away under the thwarts of the boat, in such a way that if the Mincopie showed no hostile indications, they might see nothing on our part which they might interpret as a sign of aggressive intentions. The second cutter, equipped and armed in the same way, was ordered to follow us at a short distance, in order that, if we should find ourselves exposed to a more vigorous attack than we anticipated, we might have a reserve upon which we could fall back. This second boat was placed under the charge of Mr. Cotgrove the midshipman, with strict orders not to fire at anything, unless his superior officer should consider it necessary, and direct accordingly. If no such order were given, he was to confine himself to the duty of picking up any of our people who, if we came in contact with the savages, might be wounded by their arrows, and fall into the water. This order it was of the utmost importance strictly to obey, for this part of the sea abounded with sharks, and unless they were speedily rescued, those who fell from the boats might, in their desire to escape one danger, fall into another infinitely more horrible to contemplate. Mr. Cotgrove, as we must afterwards show, with a recklessness which it is impossible to condemn too strongly, unfortunately disobeyed these directions, and his wanton act was productive of consequences bad enough in themselves, but which were very near being a great deal worse. Monsieur Mallitte was exposed to the imminent danger of death, Dr. Playfair, the coxswain, and myself were wounded more or less severely, and the boat was riddled with balls. Fortunately none of the crew were killed, owing to the fact that they were standing up at the time, hotly engaged in fight with the Mincopie, upon whom we had been compelled, by their own aggressive conduct, to discharge a fatal volley. On our return to Calcutta, Mr. Cotgrove was severely punished, for his inexcusable breach of discipline, by Commodore Campbell.

As the boats were gradually advancing towards the shore, from which we were still a considerable distance, our attention was directed to several canoes filled with natives, at a short distance from the beach. We could easily see that the reception which they were preparing for us was by no means of that friendly character we had been prepared to anticipate; and, as in all our previous interviews they had exhibited nothing but signs of the most implacable, fierce, and relentless hostility, I feared that a collision I had so much wish to avoid was now imminent, and I at once directed the men to cease rowing, to dip their oars, and to be ready for handling their arms. In obedience, however, to the strict orders I had myself received from the Governor-General, I warned the sailors that they were to remain strictly on the defensive until attacked by the natives. Although, as we drew near, we saw that their appearance was very menacing, none of our men showed them signs of hostility, or even exhibited the arms they had for their protection. As is generally the case in encounters with savages, these manifestations of a desire for peace were misunderstood, and our anxiety to avoid a contest with them was attributed to the awe with which we regarded their warlike prowess. So, the Mincopie took immediate and deliberate advantage of our backwardness, and at once became the assailants. One whom, from the position of command which he seemed to assume, and from the obedience with which his orders were received, we regarded as their chief—a vigorous, square-built, fierce-looking savage—placed himself at their head, and took the lead on their side in all the events of the fight. As the two parties came near to each other, I resolved to make a last attempt to avoid a combat which would only embitter an hostility that rendered all intercourse with the natives impossible. Standing up in the stern-sheets of the boat, I waved aloft a white pocket-handkerchief, exhibited beads of every hue, which, as they flashed brilliantly in the sun, I made them endeavour to understand by signs were to be theirs, and shouted the word *padoo* as loud as I could. The only reply was a well-directed volley of arrows, one of which was shot apparently, with well-aimed accuracy, from the bow of the truculent chief, who, in all probability, had destined it for my heart. I watched its swift flight as it came right onwards in my direction, feeling that there was no possibility of avoiding its sharp and deadly point. Providentially, at the very moment when I expected to be transfixed by it, the boat in which I was gave a lurch, and the winged messenger of death flew past me, missing Dr. Playfair also, who was near me, and went right through the thigh of Lieut. Heathcote, at a part in perilous proximity to the femoral artery. Although the wound was a very severe one, he was not the man to quit his post as long as he was able to be of any service; and he continued to discharge his duty, until, by an unfortunate accident, he was laid low by a second wound, the consequences of which were so serious that for two or three days we were very anxious as to the result. When the savages perceived the effect produced by the well-directed aim of this arrow, they gave a shout of exultation, and were preparing to send a volley of the same deadly weapons among us, when I raised my Lancashire rifle, and, covering my friend the chief, discharged it at him; but as I missed him, he escaped uninjured so far as regarded my shot. But the filibuster, who had pulled the bow oar, and marked his man, was determined to have a trial at him also, and taking a good aim, he fired and hit him, evidently fatally, for he fell amid the loud lamentations of his followers. The savage chief died almost with the dignity of Cæsar. Covering his face—not with his robe, for he had none, but with his hands, to shut out the blinding flash of the fire-arms, which we were now discharging rapidly—he sank in his canoe with a grace and dignity in which there was something really touching and melancholy. The death of a truly brave man is always a sad sight to witness; and if it could not be said of the Mincopie chief that he was *sans reproche*, he was at any rate *sans peur*.

By this time a sailor, named Johnstone, had been badly wounded by an arrow in the back, and was lying in the boat, howling lustily; and, on examination, it was found that his wound was really a very severe one. The arrow, which still remained in it, and caused him great torture, was torn out in a very rough and heedless way by one of his comrades. My Jemidar, who had distinguished himself so favourably on a former occasion, had his hand transfixed by an arrow, and pinned to the side of the boat in such a manner that he was unable to move it. By this time, although three of us had sustained severe wounds, there had been no fatal injury on our side; while on that of the savages three lives at least had been lost—one having been seen after our discharge to fall lifeless into the sea, and two others sinking dead in the canoes. These fatal results of our fire had evidently alarmed the natives, and they no longer displayed that bold, boasting, and defiant manner with which they had at first received us. There was now more than usual agitation in their canoes, which they were all at once seen, as if by some preconcerted agreement, to abandon, and jumping into the sea, though they were still a considerable distance from land, swim towards the shore. The instant I saw that all opposition to our advance had ceased, I directed, by a wave of my hand, the crew of my boat to cease firing; and, notwithstanding the exasperation of the men at what they considered the cowardly and unnecessary attack made upon them by the Andamanese, the order was obeyed without the slightest hesitation.

It was at this moment that, to our inexpressible amazement, we were exposed to a new and more formidable danger, altogether unexpected, and against which we could make no defence. While we were congratulating ourselves that resistance on the part of the natives had ceased, a withering volley of firearms was discharged into our boat, inflicting serious injury on several of our party. We were at first thrown into such a state of stupor by an event so unlooked for, that we were unable to imagine whence the alarming discharge had come; but recovering ourselves in a moment, we looked round, and saw that it had proceeded from the boat under Mr. Cotgrove, which was following as our support. As we afterwards learned from himself, he had fired at long range at a canoe full of savages, which he had observed between himself and us, but by some miscalculation or misarrangement, his shot had passed over the object at which it was aimed, and fallen direct into our boat, where it inflicted the injuries on Dr. Playfair, Lieutenant Heathcote, and others, already alluded to, for which Mr. Cotgrove was afterwards punished at Calcutta by Commodore Campbell.

Thus ended the fight of Long Reef Island, an incident which, though it ended to our advantage, I most deeply and unfeignedly regretted, as, after we had reached the last day of our expedition without coming into serious contact with the natives, I had hoped to be able to leave the islands without being under the necessity of reporting any such *contretemps*. The wounds of Lieutenant Heathcote and the sailor Johnstone, caused by Mr. Cotgrove's unlucky escapade, proved very severe, but after suffering much pain and uneasiness from them, they ultimately recovered. My poor Jemidar, also, was an object of great anxiety to me, for his wonnd was of such a nature that I feared the possibility of its ending in lock-jaw. For twenty-two days he remained in a very precarious condition, but by the end of that time his dangerous symptoms gradually disappeared, and I am happy to say that, like the others, he recovered his usual health and strength. In spite of the constant exposure to which we had been subject, during the whole period since we had first landed on the Andamans, we had the inexpressible happiness of bringing back the whole of our party safe and sound, without the sacrifice of a single life—an incident, I believe, unparalleled in the history of similar expeditions.

But to return to our position after the fight. When our men saw the savages, at a distance of two miles from the shore, betake themselves to the water, they were very anxious to have some pot shots at them, as if they had been so many water-fowl, but this I at once strictly prohibited. Their swimming capacity was truly remarkable. They made their way through the water with the greatest velocity and ease. They swam hand over hand, diving every two hundred yards like ducks baited by water-spaniels. Mr. Cotgrove pursued in the second cutter, in which, as the crew had never been in immediate contact with the savages, there was not a single man hurt. So swift was the flight of the natives that, with one exception, they all succeeded in making their way safely to the shore. The one exception was a lad of about twenty-two years of age, whom Mr. Cotgrove picked up as he was using his utmost exertions to escape, and brought safely on board the *Pluto*. In the meantime, Monsieur Mallitte, who had also received a severe wound in consequence of the discharge from Mr. Cotgrove's boat—indeed, from his profuse bleeding at the mouth, we thought, at first, he must have been shot through the head—threw himself into my arms, covering me with blood, and exclaiming, with all the vehemence of an agitated Frenchman, "Monsieur, je suis mort!" "Pas encore, mon ami," I replied, "car les morts ne crient pas."

Instead of persevering in our desire to land, we returned to the ship, that our wounded comrades might be properly attended to. We accordingly rowed back with all the speed possible, and Monsieur Mallitte, who made the greatest noise, although his wound was by no means the most serious, being put into an arm-chair, he was hoisted on deck, and at once safely stowed away in his cabin. The wounded man Johnstone was taken up and laid on a mattress on the quarter-deck. His wound was really a very serious one, and he was at once put into his hammock, and tended with the greatest care. Lastly came the Jemidar, with the broken head of a barbed arrow stuck in his hand, from which he suffered great pain, but which he endured with remarkable patience and fortitude. When they were all got safely on deck, M. Mallitte, who as a stranger was tended with great care, being put under the influence of chloroform, it was found that he had been wounded in the shoulder, the course of the ball through which could be distinctly traced. It had narrowly escaped injuring the joint in its progress, and had run along the dangerous region of the neck, and impacted itself in the occipital bone. Dr. Playfair traced its course with all the skill and sagacity of an experienced naval surgeon, to whom such wounds are familiar, and he succeeded, without much trouble, in extracting the bullet by means of the strong bullet forceps. When Monsieur Mallitte returned to consciousness, the bullet was presented to him as a trophy of his courage and prowess, at which he was greatly delighted, rejoicing particularly in the fact that he considered himself to have maintained the reputation for courage attributed justly to the great nation to which he belonged.

The Jemidar would not submit to take chloroform, although it was the only way by which he could be saved the necessity of enduring long and protracted pain, which, with that stoical power of endurance often manifested by his race, he seemed rather disposed to face boldly, however severe it might be. The crooked nail, forming the barb of the arrow, was so firmly impacted and entangled in the small bones of the hand, that dissection had to take place before it could be removed; and even after this operation had been accomplished with the greatest care, it required two strong men to extract it by main force. Johnstone, also, was still suffering a great deal, of which he kept us mindful by the loud lamentation which he never ceased making until his pain was somewhat relieved. His arrow must have been as jagged as that of the Jemidar, and had also to be drawn out by main force, tearing and lacerating the flesh very much before it could be extracted. But though the greatest care was taken of him, the doctor being unwearied in his attentions, and his comrades ever ready to render him any services, he suffered very much for some time. The fact was that his wound had assumed a very threatening appearance, and the only means by which his suffering could be in some measure relieved, and continuous periods of rest secured for him, was by keeping him under the influence of opium, which was frequently administered in such doses as were found necessary to produce the desired result. It was also considered advisable, especially when dressing his wound—an operation during which he suffered a good deal of pain—to put him under the influence of chloroform. No man could have had more care bestowed upon him, for not only was he assiduously nursed by his brother seamen, who manifested the greatest sympathy when they saw the suffering he was compelled to endure—but as there were three medical men on board, he was visited by one of them every half hour, so that all the phases of his illness were distinctly marked, and the necessary remedies at once applied. It may be observed, indeed, as a fact, the truth of which will be generally acknowledged, that no men are more carefully tended during illness, or when suffering from wounds, than soldiers and sailors, for whose care the most ample provision is made, and that not only to tend them when actually attacked by disease, but even to guard them against its approach. It has often been noted that, while cholera or some other fatal malady has been raging in a town, the garrison has been preserved entirely free from its approach; or if a solitary instance or two unfortunately occurred, the remedy was so immediately at hand that the disease was arrested before it had time to spread and cut down its tens and hundreds. So it was with this man Johnstone. No nobleman could have been more assiduously cared for; and the result was that, threatening as his symptoms for a time were, he ultimately recovered, and was able to resume his duties.

We had picked up two of the bodies of the three Mincopie who were killed during the fight, and, in obedience to the orders I had previously given, they were now laid out on deck, and decently covered over with matting.

While I was standing on the quarter-deck in the course of the day, the coxswain came up to me with that swaggering roll of the body peculiar to seamen, and, addressing me, said:

"Please, sir, Dr. Playfair wants their heads."

"Their heads!" I said; "what does he want with them? We are not here as kidnappers, so they must be left for their friends."

We examined their bodies very carefully and minutely, for the purpose of observing any peculiarities by which they might be distinguished. The two men were, like all of their race whom we had seen, of short stature, but their conformation appeared to be remarkably robust and vigorous, and the muscular development of their arms, legs, and chest was very considerable. Their countenances were anything but agreeable, pleasing, or attractive. Their expression, as it had been settled by the hand of death, had something in it that was truly repulsive and frightful. Their features, distorted as they appeared by the most violent passions, were too horrible for anything of human mould, and I could regard them only as the types of the most ferocious and relentless fiends. If the whole race resembles these two men, we had no reason to be surprised that we had failed in every attempt to arouse friendly and hospitable feelings in a tribe whose aspect was really that of demons. I doubt if Fuseli, in depicting the worst or most violent passions of humanity, ever conceived anything so horrible as the visages upon which we now looked. When we had concluded our examination, and taken note of all we wished to remember, suffering nothing to be done inconsistent with that feeling of respect and awe with which I think death ought ever to be regarded, they were put back gently into one of the canoes which had been brought in by our boat, and, the tackling being loosed, it was allowed to drift with the tide towards the shore, where it would doubtless soon be picked up by some of the natives who still lined the beach, regarding us and our vessel with more awe than they had manifested previous to the fight which had cost them the lives of their three companions.

All this time the young Andaman who had been taken captive was leaning, in a very dejected and hopeless state, against the paddle-box. The sailors had already christened their native *protegé*, the name by which they chose to distinguish him being the generic one of Jack. We could easily divine that the poor fellow was thinking of the home, poor though it was, from which he had been torn, and of the friends from whom he was separated. He had already experienced what he no doubt considered one of the hardships of a captive's lot, the sailors, scandalized, as they jokingly said, by his naked condition, having rigged him out in an old pair of trowsers and a jacket belonging to one of them. The poor fellow, whose limbs had ever been accustomed to the unrestrained and untrammelled state in which Nature had given them to him, evidently felt very uneasy in his confinement, and exhibited in his countenance an expression of hopeless misery. Seeing how desolate and dejected he appeared, the kind-hearted coxswain, who had his own rough way of expressing sympathy, went up to him, and giving him one or two of those friendly taps that were sufficient to drive a man's breath out of his body, he addressed him in English, a language which it was evidently his opinion every man ought to understand by nature. "Come, cheer up, my good fellow," he said, "don't be afeard, we ain't a-going to hurt you"—a friendly assurance from which to his surprise the young savage appeared to derive no consolation, and to which he gave not the slightest heed. Others of the crew collecting round him, they began to take liberties with him in the way of playing all sorts of tricks. One presented him with a quid of tobacco, which, notwithstanding his dejection, he at once conveyed to his mouth, and swallowed without exhibiting any of the usual symptoms of nausea, at least so far as regarded external signs, for not a muscle of his face seemed to wince as the not very choice morsel descended. Another brought a pipe, with the intention of giving him some elementary lessons in the art of smoking. He appeared to submit to all his trials very patiently, as if he considered them necessarily involved in his captive lot. His first attempts at smoking a long clay pipe were not very successful. Instead of inhaling the smoke he blew it outwards, and as he saw the curling cloud, accompanied with sparks of fire, issuing forth, he thought he had set himself on fire, and for a short time nothing could induce him to repeat the experiment, when the sailors, after showing him by example how it ought to be done, urged him to make a second attempt. As they, determined not to be beaten, would not give in, but persevered in forcing their unwelcome instructions upon him, he, apparently still in the belief that he was only undergoing that slow torture to which, as a captive taken in war, it was his lot to submit, was at last induced to comply, and was rewarded with success. This time he succeeded in making the inhalation properly, but as he closed his mouth tightly, instead of leaving a small aperture for the emission of the smoke, such as he had observed made by the sailors when enjoying their pipes, the smoke, finding no other means of issue, nearly choked him as it made its way out by his nostrils.

It was at this moment that I arrived on the scene. As I could not approve of such conduct, nor even pretend not to observe it, I at once sternly prohibited any further attempts of a similar kind. As I knew that a Maltese sailor who formed one of our crew, was of a very kind and considerate disposition, I entrusted the poor solitary Andaman to his care, with directions that he should allow no one in any way to molest the captive, and at once to inform me if any one attempted to disregard that injunction. I have every reason to believe that my directions were strictly attended to, for I neither heard nor saw any more attempts to play the same or similar thoughtless tricks upon him. Humanity was a feeling I was ever anxious to encourage, and both by precept and example I endeavoured to manifest to the crew the estimation in which I held it as one of the cardinal virtues of a truly good and brave man. He who is oppressive to the helpless has always more or less of a coward's nature in him.

My observation was drawn almost immediately afterwards to a strange circumstance, which I noticed with a good deal of interest and amusement. Our dog Neptune, a large and stately animal of the canine tribe, as soon as he knew there was a stranger on board, instigated by some such feeling of curiosity as that which in similar circumstances animates his betters, came marching deliberately along the deck until he reached the place where Jack, to adopt the name given him by the sailors, was standing, the observed of all the more curious amongst our crew. From the expression of astonishment which his face exhibited the moment his eyes fell on the noble animal, it was evident that he could never have seen anything larger in the shape of a quadruped than Mr. Blythe's *Sus Andamanensis.* The savage, with the true instinct of his unsophisticated nature, at once concluded, from the manner in which Neptune was caressed by all, and from the sensible way in which he received these manifestations of good-will, that he must be the friend and companion of man. Accordingly, as he also inferred that he, too, ought to manifest his good feeling to the dog, he did so by throwing his arms round his neck, clasping him in a friendly embrace, and lying down with him on the deck. Neptune received these unusual attentions apparently with great satisfaction, and a league of amity must have been agreed to immediately by the two, for ever afterwards they were inseparable companions. At night, it was considered necessary, as a measure of precaution, to put an iron ring round Jack's leg, so as to render any attempt at escape, by swimming ashore during the darkness, impossible; for we were anxious to convey him with us to Calcutta, as the only specimen of a native Andaman who had, at least in recent times, been seen in a civilized city. The last thing we did, before retiring to our hammocks for the night, was to give him a supper of grilled pork, which he enjoyed with all the gusto of an epicure. Every one then turned in for a night's rest, except the solitary watch who paced the deck for our protection.

Thus ended with us the eventful year of 1857. On the first day of the new year we sailed towards the entrance of one of the harbours, where Blair, generally so careful and accurate in all his observations, had marked nine fathoms. As we had perfect confidence in his recorded statement, we steamed right on, unapprehensive of any danger. But it was not long before we were made aware, by sad experience, that in this case at least our confidence had been misplaced, for before five minutes had elapsed the vessel received a shock which convinced us we had steamed right upon a coral bank, of which Blair can have had no knowledge, as he gives not the slightest indication of its presence. It could scarcely be that it had risen, since his time, to such an elevation, as to render a place where there had then been nine feet of water, now too shallow to allow a vessel of so light a draught as the *Pluto* to sail over it; for if that were the fact, the growth of coral must be much more rapid than by the best observers, and by those who have had the most favourable opportunities of considering the phenomena that mark its progress, as it gradually extends and rises, it has generally been supposed to be.

The shores of the Andaman Islands are skirted continuously by these coral reefs which are the source of so much peril to all mariners who approach their coasts. There is not a bay in which it is not found, forming a barrier between the approaching vessel and the shore, and fragments of it, in pieces of various sizes, are strewn on every beach. On the west side of the Great Andaman these reefs are far more extensive than they are on the east; and at a much greater distance from the land, they threaten the approaching vessel with perils which it requires all the skill and experience of the most accomplished seamanship to avoid. On the eastern side of the island there are many places where the depth is so considerable that the largest vessels can float in safety on the bosom of the deep, depths of a hundred fathoms being found at many places within three miles of the coast, and generally at a distance of five miles; whereas, on the western shore, the coral reefs extend out to a great distance, and form dangerous patches of rock, at a distance of twenty and twenty-five miles from land, a fact which any careful observer would be able to infer from the geological features of the island, the general dip of the stratified rocks being to the eastward, and at a high angle, sometimes as much as seventy-five degrees.

In consequence of the extent to which our time was occupied with the immediate object of our expedition, we were unable to make any particular observations on the growth of coral, a subject in many respects interesting and attractive to all the students of natural history. It deserves particular attention, both in a scientific point of view, and in the interests of our mercantile marine. Exposed to so many serious dangers, in consequence of the elevation of these beautiful but dangerous constructions, navigation among coral reefs must at all times be hazardous, and the most minute observation may sometimes fail to detect some of the isolated rocks formed by the ever-continuing labours of inconceivable multitudes of the insect. Vessels, with valuable lives and cargoes, are thus often exposed to the danger of approaching some unknown and hitherto unmarked reef, without anything to give them the slightest warning against the perils into which they are running. These extensive banks which exist so far to the westward must always prove an impediment to the prosperity of any colony which may be established in their vicinity. On that account, the hope of forming successful settlements on Interview Island, or on any part of the westward coast, must be considered as an attempt which would almost certainly end in failure.

In the course of our wanderings among the Andamans, we made passing visits to many of the smaller islands of the group, to which, in the main course of our narrative, we have made little or no allusion, as we saw nothing in them calculated to further the main object of our expedition, and in their general features they were only smaller copies of the larger and more important islands. In concluding the narrative of our visit to the Andamans, so far as the choice of a locality for a convict settlement was concerned, we may here give a hasty glance at some of the less important points where we occasionally anchored or landed. After our visit, already recorded, to Craggy Island, where we saw the first native group, we proceeded to Sound Island, which is situated on the east coast of the larger island, and, as we had been given to understand, might possibly afford an eligible site for the purpose we had in view. Proceeding through Steward's Sound, we then steamed right round the island, which we found to be of an irregular quadrilateral form, constituting one side of a large land-locked bay, and at all seasons accessible to vessels of every class. The island appeared to consist of ridges of high land running through it in all directions, and prolonged in spurs to the points of the bay, indenting its margin. Belts of mangrove, similar to those by which the other islands were fringed, grew in profusion along the coast;

and it was almost completely surrounded with coral reefs, except where, here and there, fine sandy beaches occasionally intervened. Towards the south-western extremity we discovered a spacious harbour, presenting in its conformation something of the appearance of a horse-shoe. On sounding it in several directions, we found that the water was very deep; in some places nearly three quarters of a mile. We spent two days in exploring its shores. It is rather more than half a mile across, and on the northern and eastern sides it is skirted by coral banks and rocks, but in the rest of its extent it affords good anchorage ground even for ships of a large draught. There is a great ridge which goes completely round it, rising to an elevation of about one hundred and twenty feet. We observed the same description of jungle and underwood as that of which there is such abundance on Chatham Island; but there is not nearly the same quantity, and consequently it is much less dense and tangled. The ridges also contained small plateaux of level ground, with good drainage, and sufficient in extent to form a very large settlement, with an abundance of clay and coral for building purposes. The soil also, to the best of our judgment, appeared to be very rich, and if subjected to cultivation would, in all probability, soon reward the industry of the agricultural settler by the production of abundant harvests of grain.

In one very important respect, however, it presented a very great deficiency—namely, in the want of a good supply of water. We examined in every direction for about a mile and a half, and were unable to discover a single running rill, even of the smallest dimensions. Attempts were made in some places to dig and bore; and although we descended to a depth of eleven feet, we were unsuccessful in our endeavour to discover any sign of water. The only moisture, therefore, that the island can be said to possess, is that resulting from surface drainage. The deficiency of forest trees adapted for building purposes was also at once noticed. These two defects alone would seem to render the island undesirable as a locality for a settlement of any kind. But, in addition to such deficiencies, there are certain peculiarities by which it is unfortunately rendered liable to the generation of enfeebling and even fatal disease. Not only are there belts of mangrove encircling it in all directions, but in attempting to ascertain the existence of a navigable strait between the Northern and Middle Andaman, we discovered an extensive tract of the worst description of Sunderbund, ending in such horrible putrid shallows as those we have already described, apparently running towards the interior of the island. In hot weather the pestilential emanations proceeding from these masses of decaying vegetable matter must be of the most fatal description—the very vapours of death—and every wind that blew over them would carry the poison of pestilence, the seeds of death, to every locality exposed to their disastrous influence. The extent of the pestilential Sunderbund was not ascertained; but that no navigable passage existed, and that any settlement in its vicinity would be undesirable, are points on which it is scarcely possible there can be two opinions.

In the course of our peregrinations among the smaller islands, we determined to direct our course towards a large cluster on the eastern coast, known as the Andaman Archipelago. The land of which they consisted was in many places bold, diversified by high undulating hills, and more of those belts of mangrove than any part of the islands yet visited by us. We passed round two sides of Long Island to the bay lying between it and the shore of the Great Andaman, but as no indication of running streams were seen, as the island itself was low, and as the opposite shore was skirted with a thick belt of mangrove, we did not consider it worth while to waste any time in landing to explore a place so obviously unsuitable. The remaining islands of the archipelago we did not look at; most of them were low, the absence of safe ports or harbours was evident, and the navigation among them too dangerous and intricate to permit of their being occupied as a penal settlement, according to the instructions by which we were to be guided in the selection of a suitable place. Even had some of the larger islands of the archipelago proved eligible in themselves, they would not have allowed of sufficient subsequent extension to permit of their occupation on an extended scale, with reference to the amount of culturable land near the settlement.

Ross Island, situated at the entrance of Old Harbour, was also visited. It is about three quarters of a mile long, and about half a mile broad at its widest part. On the western side it is low, but gradually rises to an elevation of about sixty feet on the eastern shore. The rock of which it consists is sandstone. It acts as a breakwater against the north-west monsoon; and as the hospital was placed there formerly, no doubt it must have been used by the settlers under Blair as a sanitarium, a purpose for which its position and appearance seemed to render it, in our judgment, well adapted. Towards the sea it is bounded by smooth rocks; the vegetation is, as usual, very vigorous, although not so rank as in some of the other islands, and the forest trees which grow in its soil are of very large dimensions.

We found no vestige of its former occupation, nor could we discover any indications of the existence of fresh water, although, from the character of the adjacent land, and the shallowness of the bay separating it from the larger island, we entertained no doubt that, if boring had been attempted and persevered in, it would have been discovered. It is more than probable that when the hospital existed on the island, the supply of water was obtained from a well; but on this, and many other points of interest and importance, we had no means of coming to a decision.

The Cinque Islands are in the vicinity of Rutland Island, our visit to which has been already alluded to. The second island of this group would form an excellent isolated station for very refractory convicts, for whom entire separation from their more tractable comrades would be considered advisable. It is three miles in length by one in breadth, at its broadest part. It is usually well supplied with water; and a circumstance of importance, when regarded as a locality for the reception of the more restless and troublesome class of convicts, it is sufficiently separated from all other land to render any successful attempt at escape an utter impossibility. In some parts the soil appears to be of a fertile character, and, if cultivated, would no doubt produce fair crops, but the extent of such land is scarcely sufficient to maintain a settlement. Its situation and general appearance would incline one to believe that it would be more than usually healthy if a colony were established on its coast. During the north-east monsoon it is easily accessible, but I am inclined to think that, during the south-west monsoon, approach to it would be somewhat more difficult. A landing, however, could always be effected, with a little care, at its north-east corner. As it is only about twenty-four miles distant from Old Harbour, it could be readily superintended from any settlement established there, and, if necessary, it could be supplied with provisions from that place at all times of the year.

Although we were in their neighbourhood, we did not consider it either necessary or advisable to visit the Labyrinth Islands. Being closely surrounded by reefs, they are at all times difficult of access, and consequently would be altogether unfitted for the establishment of a settlement of any kind. They lie very close to each other, are flat in appearance, and are probably not abundantly supplied with water. They are covered, however, with a dense, lofty, and luxuriant vegetation. As, from their situation, there is every reason to believe they must be healthy, it is within the bounds of possibility that they may prove valuable at some future time.

Nor did we consider it necessary to explore either Landfall Island or the Cocos. As we passed them in the steamer, we took a hasty look at the former, but remarked nothing demanding particular observation. Although they both lie directly in the path of commerce, yet, being destitute of harbours, they were evidently not suited for convict settlements.

When we came to the determination to recommend Old Harbour as the only place possessing the greater number of requisites for a penal settlement, we resolved also to take advantage of the opportunity to place on record, in our report to the Governor-General, our admiration of the great judgment displayed by Captain Blair in originally selecting that spot, and of his general accuracy as a hydrographer, as we had had so many opportunities of testing the results of his operations. We also suggested that, as considerable practical inconvenience might hereafter result from the identity of names in the two former settlements, the name of Old Harbour should be changed to Port Blair, in honour of that distinguished officer.

The capture of a live native of the Andaman Islands, and his introduction to the scenes of civilization, is a circumstance of so unusual occurrence, that we have scarcely any records of such an event. There are, however, one or two, and their paucity renders them all the more interesting and curious. Our friend Jack was regarded by all who had an opportunity of seeing him as an object of great interest, such as the contrast between the extreme barbarism of savage life and the highest state of civilized existence must ever excite. Among the few previous accounts we have of any Andamans who have been captured alive, is one published in the *Penang Gazette*, in the year 1819. For the following record of those individuals I am indebted to Captain Anderson, of the Bengal Army, who, as well as Mr. Anderson of the late Penang Civil Service, in whose employment the youngest of the savages died, communicated to me some of the following interesting particulars concerning them.

It appears that, about the date mentioned, a Chinese junk, manned partly by Chinese and partly by Burmese, proceeded to the coasts of the Andaman Islands, in order to collect *bêche de mer;* and while they were lying about two miles from the shore, where the crew were engaged in that operation, they observed eight or ten savages approaching the junk, not in a canoe, but by the more simple and primitive method of wading through the water. It was at first uncertain whether they were coming with a friendly intent or the reverse, but as the character attributed to them was well known, their proceedings were closely watched. It was not long before all doubt on this point was removed, for as soon as they came within a short distance of the vessel, several flights of arrows were discharged at it in succession, and not without effect, as no fewer than four of the Chinese were wounded by their barbed points, which, as in the case of our own people, caused considerable pain before they could be extracted. The Burmese immediately gave chase in their boats, and the Andamans, having no desire, to come to a hand-to-hand encounter, immediately set off to the shore with as great speed as they could keep up in their progress through the water. Their flight was so rapid that it was not without considerable difficulty the boats were able to come up with them, and, after the show of some resistance on the part of the savages, they succeeded in taking two of them prisoners, and carried them off in triumph to Penang. During the chase, it was observed that they occasionally came to deep water, in which they dived, disappearing for some time from the view of their pursuers, and baffling them in their attempts to overtake them by again appearing at a considerable distance from the place where they had disappeared, and in a direction in which the crew of the pursuing boat were not looking for them, thus for a time completely baffling them, and, with the slipperiness of eels, escaping from all attempts made by the Burmese to get them safely in their grasp.

Several of the arrows discharged by the aggressive Andamans were picked up by the Chinese left in the boat. On examination they were found to be made of rattan, a piece of hardened wood serving for a point, and a nail or fish-bone being fastened to the end in such a manner as to render the process of extraction, when they had once entered the body, extremely difficult, requiring the exertion of great force, and causing the infliction of much pain. Like our friend Jack and the natives of the island generally, these savages were diminutive in stature, and apparently well formed, though their limbs were uncommonly small. One of them was not more than four feet and six inches in height, the other might probably be about one inch more. The weight of the two was as nearly as could be the same—about seventy-six pounds. One distinguishing feature about them was the unusual prominence of their paunches, which was the more remarkable from their diminutive stature, and gave them rather a strange appearance. They seemed to be both in very good condition, free from disease, and in the enjoyment of vigorous health. One of them was an elderly man, with a face the features of which were so distorted, and with eyes glaring so fiercely, that his aspect had always something extremely unprepossessing, repulsive, and ferocious in it. This man was afterwards taken to Calcutta, but on the voyage was seized with cholera, and died before reaching that city. The other was a mere boy—at the most, not more than seventeen years of age. His aspect presented none of that ferocity by which his companion was distinguished—the expression of his countenance being good, and in some measure attractive. Both he and the elder man appeared dull and heavy, which might arise from the reflections caused by the state of captivity in which they found themselves, and their removal from their usual haunts and home. They were almost always remarkably taciturn, scarcely ever opening their mouths; and it was only at occasional intervals that they conversed with each other, and only when they were alone, and, as they imagined, unobserved by any other person on board the junk. Their language appeared to be very peculiar in its phonetic elements, the sound, to those who did not understand the sense, resembling the cackling of turkeys more than anything else. The crew of the junk, influenced doubtless by prevalent reports, looked closely after them, in case they might commit any mischief. They were particularly timid with regard to some of their children whom, with their wives, they had on board; and as they were fully convinced the Andamans were cannibals, and, if a favourable opportunity presented itself, would sacrifice the lives of the young and tender for the gratification of their monstrous appetite, they compelled them to sleep in a berth on deck, where during the night they were carefully secured.

One day the old man indulged in a strange freak. He appeared on deck a most remarkable-looking object, having, under the influence of some unaccountable fancy, shorn off his woolly hair. As they were never allowed to have a knife, or any dangerous weapon in their hands, except when they were in the presence of others, no one could imagine how he had managed to deprive himself so completely of his stiff and strong locks. On inquiry, it was ascertained that he had appropriated and secreted a piece of broken plate, with which he had succeeded—it could not have been without considerable pain to himself—in depriving his bullet head of its natural covering. The younger lad, who was christened Tom, was much more docile and tractable than his senior. He took an interest in all he saw—in the vessel, the crew, and the family of children on board. He even displayed considerable aptitude in receiving instruction. He succeeded in learning the Hindoo and Malayan languages, in both of which he could make himself understood, and comprehend what was said to him. Unfortunately he was exposed to bad example. He was unavoidably much in the society of sailors, and persons of the same class, who were accustomed to treat him to drink, for which he gradually acquired such a liking that it became necessary to him, and he would sacrifice anything to obtain it. He became a confirmed drunkard, and that train of ills which follows habitual intoxication was soon experienced in their horror by the young Andaman, who at last died from the effects of *delirium tremens*.

The skins of these men, like that of our own Andaman Jack, were of a deep jet black hue, exceedingly shining and lustrous in appearance, but deeply scarred. Their appetites, for men of such scanty proportions, were truly voracious, and it was impossible to imagine how they disposed of all they devoured. They were exceedingly fond of fowls, the hardest bones of which they would crunch with great satisfaction, pounding them with their sharp teeth, white as ivory, with the greatest ease imaginable. Their agility, like that of all savages, was remarkable; and in the quickness of their movements, and the tenacity of their grasp, they resembled so many monkeys. Their captors often took great pleasure in observing the feats which they seemed to take so much delight in performing. Their manner of ascending trees, a feat which they accomplished with greater ease than the most agile and practised acrobat, was remarkable. They would mount up the trunks of the cocoa-nut trees, and run along their various branches with the agility of monkeys; and when we thought the slender support would scarcely sustain the weight even of their slight figures, they would maintain their hold with the greatest security, never manifesting the slightest sign of uncertainty or fear.

When they were examined by the medical or other scientific men of the time, the conclusion to which they came was that they were a degenerate race of negroes—an opinion with which we do not agree, although no doubt there are some arguments which can be adduced in its support—particularly their resemblance to the standard negro type. Their hair was of a woolly texture, and their noses of the orthodox flatness. Their lips were thick and projecting, giving an animal-like expression to their unpleasing countenances, which were rarely seen to be lighted up by any amiable feeling. The large head, projecting from between high and ungainly shoulders, added to the general ungracefulness of their appearance; while their slender limbs seemed scarcely able to support the protuberant paunches with which they formed so ridiculous a contrast.

To return to our own proceedings. After we had steamed to Landfall Island, and taken a look at its coast and high lands, we considered there was nothing more to detain us, and determined to proceed at once to sea, with the view of sailing direct for Calcutta. We therefore took a last look at the remarkable group which had been the scene of our labours for some time; and the steam having been got up, we turned the head of our vessel homewards, and bid farewell to the Andamans. Poor Jack was on deck when we took our departure. Savage as he was, he evidently regarded the gradual disappearance of his native shores with feelings of a melancholy nature, remembering, no doubt, as we should do, the friends he left behind, and the scenes of infancy and boyhood he might never see again; for the future could be only dark and mysterious to him, as he understood nothing of the character, motives, and purposes of the people who were carrying him away. As the poor fellow continued gazing with such a sad and wistful expression at his native shores, until they completely disappeared from sight, I could not help regarding him with an eye of pity, and asking myself if the change would really be one for his benefit; for has not civilization its dark and appalling sides as well as that uncivilized state of life in which he had been brought up, and which he might very probably regret amid the attentions he would certainly receive at Calcutta, as long as he remained an object of interest sufficiently strong to gather about him a curious and wondering crowd? Such thoughts, however, are no sooner suggested than they are dismissed, as partaking too much of the dark and moody anticipations of those who take only the most unfavourable view of human affairs, and of those influences which are gradually and certainly widening the sphere of civilization, and either changing the savage into a civilized being, or annihilating him—for it is written in the book of Destiny, that man must constantly advance or perish.

The first land we saw, on our return, was that known as the Sand Heads, which presented a scene of considerable activity and animation, several of the Bengalee fishing boats being out at sea, the crews of which were plying their occupation busily, and enlivening it with their native songs. Their appearance excited Jack very much, and he was anxious to hail them; but when he endeavoured to draw their attention to himself, he could not succeed in his attempt to attract their observation. We reached Kedgeree at dusk, and I immediately telegraphed to the Secretary of Government, for the information of the Governor-General, to the following effect:—"Expedition returned—object successful—report ready."

Lord Canning, as I was afterwards informed, was at dinner when it was brought to him, and, on perusing it, had a hearty laugh at the laconic brevity of the expressions in which it was conveyed.

The next morning we landed, and I delivered my credentials at once to the Secretary of Government, and the same evening the several members of the expedition were invited to dine with his Excellency the Governor-General. Both Lord and Lady Canning received us with marked kindness, and, in the course of conversation, manifested the greatest interest in the object of the expedition, congratulated us on the success with which we had brought it to a termination, and expressed much pleasure that we had been so fortunate as to have gone through so many toils and dangers without the loss of a single life, or, except in the cases already mentioned, any injury to our health or persons. They also expressed the greatest sympathy for Lieutenant Heathcote, who, in consequence of the severe wound he had received, was the only one of my colleagues who found it impossible to be present. Their interest was expressed not only on account of the object for which we had undertaken our voyage to the Andamans, but also for the sake of the unhappy natives, for whose present and future welfare they felt great anxiety, and were disposed to concur in any measure by which their material and spiritual interests could be advanced. One of Lord Canning's remarks was that a great load had been removed from his mind by the result of the researches in which we had been engaged, as he had felt uncertain as to the manner in which those mutineers who, however guilty, had not deserved capital punishment, should be disposed of; but now that he was satisfied Old Harbour could again be made a convict settlement, that load of anxiety under which he had for some time suffered, was completely taken off his mind. We were examined and cross-examined in the most minute manner regarding all the incidents of our romantic voyage, and their Excellencies thanked us most cordially for the promptitude, courage, and self-denial, as they were pleased to express themselves, with which we had devoted ourselves to the discharge of duties the more laborious and difficult on account of their great importance, and which, if it had not been for the zealous manner in which we had devoted all our energies to the success of the expedition, we could not have so speedily accomplished. They then requested me to send such instruments as we might have collected in the course of our voyage and researches, illustrative of the habits and modes of life of the natives, as Lady Canning was anxious to select a set for her own museum of Indian curiosities and antiquities. Although we had not made such a collection as we desired, our attention having been so much devoted to matters more immediately pressing in connection with the duties imposed on us, still we had managed to bring back a few articles of interest. Among them were a couple of large, red, wooden shields, as we imagined at the time, but which we afterwards found out to be a peculiar musical instrument; Jack having been one day observed on the top of my house, standing on one foot at one end of this curious instrument, and with the other beating at the other end a peculiar melancholy air, which he accompanied with an equally melancholy song in his native dialect, of which we could not understand a word.

On learning that we had brought back a living representative of life in the Andamans, in the person of our friend Jack, Lord and Lady Canning at once expressed their anxious desire to see him. He was accordingly invested with a becoming suit of clothes, and taken to Government House, where he was treated with the utmost kindness by their Excellencies, which perhaps induced him, on a subsequent occasion, to attempt to salute her ladyship in the native manner, namely, by blowing in the hand with a cooing murmur; but, however kindly disposed, her ladyship preferred to reject the offered civility. Most of the time Jack spent in their presence he was greatly absorbed in self-admiration. Observing his figure at full length in the large pier-glasses with which the apartment was adorned, he stationed himself before one, and, regarding his own image with undisguised satisfaction, he continued grinning at himself with a leer expressive of the utmost self-admiration, constantly repeating, with a strange chuckle, as if speaking to himself in the glass—"Jack! Jack!" and then bursting out, in violation of all good manners, into an irrepressible fit of laughter, in which we found it difficult to prevent ourselves joining. After he had sufficiently admired himself, and Lord and Lady Canning had repeated to me the gratification which they felt at having had an opportunity of seeing poor Jack, they expressed their determination not to forget him, but, if he should remain in Calcutta, to keep a watchful eye on him during his future career. The interview was then considered at an end; and having been removed from their presence, he was taken back to my house, where quarters had been provided for him.

When the news spread in the city of Calcutta that a native of the Andamans had been brought back with the expedition, it was astonishing with what rapidity the report, which, at such an exciting period, one would have considered of little importance, spread from mouth to mouth, creating an amount of excitement we had never ventured to anticipate. Jack became a sort of nine days' wonder, and in their intense desire to see him, the inhabitants, both native and foreign, came crowding in hundreds in front of my house; and at last they became such a nuisance, that I almost wished Jack had been at Jericho when it came into my head to bring him with us. However, there was no help for it now, and we had to endure the consequences of our own act. The multitude drawn together was, on some occasions, very inconvenient, until, like Macbeth, when the descendants of Banquo were passing in review before him, I was inclined to exclaim, "I'll see no more," as one party of curious sight-seers succeeded another, eager to get a glimpse of the monstrous Anthropophage. The stories, too, that were circulated regarding Jack, who had now assumed a very quiet and composed air, were such as demanded a considerable amount of faith, a commodity which is always ready for any absurdity. That Jack was a cannibal was a point no one ventured to deny, while the common reports about his teeth, his feet, and other parts of his body, were so monstrous that I will not violate probability by stating them. His appetite was said to be amazing. A whole fowl was an agreeable *bonne bouche*, with which he diversified the other substantial viands laid before him at the breakfast table. In fact, the absurdity of the exaggerated stories that were everywhere circulated was such that it would be almost equally absurd to repeat them. They were the means, however, of keeping alive the general curiosity to see so rare a monster as they assumed poor good-natured Jack to be, and the crowds increased in number every day and every hour, until the whole neighbourhood was in a state of excitement.

The importunity of the people who crowded every morning about my residence was so intolerable, and, instead of diminishing, it kept on increasing at such a rate, that I would gladly have given anything to get quit of the constant annoyance and trouble they caused me. At last a plan was devised, which, if it did not entirely remove the evil, I hoped would tend in some measure to reduce it. I happened, at this time, to have a visitor staying in my house, a friend of long standing, with whom I concocted a plot, which I earnestly prayed might be the means of delivering me from the constant trouble and noise to which I was exposed from the daily assemblage of so many curious people, who would remain for hours staring at my windows with as much pertinacity as if they had been nailed to the spot. This gentleman possessed certain amusing talents, was fond of mystifying his friends, and I had no doubt could soon mystify and disperse the multitude assembled before my house. He happened to be an admirable ventriloquist; his powers of vocal mimicry were unrivalled; and he could make his words appear to proceed from any object he chose to fix upon. I therefore had a sort of mannikin prepared, in some measure resembling the popular notion of the Andaman islander. The head was composed of black silk, to represent the dark native complexion. It was surmounted with a thick woolly covering to resemble hair, and provided with a pair of eyes, the constant savage glare of which could outstare a whole crowd. The mouth was provided with a most formidable set of grinders, sharpened at the edge, a mere glance at which was sufficient to inspire a large portion of the assembled multitude with a salutary fear for their arms or legs. This atrocious-looking figure being set up at the window, the head was moved backwards and forwards by a very simple contrivance, and it occasionally appeared to emit a sort of savage howl, so ferocious that every one who heard it trembled with fear and agitation. It only required two or three repetitions of this simple contrivance to rid us completely of the annoying assemblage, who had become a nuisance to all who lived in our neighbourhood. They looked at the hastily-constructed mannikin as a real Andaman, and at once attributing to it all the ferocious characteristics by which they considered the tribe to be distinguished, they invested the figure, that was entirely the creation of our hands, with qualities which were the embodiment of their own imaginations, and so formidable, that it was regarded as a test of prudence to keep at a reasonable distance from a shape so horrid. The success of our imposture, however, was only temporary. By some means or other the trick was discovered, and the crowd, among whom it must have spread with great rapidity, began to assemble in as great numbers as before. They laughed heartily at the trick that had been played upon them—for a Bengalee crowd is ever good-humoured; and at once divining the object of our deceit, they delivered us, henceforth, from their presence, and we were allowed to dwell in peace and quietness, although not until they had had a good roar of laughter at their own expense.

We resolved to have a photograph of Jack taken; and as we were desirous that it should represent him in his native and original state, we requested him to strip, in order that we might have a *fac simile* of him exactly as he appeared at the time of his capture. It will scarcely be believed, however, that so great was the change already produced in him by his new ideas and associations, that he seemed utterly shocked at the very thought of appearing naked, even before individuals of his own sex. It was by no means an easy matter to prevail upon him to take off his clothes; and the process was very slow, as one by one he divested himself of his divers garments, not without many earnest remonstrances against such a display of himself in his natural state. While the operation was going on, it was extremely difficult to keep him quiet. The camera in particular excited his unbounded curiosity, and, if he had not been restrained, he would have broken it in pieces, in order, like a child with a drum, to see what was in it. When the operator had succeeded in taking the likeness to his satisfaction, Jack was dressed again, and manifested much joy at the restoration of his habiliments. The likeness was certainly not a very satisfactory one. From the powerful effects of the sun's rays at the time the photograph was taken, it had a very hard and unpleasing expression. A second photograph was attempted by Mr. Pilleau, which, although Jack was in a state of sickness at the time, gives by far the best representation of him. A portrait was also taken by Mr. Grant, in which his mild, gentle, and benevolent expression is very faithfully and accurately rendered.

He was altogether a young man of a very kind and amiable character, extremely regular in his habits, generally subdued and composed in his manner. Living constantly amongst us as a member of my family, he was very much liked by every one, in consequence of his quiet and unobtrusive disposition, and he seemed to regard them with an equal amount of affection and esteem. The best way to diet him became a subject of anxious consideration, and the conclusion to which we came was, that his food should be adapted as much as possible to the previous habits of his life, at least for a time, until by degrees he became familiarized with our modes of living, a change which was only gradually effected. Pork and fish were given him every morning. To tea he was very partial, and every evening he might be found in our family circle partaking of it with an appreciation of its excellent qualities that only required time and experience to render him an epicure in his choice of that article. All the inmates of our house, however, were not on equally good terms with him. Nothing could reconcile our native female servants to his presence. They avoided him as much as they could, and would run any distance to get out of his way. What was the cause of their timidity or aversion I am unable to say, unless it was that the absurd stories current regarding him and his race had reached their ears, and made them indisposed to the indulgence of any intimacy with him. It is certain that he was never annoying to them in any way, nor am I aware that he ever took any liberty at which even the most prudish had any reason to conceive the slightest alarm. We happened to have two babies in the house at the time, of both of whom he was extremely fond, although the manifestation of his kind feelings caused much annoyance and alarm to their mothers, who were never well pleased when he happened to touch the children. When they were first shown to him he became more than usually excited, regarded them with looks expressive both of curiosity and affection, and, holding up several of his fingers, pointed towards his distant home with an indescribably sad expression of countenance, from which we surmised that he might have a family of his own, of whom he was painfully reminded by these two, for whom his heart yearned, and whose number he was indicating by the fingers he elevated.

We left no method untried by which, through his means, we might hope to learn any fact regarding the tribe or nation with which the Andamans were allied. Among other places, we took him down occasionally to Garden Reach, to the Peninsular and Oriental Company's Steam Depôt, in order to ascertain if he spoke or understood any of the African dialects heard among the individuals of sable race who frequented that locality. Captain Hall, the superintendent of the Depôt, who was willing to render us any service for this purpose, collected together for us representatives of every African tribe he had ever seen about the place, and made them speak in the hearing of our Andaman; but the experiment proved useless, as he did not seem to understand a single word that was uttered by one of them, not even when their remarks turned on the most simple and common-place objects, or had reference in any way to himself.

About this time a very amusing circumstance occurred, and, so far as it affected Jack, it was the only occasion on which he ever expressed any astonishment. As he was out in the carriage one day, proceeding to Captain Hall's, another gentleman with whom we were acquainted followed us on horseback, riding at the side of the carriage. As Jack had never seen any one on horseback before, he stared in undisguised astonishment at the unknown object of his wonder, his countenance expressing the profoundest feeling of astonishment at what he evidently regarded as some remarkable monster with two heads and six legs. When the gentleman, on reaching Captain Hall's house, descended from his seat on the horse's back, his amazement—hitherto kept somewhat in restraint—transcended all bounds; the wonder he was unable to express in words was legible in his eyes; he leaped at a single bound out of the carriage, and in a state of irrepressible excitement approached the double monster. Going up to the horse, he rubbed his hand along its back, with the view, apparently, of discovering the place at which the spontaneous disruption had taken place. While he was engaged in this examination, the horse happened to yawn, an operation which greatly amused Jack, and set him off in an unrestrainable burst of laughter. Alas! how little we thought, as we watched the amused expression of his countenance on that day, and enjoyed his hearty and free peals of laughter, that he was so soon to be prostrated on the bed of sickness, and that, although he ultimately recovered, it was only in so enfeebled a state that it was found necessary to remove him from Calcutta. That very night, as he was sleeping in the same chamber with Mr. Pilleau, he was seized with severe internal pains, and, on being called to his bedside, I found that his case exhibited all the symptoms of cholera in its most decided form. To judge by his appearance, he was evidently in a state of great suffering, the pain and torture which he endured were apparently very severe, and he moaned most piteously. It seems that when he first awoke with a feeling of severe pain and agony, he put his hand inside the mosquito curtains for the purpose of rousing his companion, Mr. Pilleau, who, at once perceiving he was very ill, and probably suspecting the malady by which his agony was caused, summoned me immediately to his bedside. Without loss of time I applied the usual remedies, and was happily successful in relieving him in a great degree from the pain he suffered; and by constant care and attention during the period he was confined to bed, he soon became again so well that he was able to rise and walk about. But although the disease was so far conquered, he still continued in a very feeble state. The greatest anxiety was manifested on his account, and as much attention was bestowed upon him as if he had been one of the greatest in the land. Still he did not seem to recover his strength; and after his languid and ailing condition had continued for some time, every remedy having failed in restoring him to his former health and vigour, the other medical men who saw him, as well as myself, came to the unanimous conclusion, that his only chance of ultimate recovery lay in restoration to his native air.

Accordingly, he was informed of our view of his case, and of our intention to send him back to his native islands; but he had now fallen into such an enfeebled condition, that everything seemed to be a matter of indifference to him. He was loaded with presents of all kinds, by order of the Governor-General, and especially with many things of a useful and improving nature, the purpose of which, if he was restored to health by means of his native air, he might be able to teach his countrymen; for he was naturally quick in his perceptions, and had become very observant during the latter portion of his sojourn in Calcutta.

We were at last reluctantly compelled to part with him; and, placing him under the charge of a person in whom we had entire confidence, he sailed from Calcutta, and, in due time, once more arrived within sight of the Andamans. As he had been captured at South Reef Island, we had made arrangements for putting him ashore there, as the place where he would stand the best chance of being immediately recognized by former friends and relatives. He was at first conveyed ashore in the clothes he usually wore at Calcutta, but the reflection immediately occurred to those in whose charge he was, that in that condition it might not be possible for any of the natives to recognize him. He was therefore stripped, with his own consent, and left naked on the shore, a condition to which he had been accustomed all his life, except during the short period of his sojourn at Calcutta, and from which, therefore, it was probable he would suffer no injury. None of his fellow-countrymen appeared to claim him while any of the men belonging to the *Pluto*, by which he had been carried back, remained with him on the island. It was therefore resolved to bid him farewell, leaving his clothes by his side, with the hope that when they had left, he would be claimed by his kindred, or that he himself would be able to find them out. He took an affectionate leave of all who had accompanied him, appearing very dejected and low. The crew of the boat were very unwilling to leave him behind, and were it not that they believed it was for the benefit of his health, they would not have done it, so lonely and sad did the poor fellow appear. After taking a last farewell, they rowed out to the ship, gradually losing sight of him, still standing silent and melancholy in the same place; and, as soon as they had got on board, they steamed away from the Reef Island on their return to Calcutta. After this sad parting nothing was ever seen or heard of our captive again. Alas, poor Jack!

CHAPTER VII.

Manners and Customs of the Mincopie—Colonel Syme's Account of Two Andaman Females—Statements of a Brahmin Sepoy Mutineer—The act of Parturition—Parents and Children—Amusements of Children—The Mincopie Boys—The Marriage Union—Support of the Population—Their Migrations—Unsociable Disposition—Want of Religious Ideas—Mincopie Barbers—Medical Practice—Native Huts—Method of Maintaining Fires—Protection against the Mosquitoes—Fishing—Pigs and Pig-Hunts—Mincopie Migrations—Number of the Population—Manufactures—Formation of their Canoes and their Buoyancy—Management of their Canoes—The Paddle—Speed of the Canoes—The Mincopie Bows and Arrows—My Jemidar's Vengeance—The Harpoon—Water Vessels—Burial of the Dead—Ethnology of the Mincopies—Professor Owen's Paper—Their Osteological and Dental Characters—Geological and Geographical Observations.

THE Mincopie are a race of whom, till very recent times, very little was known by the rest of the world; for, although the ships of all nations were constantly passing within a certain distance of their shores, the reputation they had acquired was so unfavourable that few felt tempted to land on what appeared little better, with one exception, than a group of barren rocks. Previous to the year 1857, we cannot be said to have any account of the customs and manners of the Mincopie, on which we can depend as a faithful representation of their daily and habitual life. Perhaps I ought to except the statements of Colonel Syme, contained in the account of his Embassy to Ava, in 1794, in which he communicated to the world several interesting particulars regarding this very curious and remarkable race. He states, among other particulars, that, when at Port Cornwallis, two Andaman damsels, who had been captured by some individuals on board the vessel in which he sailed, were brought to him for inspection. They presented the usual appearance of the native women, being, from the want of hair, by no means attractive, and with faces dark, polished, and lustrous as a life-guardsman's boots. When they were brought on board his ship, he had them put into an empty cabin, where it seems they passed their time very quietly, being harmless and silent, and generally remaining unmolested. They had good appetites, which their captivity and separation from others of their own race in no wise seemed to affect, for they ate and drank freely all that was given to them. The only thing remarkable was that they kept a strict watch over each other, apparently for the purpose of preserving a virtue which neither possessed, and which, if they had, no one would have been anxious to deprive them of. However, they guarded it as a jewel of genuine water and rare value, the two never sleeping at the same time, but one always remaining on guard while the other sought repose in the land of dreams. They were kept thus for two nights in perfect safety, but on the third night, apparently longing for the recovery of their liberty, and their usual free and unrestrained habits of life, they succeeded in making their escape at a moment when no one entertained any suspicion that such an attempt would be made. Notwithstanding the number of sharks that were constantly swimming about the ship, they passed through the port-hole of the small cabin appropriated to them, as it was believed, at midnight, and, great as was the risk they ran, succeeded in reaching the shore—for they were dexterous and rapid swimmers—where they disappeared, and were never heard of again. There is some reason, however, to believe that this story is apocryphal.

In more recent times we possess an account of a Brahmin Sepoy mutineer, belonging to the 14th Regiment of Native Infantry, at Sealkote, in the Punjaub, who, being sent as a convict to these islands, escaped and joined a party of the natives, among whom, according to his own statement, he lived for some time, and acquired a considerable amount of information regarding their habits, manners, and customs. We derive a few curious particulars from the narrative of his captivity, which he was ever ready to relate for the benefit of the curious.

His most remarkable information relates to the act of parturition as performed by the Andaman females.

It appears that this important act must be performed in public. When the birth of a child is expected, the parturient woman is held up, and the child is received, immediately after it is born, by a relative of the mother. The umbilical cord is cut, about a finger's length, with a knife, but no ligature is applied. The after-birth comes away without assistance, and the mother receives no particular treatment, but after confinement continues her usual mode of life, eating and drinking as before. Some hours afterwards she is anointed with the usual unguent of red earth and turtle oil, which, being much more frequently applied as a pigment on festive occasions than in the treatment of the sick, can scarcely be regarded as a medicinal application, although it is evidently so considered by the aborigines, who attribute some unknown virtue to it. Convalescence is very rapid, and if the party to which the newly-made mother belongs should be on the move the following day, she must accompany them, like the other females of the tribe, on foot. No exhibition of rejoicing is made on the birth of a child, whether male or female. As soon as the child is born it is taken from the mother, and immediately washed in cold fresh water poured on it from a vessel made of bamboo twigs, or the shell of the nautilus. This operation being accomplished, the body is then dried by the very simple process of friction with the palm of the hand, which is heated before a fire, and quickly and repeatedly, though, at the same time, with the utmost gentleness, applied to the infant. Any other woman, who may happen to be nursing an infant of her own at the time, nourishes the child until the mother is able to do so—a kindness which the latter in her turn is expected to render to others who stand in need of like assistance.

Children among the Andamans are never weaned. As long as the bountiful source of nourishment provided by nature can supply them with sufficient to allay the calls of hunger, the mother is expected to sustain her children, until utter exhaustion renders it necessary to have recourse to other means of support. As no clothes are at any time used by the aborigines, who go about in a perfectly naked state, no sort of garment is provided for newly-born children, who also remain naked from the first day of their existence. If it should rain, however, while the party to which the mother belongs are on a march, some consideration is shown for the tenderness of the infant frame. A few leaves are collected, and sewed together by means of a kind of thread prepared from rattan, and, with this primitive and scanty garment, some slight protection is afforded the tender infant. The leaves of which this covering is made, as well as the covering itself, are called *kapa*.

Mincopie parents show their children the utmost tenderness and affection. Their fondness for their offspring is manifested by means of those significant gestures and modes of treatment which nature ever suggests to those who have no other instruction. Even Hindustani parents, who are remarkable for the warm affection with which they regard the children to whom they have given birth, cannot surpass the Mincopie in their manifestations of an ever-watchful love and care. On the other hand, the children appear to be equally devoted to their parents, whose love they reward with the warmest affection in return, and in no case can they be said to be inferior to any other race in this respect. The boys and girls may be seen running about on the beach, or on the entangled vegetable flooring of the eminences that rise above it, just as children are seen amusing themselves in Calcutta or anywhere else. The girls have some amusements in which they appear to find special delight. The sandy patches on the coast they particularly choose as the scene of their simple and innocent games. Here they raise the sand around them in the form of square or circular walls, and when they have succeeded in elevating it to the height they desire, they seat themselves in the centre, and consider themselves in their own house—a kind of amusement very similar to that in which girls and boys of tender years, in more civilized lands, delight at all times to indulge. Is it not strange that on the beach at Brighton and the shore of the Andamans scenes so precisely similar should be enacted by the rising generations of the savage and the civilized? In this and other games they attempt, in the most simple and amusing manner, to imitate the customs of their grown-up parents and relations.

Boys, too, exhibit the same propensities, although the manner in which they are manifested is somewhat different. As our own combative youth are especially fond of playing at soldiers, and having their little swords, guns, and pistols, thus exhibiting a tendency to a sort of premature volunteering, so the little Mincopie boys, with their glancing black skins, and their lustrous jet eyes, have, at as early a period as three years of age, their little bows and arrows, which they proudly display and exercise themselves in the use of. They have their little mimic hunts, and they may be seen on the reefs by the sea shore, with their small lines, attempting to catch some of the more diminutive kinds of fish that frequent the surrounding seas. Thus they gradually acquire strength and dexterity, and, by the time they are eight years of age, when they are allowed to accompany their elders on their hunting expeditions, they are able to bend a larger bow, and to take a sure and steady aim at any object they may desire to bring low. We found many of their little bows and arrows, which we picked up while wandering about on the beach or in the interior, and brought back with us to Calcutta. Several of the most perfect specimens of them were presented to the late Lord Canning, by whom they were placed in his admirable collection of Eastern curiosities. The boys at a very early age also acquire great skill in swimming, and are particularly fond of disporting themselves in the cool waters surrounding their island homes. We have frequently seen large groups of the little black imps, mere piccaninnies as to size, running about among the sunlit sands, dashing headlong into the water, and in some sheltered spot, where there was scarcely a ripple on the surface, diving to the bottom or swimming about, appearing and disappearing, their little black bullet heads soon emerging again in some distant and unlooked for spot; while their screams of laughter, pealing in echoes from rock to rock, and their treble voices, as they addressed each other in Mincopie exclamations, showed that they delighted in the water almost as much as if it was their native home.

The marriage union is one very easily contracted among the Mincopie, who have never burdened themselves with such luxuries of our civilized system as registrars, parsons of all sects, and fees of all amounts. The knot tied at Gretna Green is no doubt comparatively a very simple one, but the courting and marriage ceremonies of a couple of Andaman lovers on Interview Island would be considered by our ambitious brides and bridesmaids as absurdly so. The arrangements of the former are very soon made, and without all those doubts and perplexities that often render the course of true love so difficult, the union is effected with a rapidity that would shock a well-educated young lady in England.

Our Burmese soldier stated that he had scarcely been four months among the aborigines, when the kindness of one of them was displayed to him in a very remarkable and unexpected way. A man named Pooteeah, who doubtless considered him a desirable match, offered to bestow upon him, in what they called wedlock, his daughter Hessa, a young woman of twenty years of age, whose attractions were doubtless regarded as considerable among her native tribe, and a mere girl named Zigah, a daughter of Hessa, who in that eastern part of the world was considered quite old enough for the state of marriage. As they were by no means troubled with an uneasy amount of virtue, they made no objection to being assigned to the Brahmin soldier in the most unceremonious manner. The two, mother and daughter, at once recognized him as their husband, and entered in a friendly manner on the discharge of the duties pertaining to their new condition, remaining faithful to him, and flirting with no other gentleman who might be inclined to pay them attentions. The Brahmin, however, ultimately abandoned them, and one of them was in an interesting condition when he thus left her to take care of herself. It would have been amusing to see the offspring of the giant Brahmin and the tiny Mincopie.

The whole population is found scattered along the sea coast. In the jungle, which extends down almost to the beach, they find desirable shelter and convenience for the erection of their simple habitations. Besides which, as the sea is the main source of their support, their dwelling on the coast affords them facilities for catching fish and collecting cockles, oysters, and other shell-fish, on which they are compelled to sustain their existence. The most abundant and accessible sources of fresh water are also found near the shore. The interior of the larger islands is occasionally inhabited by some parties who resort thither for the purpose of collecting such fruits as the soil spontaneously yields. As the pig is found in the central parts of the country, hunting parties proceed thither in search of that animal, which, on the supposition that all the stories of their cannibal propensities are untrue, must be almost the only kind of animal food in which they indulge, or which they are able to procure.

Those who are in the habit of dwelling much in the interior frequently return to the neighbourhood of the coast, especially when they are travelling from one place to another. The whole population is of a migratory disposition, moving about incessantly from one locality to another. They rarely reside long in the same district. When the resources of one place are exhausted, they proceed at once to another, and, having few preparations to make, their constant movement is attended with little inconvenience. They are generally divided into small groups, the numbers of which vary considerably, some not containing more than ten individuals, while in others as many as two or three hundred may be found. The great majority of these groups of the natives consist on an average of from thirty to fifty men, women, and children, although sometimes as many as three hundred are found together. In the Great Andaman there is only one tribe, the similarity between all the members of which is so great, that there can be no doubt of the unity of the race to which they belong. The features present almost the same unvarying cast. The complexion is the same lustrous jet black. Their eyes are universally the same in colour and in form. Their manners are marked by no appreciable differences, and the routine of their daily life is confined within the same limited and narrow sphere. The language which they speak, as far as we can judge from the sounds made in its utterance, appears to be fundamentally of the same peculiar character all over the island.

The proportion between the males and females, as far as any reliable data could be obtained, was ascertained to be much the same as in Hindostan. Although it is probable that a great many infant lives must be annually sacrificed by the exposure to which they are at once subjected, there is no reason to believe that any desire is shown to limit the number of their offspring by violence. Hence infanticide is a crime that may be considered unknown. Indeed, it is said that, on the whole, the mortality of children among the Mincopie is no greater than in places where they are treated more tenderly during the first period of their existence. There are no data on which any statement regarding the number of adult deaths can be founded.

Deaths and births appear to take place in much about the usual proportion, the former on the whole being less numerous than the latter, a fact from which we may conclude that the population of the Andaman Islands is rather increasing.

The aborigines are certainly a very uncivilized people. Perhaps there is no other savage tribe that we must place at a lower stage on the ladder of civilization than the Mincopie; and their aversion to mingle with strangers, or even to receive them kindly, must tend in a great degree to prevent their advancement in the social scale. It is certainly a remarkable fact that this little group of islanders, their sea-girt homes lying in the great pathway by which the civilized nations of the earth carry on their commercial communications with each other, should still remain in a state of such degraded barbarism. We may surely venture to express a hope, now that the claims of the savage world is so loudly urged, and that such devoted and self-sacrificing pioneers of civilization are going forth to labour among the most remote and obscure dens of heathendom, that this interesting little race, at our very doors in India, will not be suffered much longer to remain in the degraded condition in which it is really a disgrace that it should have been allowed to exist so long. The very worst that can be said of the Mincopie is that they are more than usually savage and unsociable; and as so many travellers have united in blackening their character in this respect, we must assume that there is only too much truth in their statements. But they are certainly not so bad as they have been described. The statement that they are cannibals is unworthy of belief, for it rests on no trustworthy foundation. No one ever saw them indulging in those horrid banquets which have been attributed to them. Any case of their actually devouring human bodies is unknown, and we have no reason to suppose that they even devour raw flesh of any kind. They are certainly a wild, restless, and untameable race of mankind. Strangers who venture among them are not received with the open arms of friendship. They may have displayed a savage and inhospitable disposition when mariners were cast friendless and helpless upon their shores; and they are not easily induced to favour those whom accident has thrown into their power.

But in opposition to this dark side of the picture, there is at least one phase of their character which represents them in a more favourable point of view, and that is, that they are kind and friendly with each other. In all that regards religious faith, it cannot be denied that they take a very low position in the family of mankind, for there are few tribes, races, or peoples who are altogether strangers to all ideas of religion. Yet this is the case with the Andaman aborigines. They have no conception of a Supreme Being. They have never risen from the effects they see around them even to the most imperfect notion of a cause. They have never ascended in thought from the works of creation to the idea of a Creator, or even of many creators, that is to say, polytheism. Now, there are few savage tribes so low in intellect as never to have embodied some conception of a deity whom it was their duty to worship and adore. Even in the central plains of Africa, far removed from the great centres of civilization and knowledge, we find tribes of men in a very imperfect state of development, but still with some rude kind of religion; and it is a great point to possess even the mere rough undeveloped outline of such a thought, for it denotes that, though these ideas may have taken form in idols of wood and stone, intellect has still been active even in their unfavourable circumstances, and has carried them beyond themselves and the limited sphere in which they move. The growth even of imperfect religious ideas always indicates that the intellect has been awakened, and that some idea of moral obligation, on which all religious truth is founded, has been formed and comprehended. The household *penates*, even though only little figures of wood, rudely shaped, and ridiculous in form, show that man's ideas have travelled beyond the notion of self, the house, the hut, the home, and the world in which he dwells. But the poor Mincopie, small in form and stature, are also small in intellect. Their world is limited, for it is centred in themselves, and they appear never to have asked themselves those questions which occur to every child, once the understanding begins to operate upon the conceptions it receives—Who am I?—How came I here? and whither do I tend? The Mincopie in this respect are mere undeveloped children. They have never asked themselves these questions, and they are consequently yet without a religion. Their knowledge even of themselves is imperfect. They have no self-respect. They go about naked, and have no feeling of shame. They hear no voice in the garden, and are not afraid.

The wants of the Mincopie are few and limited, and easily supplied. If he can gratify the feeling of the moment, if he can satisfy his appetite when the craving for food seizes him, he is satisfied. He makes no provision for the morrow; he has neither the intelligence of the man, nor the instinct of the bee. He lives on wild roots and fruits, which he picks up and eats where he finds them; but he knows nothing of agriculture, and makes no attempt to cultivate the ground, that it may receive seed, and bring forth harvests at regular intervals. The only point in which he may be said to show the possession of intellect is in making provision for the wants of nature, as seen in the practice of fishing; for however humble may be the intellectual development indicated by this art, it does show a certain amount of contrivance and foresight. Where there is even the slightest germ of intellect, a wise education may elicit it still more, and gradually enlarge the imperfect mind by a process of careful and prudent cultivation. The poor Mincopie should not be despised because they are low in the scale of intelligence, but this should rather be considered a reason for no longer neglecting them, for wherever the germ of man reasoning, intellectual, and religious is found, there is the seed that may spring up into immortal life, yielding ten, fifty, or a hundred fold. A missionary of eternal truth, at once zealous and prudent, might in time effect an entire transformation in the condition of these poor people, and be the happy means not only of showing them how to supply themselves with their daily bread, but also of teaching them the more important knowledge of the source whence the bread of life is to be obtained.

The aborigines generally do not allow a particle of hair to remain on the head, or on any other part of the body. The women are their barbers, and very expert at the trade they are said to be. Considering the imperfect instruments they are compelled to use in the process, the nimbleness, neatness, and handiness with which they accomplish it is remarkable. Any chance morsels of bottle glass they may happen by some means to procure, or pieces of shell sharpened till they have something like an edge, are all they have to use in the practice of this primitive art. The piece of shell or glass may be no larger than a bean, but they prepare it with great expertness, striking it on a piece of hard stone to form and sharpen it. The chips which they use in the process of shaving are generally no larger or thicker than an ordinary penknife, and yet with such imperfect and rude instruments they manage to effect the operation with great adroitness and speed.

They cannot be said to have any knowledge of medicine, although there are a few remedies which they apply to almost all the ills to which flesh is heir; and they have even some followers of Æsculapius who give advice as to the times, seasons, and occasions for the application of their simple remedies, which, if their administration is only attended with that most elastic of all mental commodities, faith, may produce as much benefit to the sufferer as many of our own more elaborate remedies, although it may not be in our power to detect the hidden virtue by which they effect their astonishing cures. A mixture of red earth and turtle oil forms a sort of Mincopie Morrison's pill, and is probably quite as effective in curing the sufferings of the sick. It is a remedy of universal application, which gets the credit of the cures that may follow its application, even though the connection of the supposed cause and effect may be somewhat obscure. A few successful cases extend the credit of the Mincopie professors of the medical art, and they are consequently esteemed and honoured as men of amazing wisdom. Surgery, too, has its votaries, although the operations on which it ventures are not of a very complicated nature, being confined to the dressing of flesh wounds or sprains, and even broken bones, by means of leaves to which certain virtues are attributed. When we think of the wondrous development of medicine and surgery in the various great nations of Europe, and then turn our eyes upon the Mincopie practitioner spreading a few leaves over a wound, we may well gaze with astonishment on this picture and on that, especially when we call to mind that in England itself there was once a time when in all probability the art of medicine was little more advanced than it is at the present moment in the Andamans. Scarification is a remedy in which they have great faith, resorting to it in pains, bruises, and swellings, and using it with considerable skill, and sometimes with excellent effect—in which case they acquire a certain reputation, and are sought after as favourite, successful, and skilled surgeons.

Of all the arts of which the Mincopie has any practical knowledge, perhaps his architecture is of the most primitive and unsatisfactory character, especially when it is considered that he has only a light swampy soil on which to build his houses. The huts of the natives may be regarded as the most rude and imperfect human habitations which in any part of the world man has been found to erect. The tailor-bird and the beaver are architects from whom the Mincopie, if he were only observant, might obtain valuable hints for the construction and improvement of his bare little hut. Their habitations are the most simple that can be imagined, and it would be difficult for the most imaginative theorists to discover in their humble erections the germ of any system of architecture, either ancient or modern. Four posts, two long and two short, are fixed in the ground—it matters not whether they are straight or crooked—and are then covered with palm leaves. The leaves are connected with considerable skill, for they form a good protection against the rain, which runs down from the roof formed by them as from the talipot palm which covers the two-legged grasshoppers of Ceylon. When the natives are about to build one of these villages for the occasional reception of themselves and their families, they in the first place select a suitable locale, which must be a large space beneath great trees, and within a convenient distance of some source of water. The houses are generally erected in a circle, and in consequence of the arrangements made, and the precautions taken, are invariably well sheltered and protected. Their method of maintaining their fires for cooking purposes is very remarkable, and displays an unusual amount of ingenuity. The larger trees are charred in the interior about six feet from the ground, until, as they are very dry and gradually burn away, a great hollow is formed in the centre, in which they allow about three feet of ashes to accumulate, in such a way that, at the bottom of the heap, live fire is always found, which, with great judgment, is always so placed as to be against the wind and rain, so that there is no fear of its being extinguished by either of these causes. Over the fire in these strange ovens the Mincopie can grill his little pig, fry his fish, calipash and calipee his turtle steaks, and not improbably prepare his turtle soup, which he must be satisfied to relish without the accompaniment of any kind of pernicious condiment. Great pains is taken in the preservation of these trees, which they never entirely destroy.

At night the Mincopie puts on what may be called his full dress suit, consisting of a thick covering of yellow earth, which he allows to remain till it dries hard upon his body, in order to protect him from his persevering and annoying enemies the mosquitoes. His wife and piccaninnies are invested in a similar thick coating, the protection of which is greatly needed in that climate, for the insect world is very prolific, and the tics and other abominations of the jungle are the source of endless torture and pain. The centipedes and scorpions, which are the very demons of torture in Indian life, are harmless innocents compared with these abominable scourges of the Mincopie. When we were in the islands we were annoyed with them everywhere, and whatever pains we took to disperse and drive them away, we found it impossible to get rid of their torturing presence. It was no use swearing at them, for apparently they could not be numbered among those who have an objection to oaths, the hardest of which never seemed to move them. They followed us from place to place with a pertinacity that was perfectly annoying, so that wherever we went we found them on our course, bedclothes, and everything we possessed, becoming their select haunts, whence they issued only to annoy and irritate, murdering sleep by their sanguinary onslaughts, and keeping us in a state of constant uneasiness and agitation, more annoying than any of the Egyptian plagues of which we read.

When the savage rises at an early hour in the morning he repeats no prayers, he cleanses himself by no ablutions, but at once takes measures to gratify his appetite, which is crying for food. He proceeds perhaps to the nearest reef, where he engages in fishing, or to some inland part where he knows he can obtain edible roots or pleasant fruits. In fishing he can resort to several means for obtaining a supply of fresh fish. He is an expert diver. Familiar with the water, and capable of remaining a considerable time under it, he rarely descends without bringing with him, when he again ascends, some scaly prize. Then he has his hook, his net, or his harpoon—instruments in the use of which he is so expert, from constant practice, that he knows how to make skilful and fortunate casts with them. His choice of luxuries not being very varied, he is also fond of shell-fish, in procuring and preparing which the women and children are very clever, separating them by means of the same little adze with which they excavate their canoes. Our friend the Sepoy tells some remarkable exploits of the Mincopie in fishing, which, as they seem to indicate a Munchausen-like facility of exaggeration in the narrator, we decline to repeat. Still, it must be acknowledged that, when he was strictly cross-examined with regard to some of his statements by the shrewd and astute Dr. Walker, the most able judge of native character in India, he stuck to his stories with wonderful consistency, maintaining in particular, with characteristic pertinacity, the truth of those which even the greatest credulity found it difficult to receive.

The attempts which the Mincopie make to ornament their huts are of the most meagre description. Bundles of fish-bones, turtles' heads, and pigs' skulls, striped crosswise with red ochre, which seems to be the only colouring matter of which they make any use, are suspended from the roof, showing that their ideas of art, if such rude and simple adornment can be called by such a name, are of the most elementary nature. The pigs are of a jet-black colour, and their bristles are so thick and strong that they appear like so many fragments of black hair-pins fixed all about their bodies. The small, black, tapering tail has a facetious curl that would ravish that class of British sportsmen who delight in the manufacture of bull dogs by clipping their ears, beating in their noses, and "druving" in their unhappy little tails, a process which it affords me the greatest delight to learn the humane Landseer is about to abolish for ever. These porkers are the most curious and mischievous little animals in creation. They have a leer that makes them look like so many Mephistopheleses, who have chosen to assume that peculiar form, in many respects a very appropriate one, for if they are not so many little devils, they are certainly possessed by them. At the time of our visit to the Cinque Islands, we turned out a dozen of them, and our unwonted appearance filling them with alarm, they ran off from us with the velocity of an Indian express train, squeaking like mad. We set off and had a regular hunt after them, a hunt that beat to chalks the most exciting scene of pig-sticking ever seen in Bengal. After discharging their rifles, some of the hunters would probably find the pigs between their legs, making them measure their length on the sand. The falls were made with considerable violence, though they were not dangerous, for they only excited our risible faculties, and as each one in turn came down he was greeted with a loud and hearty burst of laughter, as a sort of congratulation to him in his misfortune. Probably the most persevering of the mighty hunters was my friend, Dr. Playfair, or "the fairplay," as we christened him for the occasion—for at such times, when even the most refined and intellectual are not very exacting, very small puns, or plays upon words, or strokes of wit, or *jeux d'esprit*, afford a great deal of amusement—who measured his length on his back on the edge of a sandhill, down which he came rolling in a manner that was irresistibly ludicrous, or perhaps I should rather say only amusing, making us and himself, when he again got on his feet, indulge in a most hearty and side-splitting burst of laughter. The doctor was, without any exception, both then and during the period of our rambles among the isles, and our voyages on the sea, the jolliest fellow in the universe, and no man who had once been in his society could desire a better companion.

The only cool hand and head in this absurd and original "Derby," was Walker the filibuster. Every shot that he fired infallibly brought to grief one of the squeaking fraternity. Indeed, he was a perfect master of his rifle, which he always had in his hand, or within convenient reach, and without which by his side he never either ate, drank, or slept. He would occasionally make the most astonishing shots, and what he said he would hit, that he invariably did hit. If he perceived, as we were moving along, a cocoa-nut hanging by its stem, he would offer to detach it without touching the nut itself, and in a moment his unerring bullet had severed it from the parent tree. He never wasted a shot, however, merely for display. It was always for some object, however insignificant it might appear. These Mincopie pigs he declared to be about as difficult game as he had ever, in the whole course of his adventurous existence, come in contact with. As he expressed himself in his own strange idiom, which he must have acquired during his residence in the Northern States of America, it was almost as easy to slide down greased lightning, or catch bottled thunder, as to touch one of these tormenting imps.

The Mincopie are a migratory race, restless in their disposition, constantly wandering about from place to place, never remaining any length of time in one settlement, generally not more than two days, or even less occasionally. They are rarely or never seen living alone, several of their little huts being raised in the same locality, where they dwell together in numbers varying between thirty and three hundred. In consequence of their unsettled disposition, and so many of them being always on the move, it has been found impossible to obtain any exact information as to their numbers, so that any attempts that have been made to give the exact amount of their population must be received with great doubt, it being generally necessary to make considerable deductions from the hasty statements which have been sometimes made. The Sepoy before mentioned, who asserts that he was perfectly familiar with all their manners and customs, and who accompanied them in their migrations, professed to have a good idea of their numbers, declaring that, although he traversed only a fourth part of the island, he was certain that he had seen men, women, and children to the number of fifteen thousand, an assertion which, considering it an extreme exaggeration, we must hesitate to accept; for those who have made any previous estimation of their numbers, and whose statement, perhaps, may be considered as below the mark, never represented the population of the islands as more than five thousand. The former number no one can hesitate for a moment in rejecting. The latter may possibly be as near a conjecture as it is possible to arrive at, for they have no conception of their population themselves. We observed, however, one fact from which we might conclude that the Sepoy's estimation was not quite such an exaggeration as it must at first appear. On one occasion, steaming rapidly round the whole island, or, at any rate, by far the greater part of it, we everywhere saw large numbers of the natives, far more considerable than we had any previous idea of, who could not by any earthly means have travelled so fast as we did, and who, therefore must have been separate parties, all seen on a single island in the group,

ANDAMAN ISLANDERS AND IMPLEMENTS

a fact which renders it probable that the population is larger than any former estimations have represented it to be.

The Mincopie manufacture various articles and implements, the construction of which is generally very rude and imperfect. We observed and examined carefully most of them, such as their canoes, paddles, bows, arrows, spears, nets, baskets, pine torches, resin, bamboos for carrying water, adzes with iron tongues, used also as axes, and various other implements for fishing, fighting, defence, and aggression. The construction of the first-mentioned of these articles, their canoes, is rather peculiar. In the first place, looking about carefully, they select one of the finest trees of the forest, that with the longest, thickest, and straightest trunk being of course preferred. As the implements they possess for felling are not of the most effective description, the process of bringing down one of these gigantic trees is one that requires a considerable amount of exertion, and is effected only after long labour. It may possibly require a week's constant work before the tree begins to totter on its mighty base, at last falling with a shock that shakes the ground all around. The next operation is to round the trunk, a process which they perform with remarkable dexterity, it being almost impossible to conceive how, with the imperfect instruments at their command, they execute their work with so much skill and neatness. Practice, however, must render them, as well as others, perfect; and hence it is that in a short time the rough and shapeless trunk begins to assume form and proportion, and when the process is ended, exhibits a finish and perfection that even a Chinese carpenter, by far the most handy and ingenious of human chips, would regard with a feeling of envy, as a work of dexterity which it would be vain for him to make any attempt to imitate. Poor Jack, when we had him on board the *Pluto*, on the voyage from the Andamans to Calcutta, occasionally showed that he was a skilful and experienced carpenter, and was very ready in imitating any operations of that nature he saw among us for the first time.

As soon as the trunk has been rounded, they commence the operation of cutting and chipping at it externally, until eventually the outlines of the elegant canoe begin to appear from the shapeless mass of the knotted trunk, just as, by the skill of the statuary, the beautiful figure gradually assumes its fair proportions in the block of marble. The shape externally is generally finished with great care and elaboration before they proceed to hollow it out internally, the next process to which they direct their attention. The interior is excavated in the same perfect and business-like manner, until the shell is no thicker than the sides of a deal bonnet-box, although it still preserves that strength which would enable it to resist successfully the utmost force and violence of the waves, should it ever be assailed by a storm, a thing not at all probable, as, unless carried out to sea by some accident, it is rare that the Andamans venture far from the shore.

The buoyancy of these boats, when they are well constructed and carefully finished, is remarkable. They float lightly on the top of the waves, and, unless they have received some injury, it is considered almost impossible to sink them. We sometimes made the attempt, but never succeeded. We fired at them repeatedly when at Port Mouat—which may be regarded as a sort of Andaman Pembroke yard, where a fleet of Mincopie men-of-war were lying in every stage of preparation—but they still floated with as great ease and buoyancy as ever. They would make most excellent life-boats, such, we believe, as have never yet been constructed by any of our most experienced boat-builders. When the Mincopie go to sea in them, they attach to some part of the boat an outrigger, in some respects resembling that which the Cingalese fishermen attach to their boats. The use of this outrigger must be a thing of comparatively recent practice among the Mincopie, for no former writers, who have given any account of them and their customs, ever allude to them. Hence many surmises have been formed as to the origin among them of this useful adjunct to their boats. But none appeared to me so probable as that which has occurred to my own mind, which easily accounts for its sudden adoption. During one of the monsoons, a Cingalese outrigger boat may have been overtaken by the storm before it could return to port, and being drifted with the currents of the Indian Ocean, from the power of which its crew must have found it impossible to escape, it may have been drifted onward at the mercy of the current, until it was, in all probability, stranded on the sandy beach of one of the Andaman Islands. On being observed by the natives, it may have been attacked by them, taken possession of, and paddled to one of their small natural land-locked harbours, where, on examining it, they would at once be struck by the peculiarities of its construction, which they would endeavour to imitate.

These outriggers enable them to proceed forty or fifty miles to sea, to one of their more productive fishing grounds. We have often seen them far out in the ocean, at the midnight hour, the pine torches which they light at such times blazing luridly, and in that distant Indian sea presenting a very curious and romantic spectacle, reminding us of the mode of salmon fishing, by "burning the water," in the rivers at home. If the Mincopie really did make such a ready adaptation of a chance discovery, they cannot be such fools as they have generally been imagined to be, and we must at least be satisfied that they possess capacities which, if cultivated and improved, would soon place them on a much higher level than that which they at present occupy.

They show great skill, too, in the management of their canoes, which must be handled in some peculiar way, for those who are the greatest adepts in rowing, steering, and guiding our ordinary boats, find themselves completely at a loss when they get into a Mincopie canoe. When any of our men recklessly got into them, and attempted to paddle out a little way to sea, they invariably succeeded in capsizing them, receiving a thorough drenching in the water as a suitable punishment for their rash and imperfect seamanship. This was a calamity that occurred almost every time they made the venture; and as, however doubtful might be the anthropophagical character ascribed to the inhabitants of the dry land, there could be no uncertainty regarding that of certain natives of the deep, who occasionally ventured near the shore, prowling for the chance of a human leg, arm, or even a whole carcass, the men were soon cured of their desire to distinguish themselves in the management of Mincopie boats. The savages, in the meantime, who were never fond of associating with us, would be watching the movements of our men from the woods where they had concealed themselves, and when any such accident occurred, the joyous peals of hearty laughter with which they greeted it first made us aware of their propinquity. On these occasions, however, they never made any attempt to molest us, and we left them, on our departure, presents of food, fruits, and the usual glittering specimens of finery which they are generally so ready to appropriate.

The paddles which they use in propelling their light and buoyant canoes, are also extremely well made, and adapted with great ingenuity to the purpose for which they are intended. The wood which they generally select, considering the simple instruments which they possess for working with, is of a very hard grain. We found that they were made of three sizes, to adapt them for boats of different dimensions used by the islanders for their sea excursions and their fishing expeditions. The smallest appeared to be about three feet long; the middle sized, three and a half feet; and the largest, four feet. The work of making them is entrusted solely to the women and children, a fact which may be worth the attention of those ladies who act as secretaries to the societies for providing more abundant employment for females. The "chips" cook the dinners for the women and children employed in this useful occupation.

With the assistance of these simple but well-shaped paddles, the canoes are propelled at such a rate that, in a fair race with one of our boats, the Captain's gig, rowed by a prize crew of Chinese and others, was completely distanced, and all attempts to recover a fair position in the race were found to be entirely unavailing. Our men and boat had no chance with that of the Mincopie, the crew of which seemed to know well their own waters, and to make their way over them with a rapidity that made us stare with undisguised astonishment. To be thus completely beaten in a fair run by these little Mincopie in their rude canoe was, as all who enter into the rivalry excited by such contests must acknowledge, a rather aggravating thing, although, fortunately, we were enabled to keep our good temper, and were even ready to laugh out our congratulations to the victors, a little, it must be confessed, with the wrong side of our mouths. Our first cutter also had a trial of speed with the Mincopie boat, but her desperate efforts to win back our character for unsurpassed speed were hopeless. The Mincopie were superior, and had it all their own way. It was very beautiful to see how the crew of the man-of-war used their oars, the long and powerful stroke they made with such regularity, propelling the boat onwards with a speed that almost merited success. Indeed, such was the effort made by these men to keep up the race for ten minutes, that they felt the effects of the unwonted exertion for some time after. As they said in their own usual exaggerated style of remark, they nearly killed themselves in their effort to maintain the credit of their ship, their cutter, and their flag.

The only arms of the Mincopie are their bows and arrows, to which we may also add their harpoons, which are capable of being used with great effect in a fight. Their bows are made of tough strong wood, and are about five or six feet in length. The Mincopie bend them with the greatest ease, the constant exercise to which they are accustomed from their earliest years enabling them to perform with facility a task which, considering their small forms, we should have thought far beyond their strength. Several of our men-of-war's men made the attempt to bend them, but the most powerful of them failed in all their efforts; from which we may conclude that skill as well as strength was required in the use of the Mincopie bow and arrow. The natives discharge their volleys of arrows with the greatest force, sending them to a great distance, and with such accuracy of aim, that they rarely fail to inflict injury on those against whom they are directed. This is a point on which we had acquired some knowledge by experience, and the wounds received by one or two of us were sufficient to show that the force with which the arrows were shot from the bows must have been very great.

Some of our men had been aimed at from a distance of forty yards, and the wounds inflicted were such that they would long remind them of Mincopie vigour and dexterity.

This was about the same range as that at which we usually discharged our fire-arms at them, when they did not appear more than usually vicious and exasperated. As we rarely took a very accurate aim, having no desire, except in cases when self-defence rendered extreme measures necessary, to injure them, our musket-balls generally fell harmless at a little distance. At this they usually laughed heartily, and sometimes derisively, as if they considered our weapons by no means very formidable. After we had exchanged shots with them, I generally sent my Jemidar, who, as a former exploit has shown, was of a disposition at once cool and adventurous, or a West-Indian Creole named Thompson, to ascertain if any damage had been done, and, in that case, what was the amount of it. They were both swift runners, in thorough wind and condition, for they took every opportunity to keep themselves in good practice. They were more than a match for any of the savages, light and agile as the latter were; but when they came to swampy ground, or those knotted arches of mangrove-stumps at low water, over which, as already described, the savages run with a velocity much greater than that ascribed by Monsieur Chaillu to the gorilla, my messengers had to slacken their speed. They frequently reported themselves as having seen small drops of blood on the route the savages had taken in their flight, tracing them for the distance of a mile or two. On one occasion, when their aggressive disposition had been displayed with such aggravating persistency that we were compelled to reply to their repeated discharges of arrows by a volley of light shot, two poor wretches were severely wounded, and they were afterwards heard, either by the West Indian Creole, or by my Jemidar, groaning most piteably, from pain and loss of blood, in a part of the jungle where they had taken refuge. My follower was a man of a very fine, humane, and, I may almost say, noble character, ever ready, when it was in his power, to render all the assistance he could to any of these poor creatures. I never wished that any of the Mincopie, when they were unfortunately wounded, should be left to linger in their pain, but always desired that they might be immediately tracked to their lair, that no one should molest them, and that any assistance they would accept from us, or which it was in our power to bestow, should be immediately rendered them. If our *rencontres* took place at a distance from any of the large villages, they were generally able to conceal themselves so completely that all our efforts to discover them were useless, and we were forced to let them go unassisted; but in the immediate neighbourhood of the villages, the trees had been cut down in greater numbers, the jungle was comparatively open, and we were thus enabled to discover their retreats, and to force upon them that aid which they were seldom willing to accept.

The arrows of the Mincopie are very formidable

weapons. Their fearful barbed points, when they once entered any part of the body, caused acute suffering, and could not be removed without inflicting severe torture. After I had become familiar with the dreadful power they possessed, when discharged with sufficient force, of inflicting, especially when poisoned, the most alarming wounds, I remembered the old lady at Moulmein, who attributed our certain death to these weapons; and though I might still consider her prophecy rash, I no longer smiled at the alarm with which they were regarded by her. The Mincopie discharge was always dreaded, for knowing their accuracy of eye, and that they were sure of hitting the object at which they aimed, we were always on our guard. On one occasion, when I was peering steadily into the dark jungle, in the thick recesses of which I could with difficulty distinguish any object, my Jemidar, whose sight was remarkably acute, quite equal to that of any of the Mincopie, communicated to me, too suddenly to be agreeable, a fact that rather alarmed me. "Sir," said he, "there is a savage concealed in that jungle, who has seen you, who has marked you out for an arrow, and now he is going to bend his bow, and fire at you;" and even while uttering these warning words, he threw himself before me with devoted gallantry, and with a self-sacrifice of which I think few similar examples could be found. Meanwhile, the arrow meant to carry death to me had winged its flight, and if I had been still standing on the same spot where I was when alarmed by the communication of my Jemidar, it would infallibly have reached me, and perhaps have inflicted a fatal wound. I thanked my faithful servant, who, under the supreme hand of Providence, was the instrument of my deliverance from a danger so imminent. The arrow alighted midway between our feet, and buried itself for half its length in the soil.

My Jemidar, whose only fault was that he had, perhaps, some share of that disposition for revenge ascribed to his countrymen, earnestly desired me at once to kill the man who had made such a resolute attempt upon my life. I declined, however, the responsibility of taking the man's life, even though he had done his best to take mine, but I had no intention he should escape scot-free. So I requested the Jemidar to hand me my Devisme, which had been given to me by a French patient whom I had attended in Calcutta, with the hope that, if ever in danger, it might perhaps be the means of saving my life. It happened, at the time, to be loaded with large shot for shooting herons. My friend, the Mincopie, foolishly thinking he had polished me off, now marched down in the direction where he expected to find my body; for as we had concealed ourselves behind some trees, he was not aware that we were near, and alive and well. When he came within a certain distance, I appeared from my concealment, pointing my weapon at him. The moment he saw my gun raised in his direction, he took alarm and fled; but I immediately fired, on which he set up a terrific howl, for he had received a quantity of the small shot. Beyond the sharp pain, however, which made him yell with vigour, it did him no serious injury, as I had fired when I knew he was at a pretty safe distance from me, and secure from the infliction of any dangerous wound. My Jemidar reproached me strongly for not having at once killed the savage who had so recklessly attempted my life, but I had constantly set my determination against all extreme measures.

The harpoon is a weapon which they use for fishing. It is provided with a moveable head, a long elastic cord being attached to it, by which it may be held when fixed in the victim at which it has been thrown. Their other fishing arrows are made of smooth, hard wood, and are merely used for transfixing the fish. Their nets, which they manufacture with great ingenuity and neatness, are beautifully made of a cord resembling small whip-cord. This cord is manufactured from the Rhœa fibre, which possesses the valuable quality of hardening in the water. The Mincopie also make small hand-nets, neat and elegant in appearance, resembling butterfly nets. The net is appended to a basket which the women attach to themselves, using it as a depôt for everything they gather during the day. They manufacture still another description of net, of exceedingly strong construction, having large meshes, the cord of which they are formed being as thick as a strong man's middle finger. Heavy stones to sink it are fastened at short intervals, perhaps about every two feet. This net is made to close like a bag, and is used for catching turtle, the largest of which, when once enclosed within its meshes, can by no possibility again escape.

The water-vessels of the Mincopie are formed of enormous joints of the bamboo. They are of very large size, and capable of containing several gallons of fresh water, the burden of which, overwhelming as it is, the women are compelled to carry every day, for a distance of many miles, from village to village.

In closing our hasty notice of the manners and customs of the Mincopie, we must briefly describe the meagre ceremonies with which the burial of the dead is celebrated. When a member of any of their communities dies, the Mincopie make little if any demonstration of grief. There is neither weeping, nor wailing, nor gnashing of teeth. The body of the dead man, while still flexible, is tied tight to the knees, and then buried in an upright position. After decay has gone on for some time, and the body is almost entirely decomposed, it is again dug up, and each relation appropriating any bone of the deceased he may be able to obtain, they all commence howling over it, although so long a period has elapsed since the death of their relative. If he was a married man, the widow obtains his skull, which she suspends by a cord round her neck, carrying it about as a lugubrious kind of ornament, which, for the remaining period of her natural life, is considered as a manifestation of the affection with which she regarded her deceased husband. But this outward display is the only way in which they are really faithful to the memory of the dead. The Nicobarians, inhabiting some islands about seventy miles or so farther south, put their dead in a bundle and bury them under trees.

Once a year the inhabitants of a village carry one of their dead relations round its precincts until the body drops to pieces. It is a curious fact that the slinging of the husband's skull round the neck of the widow is also a custom prevalent among the natives of Terra del Fuego.

Having thus depicted the manners, customs, and modes of life prevalent among the natives of the Andaman Islands, as far as we found it possible to obtain any reliable information on these points, we must now conclude our observations, which, from the hasty manner in which they have been thrown together, are much more imperfect and unsatisfactory than we should have desired to make them, with some considerations on the ethnology of the Mincopie. The geographers of almost every country without exception, including the most profound and learned inquirers of Northern Europe and Germany, have described the Mincopie as dwarf negroes, low in intellect and ferocious in disposition. In their learned works on Geography, and in their exhaustive Cyclopædias, both those intended specially for scholars and scientific men, and the more popular Conversations-Lexicons, this general statement amounts to almost all they have to say of this original and interesting race. This information was procured for me by a learned and esteemed friend, Miss Harriet Innis, a very accomplished linguist. I may add that English Geographers, and such occasional travellers as have referred to the Andamans, repeat the same incorrect statement.

Now, the Mincopie are certainly not negroes, nor in my opinion are they dwarfs. In the sense in which I understand the word, dwarfs are not only of small stature, but more or less deformed in shape. The Mincopie, on the other hand, are the most perfectly formed little beings in existence. In proportion to their size, their general framework is well constructed, and their limbs present a remarkably good muscular development. No doubt there are certain points in which they resemble the negro, but there are others by which they are broadly distinguished from him. Their hue is remarkably black and lustrous, but they are not woolly-headed. Their faces have not that projecting monkey-looking development of the lower part of the visage which is a distinguishing characteristic of the genuine negro. One never sees among them those enormous cavern-like mouths of which the poor African gives you an alarming glimpse when he opens it in a fit of laughter, or the perpetration of a yawn. The projecting heel is also absent in the Mincopie, whose whole form is as elegant as that of any European, and injured only by their own absurd fancies in the way of adornment, particularly the anointing of their whole bodies with that abominable red earth, and the removal of the hair, the want of which certainly does give their heads a bullet-like negro appearance.

In comparing them with certain other remarkable races of the black and copper-coloured varieties of mankind, we continue to be struck more by their diversity than by any analogy. They do not, for instance, possess the slightest resemblance to the Veddahs of Ceylon, the Soutals, the Coles, the Turkha Coles, who are copper-coloured, and among whom both sexes go naked. The Coles have also some knowledge of agriculture, by which they live. In fighting they use bows and arrows, the latter with barbed points, but not poisoned as those of the Mincopie, nor do they shoot with nearly the same force. It is really alarming to watch the flight of a Mincopie arrow, as it flies with the swiftness of lightning through the air, apparently destined to lodge in your iliac, and, as it were, transfixing you to the spot even before it reaches you; for you know the danger with which you are threatened, if its poisoned point should penetrate even slightly any part of your person, besides the difficulty of extracting it when the barbed end has fixed itself firmly in some fleshy part of your body. I was reminded, when I saw them, of the awe with which the old English archers were regarded, and how formidable were the steel cloth shafts with which they laid so many low at Crécy and at Agincourt. Nor do the natives of the Andamans bear any resemblance to the Garrows and the Hill tribes—the former of whom, as is well-known, live on muchauns in trees in the serail on the rapid banks of the Brahmapootra. They are equally removed in character and appearance from the Palasgie or Oceanic Pa-puans, who are all of large proportions, gigantic in size, and furnished with long crisp hair. The latter, too, if they proceed merely from one village to another, can no longer make themselves understood, each apparently having its own dialect, the difference of which is so great that the inhabitants of one hamlet are not intelligible to those of another.

It is needless to remark that their language, or languages, is strange to the Mincopie, who do not understand a single word of it. The latter are, in fact, as Professor Owen described them at the meeting of the British Association in Manchester, as also at that of the Ethnological Society of London, a "genuine aboriginal race," so distinct from all others that their relationship to any other known tribe cannot be determined. This description was based on an imperfect skeleton which was presented to me by my friend, Dr. J. P. Walker, Surgeon-Major of the Bengal army, when superintendent of the Andamans. This was the only specimen ever taken to Europe, but there is a more perfect one in the possession of the learned Mr. Blyth, Curator of the Museum of the Asiatic Society of Calcutta. Admirable photographs of the skull of this skeleton were taken by Professor Rowe, the father of photography in India, and by him sent to Professor Owen for description. From the paper read by that distinguished professor, on the Osteology of the natives of the Andaman Islands, I am permitted to make some interesting extracts, with which I conclude these notices of the Andamans and their inhabitants.

Professor Owen, as reported in the *Athenæum*, commenced by a brief notice of the geography of the Andaman Islands, and condensed an account of the physical characters and habits of the natives, from the Reports of the able superintendents and surveyors of the convict settlements recently established by the East Indian Government on these islands—quoting more particularly from the statement of a Brahmin Sepoy, one of the transported mutineers, who, after escaping from the convict establishment, passed upwards of a year (from April 23, 1858, to May 17, 1859) with a tribe of Andamaners. His statement accorded with previous accounts, that the diminutive black aborigines of these islands have no notions of a Deity, of spiritual beings, or a future state; that both sexes go naked without any sense of shame. There is promiscuous intercourse, save with the parent, which only ceases in regard to the woman when she is allotted as wife to a man, but is retained as the prerogative of the male sex.

"It is impossible," says Professor Owen, quoting some words of the author of the present work, "to imagine any human beings to be lower in the scale of civilization than are the Andaman savages.. Entirely destitute of clothing, utterly ignorant of agriculture, living in the most primitive and rudest form of habitations, their only care seems to be the supply of their daily food." *

Their chief weapons (continues the Professor) are bows and arrows; some of the males also carry a kind of spear. Scarification of the skin in certain maladies, tatooing, and shaving of the scalp, are performed with chips of glass skilfully detached from bottles cast ashore after wrecks, by sharp blows with a stone. The iron with which the arrows and spears are headed is also obtained from wrecks. The Andamaners appear to be

* Selections from the Records of the Government of India, No. XXV., "Andaman Islands," Preface, p. vi.

devoid of fear: they are powerful for their size, can carry greater burthens than the Hindoos; are swift runners, and clear rapidly, by jumping, the fallen trees of the jungle, and rocks of the tidal shore. As climbers they are little inferior to monkeys, being used from childhood to climb the lofty, straight, unbranched trees of the forest in quest of fruit and honey. They are excellent swimmers from their childhood, and wonderful divers, "fishing for shell-fish in deep water." "I have seen," deposes the Sepoy, "three or four of them dive into deep water and bring up in their arms a fish six or seven feet in length, which they had seized."—"They could perceive canoes approaching long before they were visible to me, and could see fruits and honeycombs in the jungle which I could not. Their vision penetrates to great depths in the sea, where they could see and shoot fish with arrows, when the object aimed at was not apparent to me. They see well at night, catching fish in the pools left by the tide at that season; and shooting the wild pigs which came to the coast to drink by night." By their acute sense of smell, they often detect afar off the existence of fruit in the neighbouring lofty trees. "I never met with anyone affected with gonorrhœa, syphilis, itch, piles, small-pox, or goître: but I have seen them affected with vomiting, colic, diarrhœa, intermittent fever, head-ache, ear-ache, toothache, abscesses, rheumatism, catarrh, cough, painful and difficult respiration. The only remedies I have seen used are 'red earth rubbed up with turtle-oil,' a cold infusion of certain aromatic leaves, the wetted leaves being applied to the head or other inflamed parts, and local bleedings by sharp splinters of bottle-glass." They spin ropes; make wicker baskets, large nets for catching turtle—smaller nets for catching fishes; and they scoop out their canoes by means of a small kind of adze, tipped with a semicircular blade of iron.

Thus, for all their immediate wants, invention has supplied the instruments called for by the nature of the surrounding objects and sources of food. But their life is little beyond that of the brute animal; and the low grade of humanity, with the dwarfish stature and black colour of the Andamaners, has always made a further knowledge of their physical characters peculiarly desirable.

Professor Owen was enabled to contribute the present notice of the osteological and dental characters of the Mincopie, by the opportunities kindly afforded him by Dr. Mouat, Inspector of Indian Jails, who had brought over the bones of an adult male native of the Andamans, now presented by Dr. Mouat to the British Museum. The bones presented a compact sound texture, with the processes, articular surfaces, and places of muscular attachments neatly defined. The cranium is well formed; not exceeding disproportionately in any diameter, it might be classed with those of the oval type. The frontal region is rather narrow, but not low; it passes by a regular curve upward and backward to the vertex. The frontal, much of the sagittal, and the upper part of the coronal sutures were obliterated. Part of the lambdoidal suture was very complex.

The alisphenoid joined the parietal on both sides of the head. The glabella is but little prominent; the nasals are not flat, but are moderately developed. The alveolar parts of the upper and lower jaws slightly project. The chin is a little produced, and is not deep. The malar bones are not unusually prominent. The cranial bones are not above the average thickness. The following were the principal dimensions of this cranium:

	In.	Lin.
Length, from inion to premaxillary border (178·0)	7	0
Do from do. to glabella (160·0)	6	4
Breadth of the cranium (144·0)	5	4
Circumference of the cranium (409·0)	19	6
Ante-posterior diameter of the interior of the cranium (150·0)	5	9
Transverse diameter of ditto (145·0)	5	7
Vertical diameter of ditto (115·0)	4	6

The spine of the occiput is not so developed as to interrupt the convex contour of the occipital part of the skull; the lower occipital crest is rather more developed than the upper one. The mastoids are moderately developed; there is no super-mastoid ridge. The base of the skull offers all the strictly human characteristics. There is no excess in the size of the orbits or of the auditory apertures; a sharp ridge projects from the lower boundary of the anterior nares. The lower jaw shows a variety in the shape of the coronoid process, which is occasionally seen in Europeans; it is broader and lower than usual; the front border is more convex at its upper half, and forms, with the concave lower part, a deeper and more decided sigmoid curve. The ascending ramus forms a less open angle with the horizontal ramus than in most Negro and Australian skulls. The teeth equal in size the average of those of Indo-Europeans; they correspond in this respect with those of the European figured in the author's "Odontography," plates 118 and 119. Although they are large in proportion to the size of the jaws, they are markedly smaller than are those of the Australian figured in the same plates. In the upper jaw of the male Andamaner, the true molars, as in most Europeans, diminish in size from the first to the third. The fissure which penetrates the grinding surface from the outer side to the middle of the crown, had its end unobliterated in *m* 1, and retained its whole length in *m* 2. The enamel was worn from the inner half in both teeth, but in a less proportion in *m* 2; it was also slightly worn from the outer tubercles in *m* 1. The degree of abrasion of the teeth, according to the age of the individual, is such as might be expected from the mastication of a diet consisting chiefly of fish and fruit. In the lower jaw the denture is exposed on the three outer tubercles of *m* 1; the crucial figure is not obliterated in *m* 2; *m* 3 is larger, as usual, than in the corresponding tooth above. The upper premolars are implanted by a fang which is divided at its base into an outer and an inner root. The undivided fang of the lower premolars is longitudinally grooved on the outer side. In the upper jaw *m* 1 and *m* 2 are implanted by two outer and one inner roots; *m* 3 by one antero-external and one postero-internal root. All the lower molars have distinct anterior and posterior roots. There was no irregularity in the position, nor any sign of decay in the teeth. All the bones of the trunk and limbs presented the specific and generic characters of *Homo Sapiens,* Linn. The sigmoid flexure of the clavicle was well marked. The scapula agrees with that variety of form which shows a minor extent of the supra-spinal tract, and a greater breadth of the lower part of the sub-spinal tract, with a more produced angle between the surfaces for the teres major and teres minor muscles, on the inferior costa. The inferior costa describes a continuous concave curve from the angle to the base of the coracoid, without any supra-scapular notch. The os innominatum, calcaneum, astragalus, and bones of the hallux, contrasted as strongly with the quadrumanous characters of those bones as in the highest of the human races. The first lumbar vertebra had the diapophysis, metapophysis, and anapophysis distinct, and almost equally developed, and well illustrated the true serial homology of the longer diapophysis of the succeeding lumbars. In many European skeletons the diapophysis of the first lumbar vertebra is more developed than in that of the Andamaner. The ridges, processes, and surfaces for muscular attachment are well and neatly defined on the several limb-bones of this skeleton, and agree with the character for agility in running, climbing, and swimming, assigned to the Andaman race. The following were the dimensions of the principal limb-bones :—

Scapula.

	In.	Lin.
Length from end of acromion to inferior angle	7	1
Breadth from upper and outer angle to lower border of glenoid cavity	4	0

Os Innominatum.

Length	7	7
Breadth of ilium	5	5

	Humerus		*Ulna*		*Radius*		*Femur*		*Tibia*		*Clavicle*	
	In.	Li.	In	Li.	In.	Li.	In.	Li.	In.	Li.	In.	Li.
Length	12	2	10	8	9	11	17	5	14	3	5	2
Transverse diameter of upper end	1	10	1	2	0	10	3	4	...		...	
Ditto of middle	0	9	0	6	0	6½	0	11	1	1	...	
Ditto of lower end	2	1½	0	9	1	3	2	9	1	10	...	

The above dimensions of parts of the skeleton indicate that they are from an individual of 4 feet 10 inches in height. The Andamaners, or Mincopie, are called, by most of the observers who have described them, "Negrillos," or dwarf Negroes. They have no knowledge, and appear to have no idea, of their own origin. It has been surmised that they may be descendants of African Negroes, imported by the Portuguese for slave labour in their settlement at Pegu, and which had been wrecked on the Andamans. But the recorders of this hypothesis allude to it as a mere hearsay—"We are told that when the Portuguese," &c. (*Calcutta Monthly Register, or India Repository,* November, 1790, pp. 15-17). Neither the skull nor the teeth of the male Andamaner above described, offer any of the characters held to be distinctive of the African Negroes. The cranium has not the relative narrowness ascribed to that of the Negro; it presents nothing suggestive of lateral compression; it conforms to the full oval type, with a slight degree of prognathism, and is altogether on a smaller scale than in the Indo-European exhibiting that form of skull. It is to be presumed that the Portuguese would import from the Guinea coast, or other mart of Negro slaves, individuals of the usual stature, and it is incredible that their descendants, enjoying freedom in a tropical locality affording such a sufficiency and even abundance of food as the Andamans are testified to supply, should have degenerated in stature, in the course of two or three centuries, to the characteristic dwarfishness of the otherwise well-made, well-nourished, strong and active natives of the Andaman Islands.

Professor Owen concludes, therefore, that they were aborigines; and merely resembled Negroes in a blackness of the tegumentary pigment, which might be due to constant exposure in such a rude and primitive race.

Their prognathism is not more than is found in most of the Southern Asiatic peoples, and indeed in the lower orders of these in all countries, and may be due or relate to the prolonged sucking of the plastic infant.

The observation of the hair of the scalp, which we must suppose to be unsatisfactory or insufficient in regard to a race that habitually shaves or eradicates the hair, were it exact in regard to the crisp, curly, or woolly character of the hair, would show a resemblance of the Andamaners to the Papuans and Australians, as well as to the African Negroes. But the skull and dentition of the Andaman male is still more distinct from the Papuan-Australian type than from that of the West-coast Negro. There is no supra-nasal ridge due to a sunken origin of the flattened nasal bones; neither the malar nor zygometric arches show the strength and prominence that mark them in the Australian male; there is no excessive size of molar or other teeth.

From the present opportunity of studying the osteology and dentition of the Andamaner, the ethnologist derives as little indication, or ground of surmise, of the origin of the race in question, from an Australasian as from an African continent; and there is scarcely better evidence of his Malayan or Mongolian ancestry. Professor Owen was not cognizant of any anatomical grounds for deriving the physical Andaman people from any existing continent. But in making these remarks he intended no encouragement to a belief that they originated in the locality to which they are now limited. Dr. Latham states that "their language shows them to belong to the same division with the Burmese of the opposite continent." These, however, show the average stature of the Southern Asiatic men. And it would be as pure assumption to affirm that they had been derived from the Andamaners, as that these were degenerate descendants of the Burmese.

Combined geological, geographical, and zoological researches have made us cognizant of the fact of the formation and destruction of continental tracts of land in the known course of the earth's period of existence. The Andaman Islands, like Java, Sumatra, and Ceylon, may have been parts of some former extent of dry land, distinct from, and perhaps pre-existent to, that neighbouring and more northern continent which has been the scene of the elevation of the Himalayan range of mountains, in part—perhaps a great part—within the tertiary period. The Andamans are forty miles distant from the nearest islands—the Cocos—on their north, and seventy-two miles distant from the Nicobar Islands on their south. There is a mountain 2,400 feet in height, called Saddle Peak, probably volcanic, on the main island; and there is a volcanic island in the vicinity, called Barren Island, with an active volcano. The whole of the shores of the Andamans are skirted by con-continuous coral reefs.

It is plain that the Andamans are the active seat of those causes that influence the change in the relations of land to sea. We should, doubtless, err, therefore, in any speculation on the origin of their population, if we were to assume that the Andamans were such as they now are when they received their first human inhabitants. The cardinal defect of speculators on the origin of the human species is, the assumption that the present geographical condition of the earth's surface is anterior to, or, at least, co-existent with, the origin of such species. The Monogenist, on that assumption, bent on tracing all human races from one source and one existent centre, exaggerates the application and value of casual remarks, to show, for example, that "the Australians are not a pure race, but hybrids between true Negroes and a Malayan or yellow race." (See Quatrefages, "Unité de l'Espèce Humaine," 12mo., 1861, p. 133). And the Polygenist invokes a separate creation of each race for each existing continent, or island home, of such race.

The Andamans are, perhaps, the most primitive, or lowest in the scale of civilization, of the human race. They have no tradition, and, as has been before remarked, apparently no notion of their own origin. Finding in their bows and arrows, and their hand-nets, implements that answer for acquiring the principal articles of food which their locality yields, they have carried the inventive faculties no further. At best, they may have availed themselves of the wrecks during the last century or two of their insular existence to barb their arrows with iron instead of fish-bone, and to get from broken bottles such trenchant fragments as our oldest known Europeans obtained from broken flints. The animal appetites are gratified in the simplest animal fashion; there is no sense of nakedness, no sentiment of shame. The man choosing promiscuously for one or more years after puberty, then takes, or has assigned to him a female, who becomes his exclusive mate and servant; and the reason assigned for this monogamy is that, though she be restricted, he may continue to select from the unmarried females as before. The climate dispenses with the necessity of any other protection for the body than a paste of earth and oil. Any rudiment of a cincture relates solely to the convenience of the suspension of weapons or other portable objects.

They are not cannibals. Implacably hostile to strangers, the Andamaners have made no advance in the few centuries during which their seas have been traversed by ships of higher races. Perhaps the sole change is that of the materials for weapons derived from casual wrecks, to which allusion had already been made. Enjoying, therefore, the merest animal life during those centuries, why may they not have so existed for thousands of years? The conditions of existence being such as they now enjoy, on what can the ethnologist found an idea of the limitation of the period during which the successive generations of Andamaners have continued so to exist? Antecedent generations of the race may have co-existed with the slow and gradual geological changes which have obliterated the place or continent of their primitive origin, whatever be the hypothesis adopted regarding it.

In every essential of human physical character, the present Mincopie, or Andamaners, participate with their more gifted brethren; they approach the Orangs and Chimpanzees only in their diminutive stature; but this is associated with the well-balanced human proportions of trunk to limbs: they are, indeed, surpassed by the great Orangs and Gorillas in the size of the trunk, and in the length and strength of the arms, in a greater degree than are the more advanced and taller races of mankind.

APPENDIX.

THE ZOOLOGY OF THE ANDAMAN ISLANDS.

BY EDWARD BLYTH,

CURATOR OF THE MUSEUM OF THE ASIATIC SOCIETY, ETC.

OF the *Fauna* of the Andaman Islands, we are just beginning to learn a little. Until some time after the penal settlement at Port Blair was established, nothing was known with certainty on the subject. There were merely a few loose statements of the existence upon the islands of a few animals of sundry classes, but which had not been scientifically determined. We had been informed, for instance, that there were wild pigs, rats, crows, &c; but what particular kind of pig, or rat, or crow, was thus vaguely referred to, remained to be ascertained. Of course the pigs and the rats were supposed to have found their way out of some wrecked vessel, and the crow was "the common crow of India." As if the Andamaners would not at once have speared and destroyed any tame pigs that had gone astray upon their territories, even supposing that these had comprised perfect individuals of both sexes; and as if the common Indian crow (*Corvus splendens*, Vieillot), is anywhere found in jungle, away from populous and settled human communities. One or more of the constructors of the famous edible birds' nests must needs be there, and the hawk's-bill turtle; because edible nests and tortoise-shell were known to have been collected on the Islands, although it is pretty well understood that the collection of these products was little more than a pretext, on the part of their chiefly Malayan visitors (mostly from the west coast of Sumatra), for carrying off the human inhabitants that might be captured, to be tamed and made useful as slaves. Up to the present time, the gentleman who has achieved most in collecting specimens of the animals of the Andamans, and transmitting them to the Museum of the Asiatic Society, Calcutta, is Captain T. H. Hodge, who commanded the guard-ship *Sesostris*, in 1859-60; but the first pioneer, from whose exertions in the same line we have benefited, is Dr. G. von Liebig, whose collection is reported upon in the "Journal of the Asiatic Society," for 1858, page 267. Lieutenant-Colonel Tytler, who now governs at Port Blair, is well known as an amateur naturalist, and especially as an experienced ornithologist; and he has considerably added already to the list of birds accurately determined, and has discovered some highly interesting novelties in that class: while there is reason to hope and expect that, under his auspices, the *Vertebrata* proper of the region will soon be exhaustively investigated, so far, at least, as relates to the discrimination and recognition of the species.

As might be expected, the kindred archipelagos of the Andamans and the Nicobars, with the more detached islets in the Bay of Bengal, are poor in species of mammalia, with the exception of such only as are endowed with the power of flight—the bats; and these latter have been little studied as yet. On reference to the map, it will be seen that the mountain range that separates Arakan from Pegu, and terminates southward in the promontory of Cape Negrais, there dips into the sea, and successively appears above it as different islands in the bay, forming a curved line of them to Acheen Head—the northern extremity of Sumatra—there again rises to form the spine of that great island, and is then continued onward and eastward even to New Guinea, still following about the same line of curvature. This geographical disposition of the successive islets, and groups of islands, connects the series distinctly with the existing Asiatic mainland, rather than indicates them to be the mountain-tops of a separate continent, now submerged, as has been recently suggested.* In the Bay of Bengal, the first spot of land upon that line of curvature lying south from Cape Negrais, is the islet of Préparis, situate about half-way between Cape Negrais and the Cocos group of islets; then follows the more considerable territory of the Andamans, Great and Little, succeeded by the Nicobar group; with again some islets before reaching the extensive land of Sumatra.† A little out of the line, about thirty-six

* *Vide* "Parthenon," Nos. vi., vii. (1862). This writer remarks that the *Lemuridæ* are exclusively confined to Madagascar. But there happens to be the genus *Galago* in continental Africa, E. and W.; the genus *Stenops* in S. India and Ceylon; the genus *Loris* or *Nycticebus* in E. Bengal, Asam, all Indo-China, and all W. Malasia; the genus *Tarsius* in Banka, if not also in Borneo; and the genus *Galæopithicus* in W. Malasia and the Philippines, extending northward into the Tenasserim province of Mergui. The last is at least subordinate to the great Lemurian type. Of course, the chief Lemurian genera, as *Lemur* itself (comprising so many species), *Lichanotus*, *Propithecus*, *Cheirogaleus*, and *Cheiromys*, are peculiar to Madagascar; but most assuredly not the entire family of *Lemuridæ*. Our Loris, from the islet of Préparis, is most undoubtedly a Lemurian animal! Moreover, in Madagascar, the Lemurian type does not entirely replace the Simian, as is generally supposed.

† There is a chain of small islands off and along the west coast of Sumatra, the ethnology of which is particularly worthy of study. I have

miles to the eastward of the Andamans, rises the remarkable volcano of "Barren Island;" and north-east of this, at a greater distance from the northern extremity of the Great Andaman Island, is situate the islet of Narcondam. Of the animal inhabitants of these more detached specks of land in the Bay of Bengal, we know absolutely nothing; but, small as they are, they are not, necessarily, quite deficient of the class mammalia, additional to its volar order of bats. My well-informed friend, Captain S. Hill, of the Calcutta Bank's-hall, assures me positively that he has seen the *Loris tardigradus* (popularly known as the "sloth" by Anglo-Indians) upon Préparis; and lately the Reverend C. S. P. Parish, the able botanist and chaplain of Moulmein, observed on Barren Island the half-devoured remains of some rat, which it is not likely had been carried by a bird of prey from the nearest land, thirty-six miles distant: as the carcase was much mutilated, Mr. Parish did not think it worth while to preserve it in spirit; though, had he done so, the identification of the species with the peculiar spiny-coated *Mus andamanensis* would probably have been easy: two peculiar species of *Mus*, however, I find have been discovered on the Nicobar Islands, by the naturalists attached to the Austrian "Novara" expedition; though one of them may, likely enough, prove to be no other than the *Mus andamanensis*. From the Cocos Islands I have received a pair of living young of the beautiful Nicobar pigeon (*Calænas nicobaricus*); this being probably the northernmost range of the species, the distribution of which extends thence even to New Guinea: north of the Malayan peninsula, I only know of its elsewhere inhabiting the islands of the Mergui archipelago.

Now this is a bird not at all likely to make long sea

been assured that the human race differs remarkably upon almost every one of those islands.

voyages; and I look upon it, therefore, as an additional presumptive proof of former continuity of land from Cape Negrais to Acheen Head in Sumatra.

The small Andamanese wild pig appears, at first, to be as isolated in its range as new to science; but I have been assured of the existence of a diminutive wild pig in the Nicobars, additional to the huge tame swine of undoubtedly exotic origin, which are bred by the Nicobarians of the coasts; and I have also considerable reason to suspect that it exists likewise in Sumatra (additional to *S. vittatus*), being probably the diminutive wild swine of that island noticed by Bingley in his "Animal Biography," the passage from that work being quoted in the "Journal of the Asiatic Society," for 1860, page 104. The *Sus andamanensis* was slightly noticed, and a very rude figure of the skull given, in Jameson's "Edinburgh New Philosophical Journal," vol. xvi. (1826), 27: but all that is stated occurs casually in the description of an Andamanese hut:—"Ranged in a row round the walls were the smoked skulls of a diminutive hog; the canine teeth shorter than in other species of *Sus* in Eastern countries, the jaws fastened together with strips of rattan." This was upon the *Little* Andaman Island; and the writer could only have seen the skulls of sows; for the tusks of the boar are proportionately quite as much developed as in the large wild swine of the adjacent regions.

The existence of the Loris upon Préparis affords further scope for speculation. The species may have there survived considerable geological changes in the extent of land elevated above the sea in the present Bay of Bengal. However, it is not quite impossible that a pregnant female, belonging to a party who had landed on the island (as this little animal is not unfrequently conveyed about in cages), might have made its escape, and so have founded a colony; but the former I look upon as very much the more probable theory. There is, besides, the rat (*Mus andamanensis?*) on Barren Island;* and besides the pig, there is also a Bondar (*Paradoxurus*) in Great Andaman, of which I have only seen the skull of a very aged individual, that had lost most of its teeth by decay. This skull is now in the Asiatic Society's Museum, Calcutta; and it is the animal that has been noticed in some of the newspapers as "a sort of Mungoose," and perhaps, also, that similarly mentioned as "a kind of wild cat." It would appear, however, from a letter recently received from Lt.-Col. Tytler, that a small species of true wild *Felis* exists in the Andamans, which makes only the second *carnivore* observed in the territory.†

"On the 4th July, at Aberdeen," writes Lt.-Col. Tytler, "I distinctly saw a feline animal of the size of the European wild cat. This animal walked across the road about 150 yards before me; its colour was of an uniform yellowish-brown, more like the yellow of a leopard, perhaps lighter, but I could see no marks or spots. There are several yellow-coloured domestic cats belonging to the European Naval Brigade here, but they are small—besides which, no cat from Ross Island could swim over to Aberdeen: again, where I saw it, none of the convicts' houses were within half a mile of the place. From the rapid casual view I had of it, I am persuaded that it was a wild animal, and not a stray domestic cat." Not im-

* "From the description of some of these accounts" of Barren Island, writes Dr. von Liebig, "it would appear that the high vegetation which we found on the external slope of the island, is of quite recent origin." (*J. A. S.* xxix., 7). Mr. Parish visited Barren Island in 1861, and remarked a beautiful flower blooming on the bare lava: he obtained it with difficulty, and it proved to be the fine usually epiphytic orchid, *Dendrobium formosum*, which is very common in the Southern Tenasserim provinces. I saw the specimen with Mr. Parish at Moulmein. If the general vegetation of Barren Island is really "of quite recent origin," the investigation of it would possess no ordinary interest.

† Since the above was written, I have been informed by Dr. Mouat that he found the skull of a small *Felis*, on the occasion of his visit; but that the specimen was unfortunately and unaccountably lost.

probably the *Felis chaus*, from the above description; and the *Paradoxurus* skull accords nearly with that of *P. musanga* of the neighbouring countries.

No *Quadrumana* have as yet been observed, on credible testimony, in the Andamans; nor *Insectivora*; nor *Rodentia*, besides the peculiar rat (the small mouse of India, *M. manei*, being doubtless of recent introduction): there have been seen no squirrel, nor flying squirrel; nor any muntjac or chevrotain (mouse-deer), among the *Ruminantia:* but some bones of the marine duyong (*Halicore indicus*) have been found in an Andamanese hut or lair, this being the most northern locality known for the species in the Bay of Bengal.

In the Nicobar Islands, a monkey (*Macacus cynomolgos*) abounds; and a large black species (doubtless a *Presbytis*) has been reported to exist, and which could not be obtained on account of its extreme wildness. Two peculiar species of *Mus* have likewise been described recently, as already noticed; and Captain Harold Lewis observed a large squirrel in 1846, which he said was different from any sort at that time in the Museum of the Asiatic Society.*

Certainly the most extraordinary animal known to exist in the Nicobar Islands, and which should also be looked for in the Andamans, is a species of the anomalous family of poultry-birds, known as the *Megapodiidæ;* the rest of this family being almost confined to the Great Papuan and Australian region.† These are the birds, the eggs of which are never incubated, but are deposited in a hole, either in an artificial mound, accumulated and raised by the birds themselves, or in sand, &c.; which lay most disproportionately large and thin-shelled eggs, and the young coming forth from them well-plumed and sufficiently advanced to make their way in the world.

* *Vide* "Journal of the Asiatic Society" for 1846, page 367.

† According to Mr. Wallace, the genus *Megapodius* has its "western limit in Lombok!" *Proc. Lin. Soc.* 1860, p. 173.

The *Megapodius nicobarensis* has not hitherto been met with excepting in the Nicobars, and would appear to be "common on all the islands" of that group, according to the personal observation of an excellent amateur naturalist, the late Reverend J. Barbe, of the Society of Jesus.

There are several species of birds which have hitherto been observed only on the Andamans or the Nicobars, or on both groups of islands conjointly; and several of the Andamanese races accord better with corresponding races at a considerable distance than with those inhabiting the nearest parts of the continent. Thus the *Artamus* and the *Oriolus* of the Andamans appear to be identical with those of Java, but not of India and Burma; and a shrike, common on the islands, agrees much better with *Lanius lucionensis* of China and the Philippines, than with the nearly akin *L. phœnicurus* of Bengal and Arakan, the equally akin *L. superciliosus* of the Malayan peninsula, and the representative of the same group in Martaban and the Tenasserim provinces, which is *L. hypoleucos*. Among the *Reptilia*, there is a beautiful species of Gecko (*Phelsuma andamanense*), the immediate kindred of which are only known in Madagascar and the Mascarine Islands. It is remarkable that the common black-necked oriole of the Andamans (*Oriolus horsfieldi?*), should differ from that of the neighbouring Nicobar Islands (*O. macrourus*), and both from the kindred species of India and Burma.

Reptiles are numerous in both groups of islands; but I am unaware that any crocodiles have been observed. A *Python* has been seen in the Nicobars. The marine *Testudinata* of the Bay occur, of course; and the skulls of turtles are commonly found in the huts of the Andamanese. *Ophidia* would appear to be numerous, both as species and individuals; and, as *Batrachia* are rare upon islands well out in the sea,* it is inte-

* *Vide* Darwin's "Origin of Species."

resting to the zoologist to know that the common Indian toad *(Bufo melanostictus)* is very abundant on the Andamans.

Of marine fishes, the Asiatic Society has received large collections from Port Blair, which are chiefly due to Captain Hodge; but as the marine zoology of the Andamans and Nicobars is essentially that of the Bay of Bengal, it is hardly worth while here to enumerate a long list of species. Any fresh-water kinds would possess more interest in the present instance; and of these we know only certain mud-skippers, as *Periopthalmus papilio* (Bloch, Schneider), and *Andamia expansa*, nobis *(J.A.S.* xxvii., 271). A very fine land-crab is common, and is probably much eaten by the aborigines; it differing only (that I can perceive) from *Cardisoma carnifex* of the Peninsula of India by its much larger size. Some interesting land-shells have also been described by Mr. W. H. Benson, reference to which will be given in the sequel; and a few insects have also been collected, which have been singularly barren in novelties. The large centipede *(Scolopendra morsitans)* would appear to be rather common both in the Andamans and Nicobars.

I now proceed to enumerate the species of mammalia, birds and reptiles, as yet identified from the Andamans, with an occasional reference to the *fauna* of the Nicobars, and to what very little we know of the animal productions of certain other islets in the Bay of Bengal.

Mammalia.

Quadrumana. Unobserved as yet, on credible testimony, in the Andamans; but *Macacus cynomolgos* common in the Nicobars, and a dark-coloured species of *Presbytis* apparently inhabiting the same group. The *Loris tardigradus* has been seen on the islet of Préparis.

Cheiroptera. No *Pteropus* (or "flying fox," or roussette,) has as yet been observed upon the Andamans; but a species is common in the Nicobars, which is styled *Pteropus nicobaricus* by the naturalists of the "Novara" expedition, and *Pt. melanotus* in the "Catalogue of the Mammalia in the Museum of the Asiatic Society."

Cynopterus marginatus (B. Ham.) This small frugivorous bat (or one very like it) has been received both from the Andamans and Nicobars; but should be re-examined from these localities, as the naturalists of the "Novara" expedition have described * both a *Pachysoma giganteum* and a *P. Scherzeri* from the latter archipelago (the name *Pachysoma* being a synonym of *Cynopterus*).

The *Cynopterus* is the only species of bat as yet received from the Andamans; but Colonel Tytler writes word, that "there is a great abundance of small bats on the island, and I am surprised that you have not received any." From the Nicobars have been received *Hipposideros murinus* (Elliot), and *Nycticejus Temminckii* (Horsfield); and the "Novara" naturalists describe a *Vesperugo nicobaricus*.

Carnivora. Only two species as yet; the wild *Felis* seen by Col. Tytler, which is perhaps *F. chaus*; and the *Paradoxurus* already noticed, which is apparently *P. musanga* (*vide J.A.S.* xxix., 102). No carnivore appears to have been yet noticed in the Nicobar Islands.

Insectivora. The genera *Sorex* and *Tupaia* are not unlikely to occur, but have not been observed hitherto.

Rodentia. *Mus andamanensis*, Blyth, *Journ. As. Soc.* vol. xxix., p. 103. (Found also on Barren Island?) Also *Mus manei*, Gray, the common house-mouse of most parts of India—Port Blair, where doubtlessly introduced. In the Nicobar

* Die Ausbeute der Oesterreichischen Naturforscher an Säugethieren und Reptilien während der Weltumsegelung Sr. Majestät Fregatte Novara.—Von Dr. L. J. Fitzinger. I only know of this work from the notices of it in the "Natural History Review" for January, 1862, page 9.

Islands, the "Novara" naturalists discovered a *Mus novaræ*. and a *M. palmarum;* the former perhaps identical with the *M. andamanensis*, and the latter perhaps identical with *M. nemoralis* or with *M. flavescens* of India.

Pachydermata. *Sus andamanensis*, Blyth, *J.A.S.* xxvii., 267; xxviii., 271; xxix., 103. Inhabits both the Great and Little Andamans; apparently, also, the Nicobars; if not, likewise, Sumatra. *

Syrenia. *Halicore indicus.* Various bones found in an Andamanese hut.

Edentata. Unknown; though a *Manis* may perhaps occur.

Cetacea. No special observations as yet.

Aves.

[In the following list, those species of birds, to the names of which an asterisk is prefixed, are given on the authority of Lt.-Col. Tytler. The rest have been received in the Museum of the Asiatic Society, Calcutta.]

*1. *Palæornis Alexandri* (L). "Very common on the main as well as on the smaller Islands." (Tytler.)

2. *P. erythrogenys*, Blyth (*P. nicobaricus*, Gould)—Peculiar, so far as known at present, to the Andaman and Nicobar Islands. Another species, *P. caniceps*, Blyth, inhabits the Nicobars, where Captain Lewis obtained a living male, with its wings and tail mutilated by its native captor. A female was procured by the late Dr. Cantor in Pinang; and these two specimens appear to be the only examples of the species as yet known.

*3. *Loriculus* (*vernalis?*) "Five Lorikeets, I think of this

* A full-grown female of this species is now living in the Zoological Gardens, Regent's Park, London.

species, flew over from the mainland to Ross Island. I tried all I could to examine them with the aid of a spy-glass; but their movements were so rapid, and the tree so full of leaves, that I found it difficult to determine; still, from the observations made, I think beyond doubt that they were *L. vernalis*." (T.)

4. *Hæmatornis cheela* (Latham, *vel undulatus*, Vigors). "This is not so common as the next." (T.)

5. *H. Elgini*, Tytler, *nov. sp.* A very distinct species, discovered at Port Blair by Col. Tytler. "These birds are common on the main island. I have not seen them on the smaller islands. They are not at all timid, and are found perched on the top branches of trees." (T.) Two specimens received in the Museum of the Asiatic Society.

6. *Blagrus leucogaster* (Gmelin). This fine eagle, coloured like an ordinary sea-gull, or white with ashy mantle (in the adult plumage), has been observed both in the Andamans and Nicobars. Latham well designated it the "Maritime Eagle," as it is principally observed along the sea-coast, or within the tideways of large rivers. It preys chiefly on water-snakes. From the Bay of Bengal and Straits of Malacca, the range of this eagle extends throughout the "island-world," even to the coasts of New Guinea and Australia. "There appear to be three of these splendid eagles, frequenters of Ross Island and Aberdeen; but I have not as yet observed more in this harbour." (T.)

*7. *Pontoaëtus ichthyaëtus* (Horsfield); or perhaps the smaller species, *P. humilis* (S. Muller). "A fine sea-eagle flew over my house on the 2nd of July, evidently a stranger from the number of crows which followed it. I examined him with a glass: he looked very like *P. ichthyaëtus*, but he was too far and high up to judge accurately." (T.) From Col. Tytler's description of the colouring, he is most probably right in his identification.

No Vultures have been observed either in the Andamans or the Nicobars; and of Owls the beautiful *Bulaca seloputo* (Horsf., *pagodarum*, Tem.,) was obtained in the Nicobars by Captain Lewis. Of course various other species will be found to occur; of the genera *Noctua*, *Scops*, *Ketupa*, and very probably the *Phodilus badius*. Of *Falconidæ*, we may expect *Falco*, *Pernis*, *Accipiter*, *Spizaëtus*, and others. No *Bucerotidæ* or hornbills have yet been observed; nor *Upupidæ* or hoopoes. But of *Halcyonidæ* or kingfishers.

*8. *Halcyon leucocephalus* (L). "Very common." (T.) There are three distinguishable races of this bird. One, which must be the true *leucocephalus*, has the cap albescent. It is common in the Tenasserim provinces; and from a description received from Col. Tytler, it is clearly the Andamanese race.

9. *H. coromandus* (Latham). Apparently not common.

10. *H. fuscus*, Boddäert: *H. smyrnensis* of India, *auctorum*. "Common on the main island." (T.)

11. *H. atricapillus* may be expected to occur, as a matter of course.

12. *Todirhamphus collaris* (Scopoli). "Very plentiful on the mainland as well as on the smaller islands." (T.) It is also common in the Nicobars, together with another species, *T occipitalis*, nobis.

*13. *Alcedo bengalensis* (Gmelin). "On the mainland, where they are not very common." (T.)

14. *Merops philippinensis* (L). The only bee-eater as yet received, and both from the Andamans and Nicobars.

15. *Mulleripicus Hodgei* (Blyth), *J. A. S.* xxix., 105. "This noble woodpecker is not uncommon on the mainland. I have had several shot and sent to me." (T.)

16. *Picus andamanensis* (Blyth), *J. A. S.*, xxviii., 412.

"Common." (T.) These two are the only woodpeckers as yet obtained.

No *Megalaimidæ* or barbets have yet been received; nor *Cuculidæ* or cuckoo family, though several species of this must needs occur; nor *Caprimulgidæ* or night-jars. Of *Cypselidæ* or swifts two species.

17. *Acanthylis giganteus* (Temminck). "I never see more than one of this splendid brown-backed black Swift with white under the tail. It usually, about four to five p.m., flies round and round my house like a meteor; the flight is strong and most rapid. I have watched it narrowly in flight: the head is much elevated, and tail depressed; this struck me as rather peculiar. It is a stronger bird than *Cypselus melba* on the wing, and much more rapid in flight." (T.) Since obtained and received in the museum of the Asiatic Society.

18. *Collocalia nidifica* (Gray). "More or less common everywhere, but nests are found in peculiar places." (T.) This is the most common of the constructors of the edible birds' nests. In the Nicobars a smaller, and more valuable species, the *C. linchi* (Horsfield), was alone observed.

19. *Corvus culminatus* (Sykes). The so-called "Raven" of Anglo-Indians in Bengal, and probably also the Sumatran *C. corax* of Raffles. It is extensively diffused over India and Indo-China, and specimens of it have been received from Malacca; pairs being often met with in the depths of the forest, away from human communities, which is never the case with *C. splendens*, or "the common crow of India." It might indeed well bear the name of "jungle crow," as compared with the other.—"Very abundant, on the mainland as well as on the smaller islands." (T.)

20. *Dendrocitta Bazleyi*, Tytler, N.S. "Not uncommon on the mainland." (T.) Of small size; length 13½ in.; closed wing, 4¾ in. Form typical.

*21. *Calornis affinis*, A. Hay. "Not uncommon on the

main island." (T.) Also common on the Nicobars, and on Ramree Island, Arakan.

22. *Temenuchus erythropygius ; Sturnia erythropygia*, Blyth, *passim.* "This pretty white-headed *Páwé* is very plentiful throughout the islands, and I have some pairs building in my verandah." (T.) Common also in the Nicobars, and unknown elsewhere.

23. *Gracula intermedia*, A. Hay. Received from both the Andamans and Nicobars ; a living albino specimen from the latter group.

* 24. *Gr. religiosa* (L.) "Not uncommon on the mainland. The *Gr. intermedia* I have not seen." (T.)*

25. *Munia leuconota* (Tem.) Like specimens from S. India, or darker and less distinctly striated than *M. striata* of Bengal. "Very abundant on the mainland in large flocks." (T.) No other finch observed as yet, not even the *báyás*, or "weaver-birds."

26. *Artamus leucorhynchus* (L.) The white-bellied species inhabiting Java and the Philippines, as distinguished from the rufescent-greyish breasted bird of India and Burma (*A fuscus*, Vieillot). "This graceful bird appears generally about Ross Island from about 4 p.m. to dusk. Numbers fly past the verandah of my house, and I have seen some dart through in pursuit of insects." (T.) Both species have the bill deep glaucous-blue when alive or fresh-killed.

27. *Hirundo rustica*, L. A specimen in the first plumage (*H. gutturalis*, Scopoli, &c.) was obtained at Port Blair by the Reverend Mr. Parish.

28. *Edolius malayensis*, A. Hay, *vide: J. A. S.*, xxviii., 272. "Not uncommon in the mainland." (T.) No other drongo observed ; but a specimen of the common Malayan *Dicrurus*

* There is probably a mistake here. It is not likely that both of these races of *Gracula* occur together.

balicassius (L.) was obtained at sea by Captain Lewis, when nearing one of the Nicobar Islands.

* 29. *Graucalus macei*, Cuvier. "I have seen several on the mainland as well as on the smaller islands." (T.)

30. *Irena puella* (Latham). The Indian race as distinguished from the Malayan. "Not very common." (T.)

31. *Lanius lucionensis*, Scopoli. Agrees with specimens from China and the Philippines.

32. *Hyloterpe philomela* (Muller): *Tephrodornis grisola*, Blyth.

33. *Myiagra azurea*, Vieillot. Received both from the Andamans and Nicobars. A *Tchitrea* was also seen in the Nicobars, doubtless *Tch. affinis*, A. Hay.

34. *Pericrocotus speciosus* (Latham). "Not common on the mainland." (T.)

35. *P. peregrinus* (L.)

36. *Geocichla innotata*, Blyth. Andamans and Nicobars. One obtained on the island of Pinang by the late Dr. Cantor. "I have only seen one, and that was in my garden in Ross Island." (T.)

37. *Turdus rufulus*, Drapiez.

38. *Petrocossyphus cyaneus* (L.)

39. *Oreocincla inframarginata*, Blyth. *J. A. S.*, xxix., 106.

40. *Copsychus saularis*, (L.) "Very abundant throughout the island. The males are more brilliant in colour than those generally seen in Bengal, and sing exquisitely. They are now in full song" (in May). (T.)

41. *C. albiventris*, Blyth. "Common, but not so plentiful as I expected. They are found not only on the main island, but on the smaller islands, and frequent the garden grounds. The habits of this bird are more those of *C. saularis* than of *C. macrourus*. (T.) Song deep-toned; but very inferior to that of the *macrourus*.

42. *Arundinax aëdon* (Pallas; *olivaceus*, Blyth.)

43. *Motacilla luzoniensis*, Scopoli. Common in the cold season.

44. *Anthus cervinus* (Pallas). Agrees with Peguan and Chinese specimens, and not with *A. rosaceus*, Hodgson, of the Himalaya.

45. *Pycnonotus jocosus* (L.) Malayan and S. Burman variety. "Very common on the main as well as on the smaller islands. This bird is identical with our common Bengal species, but may in some respects be regarded as a local variety. The red on the cheeks is less, and the bird is a little smaller; but the habits, notes, flight, &c., are identical. I saw a female sitting on her eggs on the 19th of May." (T.) *Hypsipetes virescens*, Blyth, inhabits the Nicobars; and these are the only bulbuls that have been observed as yet.

46. *Oriolus horsfieldi*, Pr. Bonap.: apparently this species, but I have not had the opportunity of comparing it with Javanese examples. It is distinct from the *O. macrourus*, Blyth, of the Nicobars. "Very common on the main as well as on the smaller islands." (T.)

No *Nectariniidæ* have yet been sent, though known to exist. On the Nicobars, *Nectarinia pectoralis*, Horsfield, abounds. *Zosterops palpebrosus* (Tem.) has also been sent from the Nicobars.

47. *Osmotreron chloroptera*, Blyth. Peculiar (it would seem) to the Andaman and Nicobar Islands. "Not uncommon on the mainland." (T.)

48. *Carpophaga sylvatica*, Tickell. Identical with the common species of Burma, if not also of India. The corresponding race of the Nicobars (*C. insularis*, Blyth), differs slightly but constantly. "This splendid large green wood-pigeon is very abundant on the main island. I have seen nearly forty of them together on the top branches of trees." (T.)

49. *C. myristicivora?* (Scopoli.) This is common in the Nicobars, and Babu Rajendra Mallika possesses living speci-

mens, which he states to have been brought from Port Blair. The species cannot but occur along the shores of the Andamans.*

50. *Calœnas nicobaricus* (L.) From the Cocos Islands, and also the Nicobars; wherefore, of course, inhabiting the Andamans.

51. *Chalcophaps indicus* (L.) "This beautiful green dove is rather rare, few having as yet been found; but I have no doubt that when the jungle is more cleared, we may find a good many of them." (T.) The Nicobarian race differs, and accords with the description of *Ch. augustæ*, Pr. Bonap.

*52. *Turtur humilis* (Tem.) "Several of these beautiful doves fly over from the mainland to Chatham Island." (T.) On the Nicobars, *T. tigrinus* (Tem.) exists, similar to the race inhabiting Burma and Malasia, and differing from the equally common *T. suratensis* of India and Ceylon. Another beautiful dove is also found in the Nicobars, *Macropygia rufipennis*, Blyth, which should be looked for on the Andamans.

(Here, too, must be noticed the *Megapodius nicobariensis*, Bl., which should be sought for on the Andaman Islands. No other gallinaceous bird has been observed as yet on the group.)

*53. "*Charadrius Leschenaultii*, I think; but as it was but a casual distant sight I had of the bird, I cannot at present determine." (T.) *Actitis hypoleucos* and *Strepsilas interpres* have been received from the Nicobars: the latter being, perhaps, the most universally distributed of birds, being found on every sea-coast.

* There are four nearly allied species of these white *Carpophagæ*, which frequent the mangrove swamps of different shores of the Indian Ocean. That of the Andamans and lands bordering on the Straits of Malacca is probably not the true *myristicivora* of Scopoli, which is from the Philippines.

* 54. *Numenius phæopus*, L. "Found on the beach of the main island and at the creeks." (T.)

* 55. *Herodias garzetta*, (L.) "I have seen a great many white Egrets, and from looking at them with a glass I should say beyond a doubt that they were *H. garzetta*." (T.)

* 56. *H. concolor*, Blyth. Inhabits Arakan, the Andamans, and Nicobars. "This dark Heron is commoner about the rocks on the beach, and is solitary in its habits." (T.)

* 57. *Butorides javanica* (Horsfield.) "A small dark Heron flew past my cutter on my way up the harbour, and had it been in India I should at once have pronounced it to be this: I had no glass to determine." (T.) Common in all the neighbouring countries.

58. *Euryzona Canningi*, Tytler, *n. s.* A very splendid new bird of its genus, of which only a single specimen has been obtained, which is now in the Museum of the Asiatic Society. The generic name does not felicitously apply to this species.

59. *Onychoprion anasthætus*, Scopoli.

60. *Anous stolida* (L.)—*Onychoprion melanauchen* (Tem.) breeds abundantly in the Nicobars, and must also be found on the Andamans. *Thalasseus bengalensis* (Lesson, *Sterna affinis*, Rüppell) has likewise been received from the Nicobars.

* 61 *Phaëton candidus*, (Brisson.) "I shot a fine female from my verandah the other evening. It was evidently attracted by the white plumage of some domestic pigeons near the house." (T.) I have not seen this species from the Bay of Bengal, but only *Ph. æthereus*, L. (the young), *v. Ph. phœnicurus*, Gm. (the adult,) which has been received from the Nicobars; as also *Pelicanus philippensis*. A young individual of *Ph. æthereus* I once kept alive, and it displayed in a remarkable degree the scandent propensity observed also in cormorants, gannets, and perhaps other *Totipalmati*.

(Two species of gannet, *Sula fiber* and *S. piscator*, occur in the Bay; as also two species of petrel, undetermined. One of the latter is a *Thalassidroma* or storm-petrel, which appears to have been observed only in impracticable weather; the other is a largish brown species, that was once obtained by Dr. Jerdon. The *Larus icthyäetus*, Pallas, is a fine species of gull, which will very probably be observed ere long in the harbour of Port Blair.)

Reptilia.

Testudinata. The different marine turtles of the Bay of Bengal occur of course; viz.—

1. *Couana olivacea*, (Eschscholtz). The "loggerhead" turtle. There is a particularly large skull of this species in the Museum of the Asiatic Society, found in an Andamanese hut.

2. *Chelonia virgata*, Schweigger. The edible turtle.

3. *Caretta imbricata*, (L). The "hawk's-bill" turtle, which yields the "tortoise-shell" of commerce.

(It is by no means improbable that land-tortoises, of one or more species, may prove to inhabit the islands. The pelagic *Sphargis coriacea* has lately been obtained near Moulmein.)

Loricata. Of the crocodile group, so far as I can learn, no species has been observed.

Sauria Geckotidæ. Four species have been received, two of them new; and more are likely to occur. During a recent excursion in Burma, I had occasion to remark to how great an extent the small *Geckotidæ* are conveyed about to great distances in boats.

4. *Gecko verus*, Merrem. The *tok-tou* of the Burmese.

5. *Hemidactylus frœnatus*, Schlegel. Received both from the Andamans and Nicobars.

6. *Phelsuma andamanense*, Blyth, *J. A. S.* xxix., 100.

A remarkable species, as the genus belongs otherwise to Madagascar and the Mascarine Islands.

7. *Puellula rubida*, Blyth, *J. A. S.* xxix., 109. Both species and genus new. It would seem to be of common occurrence.

Agamidæ.

8. *Tiara subcristata*, Blyth, *J. A. S.* xxix., 109. Of common occurrence. (From the Nicobars have been received *Calotes ophiomachus*, Merrem, identical with the species common in S. India and Ceylon; and *C. mystaceus*, Daudin, identical with that inhabiting the Tenasserim provinces.

Varanidæ.

9. *Hydrosaurus salvator*, (Laurenti), var. Quite similar on the Andamans and Nicobars; but differing in markings from the common reptile of the neighbouring countries (*vide J. A. S.*, xxix., 107). From the Nicobar Islands, however, the ordinary type of markings has likewise been received.

Scincidæ. As yet no member of this group would appear to have been observed.

Ophidia. Of this order eight species of snakes have been received, six of them being non-venemous, and two venemous. No sea-snake *(Hydridæ)* has yet been sent; though these are certain to be numerous; but *Pelamides platurus* (one of them) has been received from the Nicobars. On those islands, a species of *Python* (probably *P. schneideri*), was observed, both by Mr. Barbe and Captain Lewis.

The non-venemous snakes are:

10. *Lycodon aulicus* (L). A uniformly coloured variety, and an unusually much speckled variety. Common.

11. *Dendrophis pictus* (Gmelin). A remarkably rich-coloured, variegated, green variety of this exceedingly beautiful tree-snake would appear to be very common.

12. *Dipsas hexagonotus*, Blyth, *J.A.S.* xxiv., 360. Only young individuals have been received; the adult remains to be described.

13. *Herpotodryas prasinus*; *Coluber prasinus*, Blyth, *J.A.S.* xxiii., 291.

14. *Tropidonotus Tytleri*, Blyth, *J.A.S.* xxxii. A fine typical species of this genus.

15. *Cerberus boëformis* (Schneider). Common.

The venemous:

16. *Hamadryas vittatus* (Elliot).

17. *Trimesurus viridis* (Lacepede). Common, and attains to four feet in length; some of the individuals resemble those of the neighbouring countries, being of the usual bright grass-green colour; but the majority, both in the Andamans and Nicobars (*Tr. cantori*, Bl., *passim*), are singularly variable in their colours and markings, hardly two (of many that I have seen) having been alike (*vide J.A.S.* xxix., 110).

Batrachia. There has been observed only:—

18. *Bufo melanostictus*, Schneider. The common toad of India and S. E. Asia generally, which occurs abundantly.

Mollusca.

Passing over the strictly marine zoology, I proceed to enumerate a few land-shells, which have been described by W. H. Benson, Esq., formerly of the Bengal Civil Service, in the "Annals and Magazine of Natural History" third series, vol. vi., (1860), pp. 191 *et seq.*, and *ibid* vii., 82 *et seq.*

Helix helferi, Benson.

H. trochalia, B.

H. choinix, B.

H. stephus, B.

H. sanis, B.

Sreptaxis andamanica, B.

Helicina andamanica, B.

In conclusion, I must express regret that I have not been able to learn what was collected in the Nicobar Islands by the scientific staff attached to the Danish frigate "Galatea," in 1843; and I am also unacquainted with the discoveries which must have been made in the same islands by the scientific officers of the Austrian exploratory expedition of the "Novara" frigate in 1860: because it may be that I have been anticipated in the names which I have bestowed on certain species pertaining to the ascertained *Fauna* of the Andamans.

THE END.

MACDONALD AND TUGWELL, PRINTERS, BLENHEIM HOUSE.

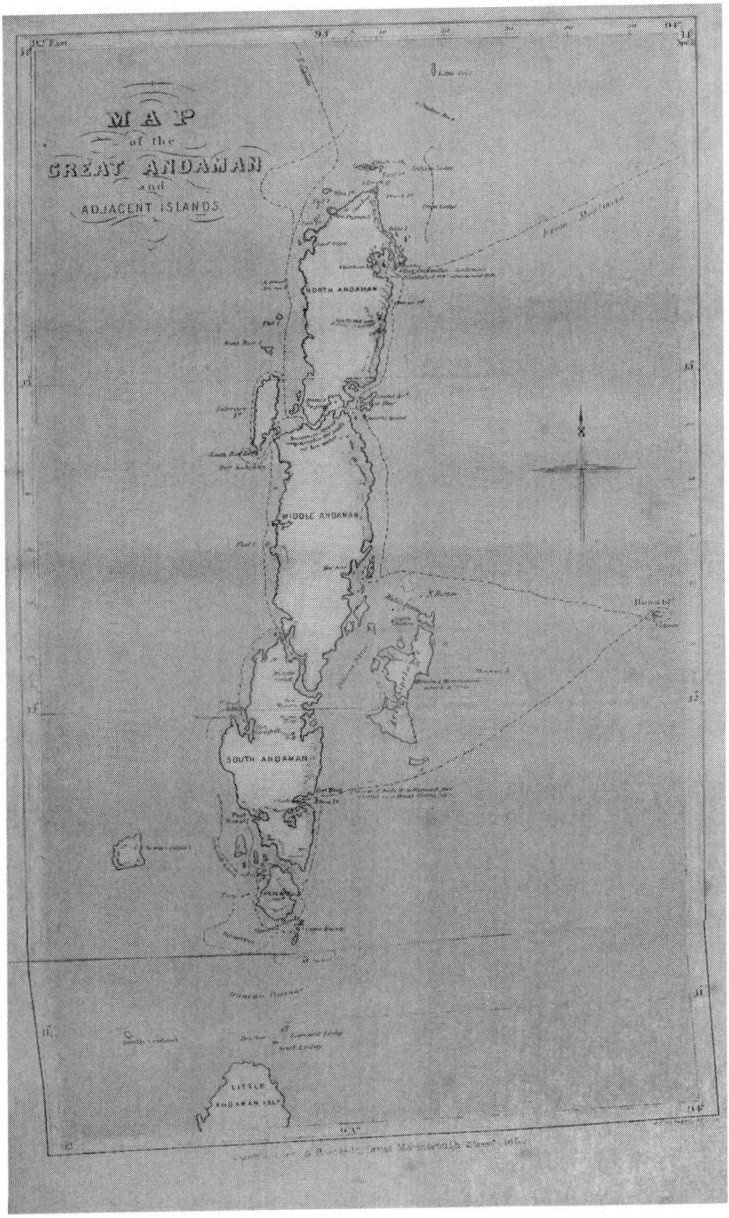
MAP
of the
GREAT ANDAMAN
and
ADJACENT ISLANDS.
NORTH ANDAMAN
MIDDLE ANDAMAN
SOUTH ANDAMAN
LITTLE
ANDAMAN ISL^D
93
94